Morning Prayer in Urumqi

Preparing Petitions When Praying for the World

— DAVID GOODACRE —

Sacristy Press

Sacristy Press
PO Box 612, Durham, DH1 9HT

www.sacristy.co.uk

First published in 2023 by Sacristy Press, Durham

Sacristy Limited, registered in England & Wales, number 7565667

British Library Cataloguing-in-Publication Data
A catalogue record for the book is available from the British Library

ISBN 978-1-78959-261-0

Contents

Preface

We have become insular in our intercessory prayer. Too often we pray only for the Church and for the sick and forget that we have a vocation to serve and pray for a range of much wider concerns. Of course many do, but too many don't—which makes me wonder what occasional visitors must think of us. So, first of all, the purpose of this book is to encourage us to widen our concern, in particular how we might intercede more for the world both in our corporate and in our personal prayer.

Some years ago, I did a survey of intercessory praying. I had retired in 2001 and, like other retired priests, was finding myself invited to take services in different churches. The research was carried out in 2008, but my impression is that what I discovered then is still as true today.

Of the 52 Sunday Eucharists of the year in question I attended 50. Of the two missing, one was in a Dorset village where there was no Sunday service until too late—even then not a Eucharist—and on the other occasion it was impossible to go anywhere. Thirty-two of the services were in one or the other of my normal places of worship (64 per cent) and the rest were in 13 other churches. Two were Roman Catholic, one Our Lady, Star of the Sea on the island of Barra, the other St Pierre Cathedral in Lisieux, where the Martin family and their daughter Thérèse used to worship—the old cathedral not the new basilica. Two were cathedrals in different parts of England, one was in a retreat setting, and the rest were in different English parish churches.

For five of the 50 services, written forms of intercession were provided on a service sheet. Of the rest, all the intercessions were prepared carefully. On one occasion, a family led the prayers, the ones spoken by the younger participants being especially meaningful. On two other occasions, the congregation sang the responses.

There were problems with the content in particular and in the length. Intercession was largely for the Church at home and abroad, for peace, for the sick and for the departed; the main emphases being the needs of the Church and the sick. There was rarely any mention of local or Newcastle concerns—Newcastle being where I live—or even much interest in problems of the country as a whole. During 2008, we were in the midst of a global financial crisis. It featured hardly at all—nor did Europe, the Law, social services, schools or universities. Since that time, and well before Brexit appeared on the scene, when there was a European election in the offing, there was rarely any mention of that either. It was the same at the time of the referendum on European Union membership—nor when we had voted to leave much about how our leaving might be accomplished. This may have been because the persons leading the prayer did not know how to phrase the petitions, fearing they might reveal their personal convictions, but help could have been given with that. A mention would have been enough with prayers suggested by *Common Worship*, or indeed the *Book of Common Prayer*. It almost makes me nostalgic for the latter's intercessory prayer with its clear concern for the wider world.

It is true of course—to take an example—that the lack of prayer for Europe did reflect a national lack of interest with the issue. Research before the referendum suggested that only 2 per cent thought it a serious matter,* so it might be that the Church was merely reflecting a national truth. Still, it was not good enough. The Church has a vocation to discern in what ways we are to engage with and work for the Common Good. We cannot do it if we do not pray about it.

For our prayer in church, there are several forms or templates in *Common Worship*. There is further help in the works of several others, Susan Sayers and Ian Black especially.** The order of prayer in *Common Worship* includes the needs of the world and the local community. Of course we pray for the Church and indeed for the sick and departed; the weakness arises when it comes to praying for any wider concerns.

Including such concerns should not make the prayer longer. The intercessory form in the *Common Worship* liturgy is about 200 words. This takes about three minutes to speak aloud, and if a brief amount of material is added, not more than a further 200 words, that will be enough.

---

* *In Touch*, the alumni magazine of King's College London (Spring 2016).

** See the select bibliography.

A sung response, or a range of voices, helps concentration. I was brought up in a vicarage family, which meant that I learnt early how to daydream my way through the duller parts of any service—and to a small child, what service is not dull! I have found the habit difficult to change. So, intercessors, please have mercy and be brief.

Arrangement of the book

The main body of this book begins with an introductory essay under a heading from the Lord's Prayer, **Your kingdom come, Your will be done**. It is a venture into the theology of intercession. This is followed by a short chapter on the practicalities of preparing an intercession. The rest of the book is made up of 52 weeks, each of them covering some area of the world, sometimes a single country, or more often a region. They are my way of introducing the reader to the world, a series of vignettes: reminiscence, stories, associations, some of them quite personal, the kind of association any ordinary person could make, as a way of focusing on a particular area. My associations, I have found having written them, have come to form a biographical sketch of my ministry over the years. Their main purpose though is to help Christians look with the Lord upon the world which God loves—in a spirit of thanksgiving.

Each week starts on a Monday after the Sunday mentioned and ends on the following Sunday in resurrection hope. Each is introduced by a fact box: an outline of the region, the population to the nearest million or so—according to the UN figures of July 2022—the dominant religion, the Anglican presence if there is one, and a note or two about important recent events. The body of the vignette then follows, each one exploring some theme which came to mind.

The arrangement of the vignettes is a scattered one; a wandering around the globe haphazardly rather than taking one continent at a time. China, India and the United States are allotted major moments of the Church's year and two separate weeks each, because of their size and significance. Jerusalem, as a major spiritual hub of Judaism, Christianity and Islam, has a week to itself—and there are one or two places where the vignette and the area chosen are related to the season.

Some parts of the world I know fairly well, Cyprus and Zambia in particular, but not much beyond that. During my National Service in the 1950s, I was for some 18 months stationed in Kenya, Aden and Cyprus. My wife Joy worked in Zambia before we were married, and we kept in close touch with the country after that. Joy and I travelled extensively during our holidays, usually with one or other of our two daughters, and I have used personal experiences of these journeys in several of the vignettes; indeed they are all constructed from the various associations I have made with the different regions.

Intercession is an imaginative exercise, a way of thinking about another part of the world, to engage with it, so that we can cooperate with Christ in God's concerns. I found I could discover some sort of association with almost every part of the world; even if in some cases it was very slight—as I explore in the **Preparing the petitions** section. They encouraged me to think around what came to mind and see where I was led. It was from this process that various aspects of spiritual and pastoral ministry emerged, a series of themes. I hope this way of doing things will encourage intercessors to adopt a similarly imaginative approach to the compilation of their own intercessions.

Political events are in constant flux. The vignettes do not therefore provide any up-to-date information. The media and internet are the sources for that. They are nonetheless suggestive. Take for example the first one. The main theme there is actually Morning Prayer, but it so happened that when I was in Urumqi in 2009, the Uighur troubles were becoming more serious. I pray, by the time you come to read this, that that particular problem has been eased in some way. If that is the case, the problem may well have shifted to some other place. Sadly, since dominant powers tend to oppress minorities that differ from them in faith and culture, similar problems constantly arise. The Nigeria vignette (Week 12), which is about trafficking and in particular the activities of *Boko Haram*, is an example. At the time of writing in 2021, it was still a problem in Nigeria, but it was also then spreading to the other side of Africa, to Cabo Delgado in the north of Mozambique (see Week 18). The material, the country or the theme explored in one vignette may well be relevant, or even more relevant, to another part of the world. The themes index is a guide to where they are.

Several themes have emerged as I have been writing the book; the dominant one is the degree of separation that exists between so many peoples. It is a problem everywhere, whether an instance of ethnic separation, of race, religion or some other source of tension—a problem addressed by St Paul in his letters where he asserts that in Christ Jews and Gentiles form one people. When things are settled, disparate peoples get on well enough; when they are disturbed, they find it much more difficult, sometimes catastrophically difficult.

A second theme is the growing background threat of climate change. While the book is primarily about praying for social harmony, for *convivencia*,* the need to think about and pray through the challenge of climate change is fundamental.

These two themes lead to a third: the challenge of religious division in the world, how peoples of different faiths are to reach a deeper appreciation of each other. As ecumenism was the Church's calling in the twentieth century, interfaith understanding is the challenge for the twenty-first.

If we are to address these challenges, we need good leadership—very much explored in the following essay: the spiritual gifts our modern leaders require if there is to be good governance, the alleviation of poverty and the building of nations. We need also to be open to the importance of vocation in all of this as we journey in Christ, listening to the movement of the Holy Spirit calling us to join with him in working for the kingdom. Pope John XXIII used to speak of such callings as "surprise".** May we all be open to such surprises.

---

* For translation of the Spanish word and definition see Week 1.

** Pope John XXIII, *Journal of a Soul*, trans. Dorothy White (London: Geoffrey Chapman, 1980), p. 329.

Acknowledgements

My debt to a range of writers who contributed so much to this work is enormous. There are some whose public writing has made a particular impression, and I am grateful to Sheila Cassidy, Roger Cohen, Aida Edemariam, James Hanratty, Kate Hennessy, Michael Ignatieff, and Malala Yousafzai for what they have shared—thank you to them all. When covering such a large canvas, it would have been impossible to write knowledgeably about the different regions, without the witnesses of so many writers and thinkers.

On a personal note, I have tried to make contact with everyone who is mentioned by name and all who have replied have given their permission. Sadly I have lost touch with one or two. My heartfelt thanks to all the following, who have been so generous with their love and friendship—and their time in helping me with this book: Musa Hassan Ali, James Amanze, Trevor Beeson, the late Chris Dalton, Sr Renate Düllmann OP, Paul Grundy, Shazad Hussain, Katja Hržić, Derek Jones, Sr Margaret Angela CSJD, Kerileng Nomalizo Moeti, R Justin Moni, Rosemary Mumbi, Rosa Neaber, Osaro Omobude, Peter Ramsden, Hayriye Rüzgar, Fr Martin Stempczyk, Obehi Sule, Fr Thomas Timpte OSB and Keith Woodhouse. Thanks also to my editor Natalie Watson.

Several of my colleagues in Newcastle diocese have generously read large swathes of the typescript: Richard Bryant, Paul Grundy, David Peel and Bishop Stephen Platten, who also guided me towards publishers. I am grateful to them not only for their comments but for their willingness to give so much time to the task.

Much of the journeying described in the book was with Joy and one or the other of our two daughters, Christine and Marie, whose love and companionship over the years has been so wonderful and enriching—a thanks that extends to their husbands Nicholas and Jon and our seven grandchildren who have afforded us so much love and joy. Thank you to them and especially to my three adult grandchildren, Ruth, Lucy and Ben, who have commented on relevant parts of the book.

Joy was my beloved companion of many years. When I was visiting one of Joy's friends, Sebastian Bakare—and his late wife Ruth—in Mutare (Zimbabwe), where he was Bishop of Manicaland, we said Evening

Prayer together in their chapel, an African conical room standing beside their home; in the intercessions Sebastian thanked God for Joy's prayers for us in heaven—Joy's intercession joining with ours and those others in Christ with whom we were bound together in the Holy Spirit, held in prayer by the ascended Lord before the Father. Let us thank God for all those who continue to hold us in prayer.

Your Kingdom Come, Your Will Be Done

Intercession for the kingdom

Rogation prayer

Ovingham, where I was vicar for 20 years, is a rural parish in the Tyne Valley. It is halfway between Newcastle and Hexham, immediately beside the river. It is largely a commuter village, most of the people working in Newcastle. There were a few who worked locally in the water industry or as farmers. There were 12 farms in my day. Several of the old farms had become mini housing estates, and even the active ones had converted several outbuildings into holiday cottages.

The Sixth Sunday of Easter and the three days that follow it make up the season of Rogation. This is the time when the Church prays that the earth might be fruitful, the sea full of fish, and the industry of the country productive. The word "Rogation" is from the Latin (*rogo*—I ask), and the day, Rogation Sunday, and the three days of fasting and abstinence that follow have been days of prayer since the fifth century. They end when the Church reaches the Ascension, celebrated on the Thursday.

Rogation prayers are provided in the current Anglican Daily Prayer, *Common Worship*.* After I had been in Ovingham some years, we decided we should make more of Rogation by reinstating the old practice of a procession through the parish so that we could look towards the fields and offer our intercession as we went around. We prayed that the fields might be blessed, that the farmers might serve "the common good", that they might sustain "the fabric of the world" by being "wise and faithful

* *Common Worship: Daily Prayer* (London: Church House Publishing, 2005), p. 537; *Common Worship, Times and Seasons* (London: Church House Publishing, 2006), pp. 609–19.

stewards of God's gifts". We prayed that there would be a good harvest. We did once walk round the entire parish, "beating the bounds", as it used to be called, but it took us all day so in subsequent years we simply walked around the church. Both church and yard were conveniently circled by a road.

We began at the North Gate, the congregation and choir filling the road. Opposite the main churchyard and across the road there was an extension yard. In the 1990s, this was used by a smallholding farmer for some of his sheep and goats. On seeing us arrive they would rush to the gate and there—to the delight of the choir—would join in, bleating their prayer and praise along with the rest of us.

Our few minutes in the road used to block the way to the village shop. Most of the casual villagers who happened upon us—on their way for their Sunday paper—would wait for us to finish, but the odd one would barge through, as though we were not really there. If I doubted in any way the wisdom of our actions this sort of intrusion was bound to make me think. What in fact were we doing? After all, in a modern farm the crops had been sown long before, usually in the previous autumn. They were now well grown. What additional benefit were we supposing would arise as a result of our prayer? Basically I was wondering what we were in fact interceding for.

We were praying that our farms, functioning as they were meant to be doing, might continue to be sustained by God. We expected, of course, that the crops were going to come up whether we prayed about them or not, but we knew too that if we were to take things too much for granted, complacently assume that all would always be well, and never give thanks for what we had been given, that we might well be the losers. We needed to acknowledge before God our awareness that all that was around us was gift—the creation, the fields, the growth. In this spirit, we prayed that God would continue to sustain our world, as God had done for so many centuries before.

The weather of the Tyne Valley is less harsh and windy than other parts of the Northeast. The villages of Ovingham and Ovington which made up the parish in the 1990s were originally founded by Saxons sometime around AD 500. They had invaded and in contrast to their predecessors, who had preferred to live on higher ground well away from the forest, its predators and the river, they had settled in the valley. They cleared the land, and over the ensuing 1,500 years they and their successors had learnt how best to farm it and in the process had transformed a wilderness into the fertile and beautiful landscape that it is today.

When the Saxons had first come, they had worshipped their gods, probably in the place where the church now stands. They hoped that their prayer would propitiate any evil spirits that might be lurking about. Roughly 50 years or so after their arrival, St Aidan had come to the village with good news to share.* Bede says that the king, Oswald, used to accompany him and translate his Scottish into Anglo-Saxon. The villagers responded by erecting a cross in their sacred space where they could continue their prayer for their land and each other—just as we, so many years later, were also doing. Many today believe that all that is needed for a farm to flourish is good husbandry supported by up-to-date science and technology, and that that is enough. We felt differently. We felt it would be a failure not to give thanks for the gifts we had received and indeed foolhardy to be unaware that as human beings we were also vulnerable. While the Tyne Valley and Europe in general is fertile, it is also like everywhere else subject to dangerous happenings; poor weather, floods, drought, disease—and now, the ever-increasing threat posed by global warming. We are faced with enormous ecological problems. The reality is that they are a threat which we must face and pray about. Thankfully, young people are proving to be much more sensitive to all this than we older generations.

Our Rogation prayer, prayer generally, had proved to be an opportunity to strengthen ourselves spiritually to recognize the immensity of the issues we faced. At the end of our perambulation, we returned to the church to complete our thanksgiving and intercession in the rest of the Eucharist.

---

* Bede, *A History of the English Church and People*, trans. Leo Sherley-Price (London: Penguin Classics, 1955), Book III, p. 142.

Eucharist

We had reached the "Liturgy of the Sacrament", as it is called in *Common Worship*, the moment when we came back into the building to rehearse together the fourfold action of the Eucharist:

> (Jesus) took a loaf of bread, and after blessing it, he broke it, gave it to them and said, "Take, this is my body." Then he took a cup, and after giving thanks he gave it to them and all of them drank from it. He said to them, "This is my blood of the covenant which is poured out for many" (Mark 14:22–24).

Coming in, as it were from the fields, we brought our offerings of bread and wine—both of them processed foods made in bakery and vinery from the produce of farms, symbolizing the gifts of creation we had prayed for. "Everything in heaven and on earth is yours", we said together. "All things come from you, and of your own do we give you."*

The President took and received the offering, and then began the great prayer of thanksgiving. The President, on behalf of the congregation, gave thanks for the creation, for the infinite presence of the Word within the finite Jesus Christ, for his ministry, his dying on the cross, his rising from the dead and his ascension into heaven—there to intercede for us. What we had prayed for outside in the earlier part of the service, we were now praying about within.

The President then broke the bread: practically to share the loaf, symbolically to represent Christ's brokenness on the cross–and our own brokenness and vulnerability and separation from God and each other. We prayed that despite this separation we might be healed and made one.

And so to the fourth part! The infinite Word of God now fully present within the finite earthly symbols of bread and wine, we were to share the simple meal. We would become one with Christ–now at this present moment, and as a foretaste of the final heavenly banquet of the kingdom. The Eucharist celebrates our hope for the fields while also giving us a

---

* *Common Worship: Services and Prayers for the Church of England* (London: Church House Publishing, 2000), p. 291.

glimpse of a future harvest, that final moment when heaven and earth are transfigured at the end of time.

Our intercession had thus become wholly interwoven with our thanksgiving. We had acknowledged and celebrated the gift of creation. Together, we had declared our appreciation of what our farmers over the years had been learning and were still doing, working sustainably within the heft of creation while innovating and experimenting for the future. We had prayed too that if there were to be problems, those who had the responsibility to do something about them might have the strength and wisdom to overcome them. Our Eucharist was ended. We were to "go in peace to love and serve the Lord: in the name of Christ".*

The Ascension

The short season of Rogation ends with Ascension Day. When I was a boy, there was still the possibility of having the Ascension as a day off from school. My father regarded this as important and used to take advantage of it; not possible now, I fear! These days the festival passes by virtually unnoticed. Perhaps the Anglican *Thy Kingdom Come* initiative, which starts on Ascension Day, will change this. For me, as it was for my father, the Thursday celebration of Ascension Day is one of the highlights of the Church's year!

The Ascension focuses on two themes: Christ as king, and Christ as intercessor before the Father. The two are intimately connected; the first offers a vision of Christ's kingly rule as something immediately present and in the future, the second our Lord's intercession towards that end. As ascended Lord, both Word of God in relation to the Father and fully human as Jesus the Word, he holds us in his priestly heart before God. As St Paul says, Christ is at the right hand of God making intercession for us (Romans 8:34; see also Hebrews 7:25); this sets our own intercession within its proper context, our prayer as a part of Christ's own continuing prayer. He calls us to cooperate with him in this prayer, to align ourselves with his will and purpose. Our intercession is thus to become incorporated within the prayer of God the Trinity, the Word

* *Common Worship*, p. 183.

holding us before the Father, the Father empowering us by the Holy Spirit that in Christ we may become workers with him for the kingdom.

Jesus spoke continually about the kingdom, a term which we might now translate as a society ordered within the loving kindness of God towards the Common Good. In the many encounters Jesus had, he intimated what this would mean in the stories he told and in his actions: accepting people as they were, forgiving them their sins, healing them of their ills and challenging them to live fuller lives. They were to know what living in relationship with the Lord would be like. We had had an earnest of this in the Eucharist described above when we received the sacrament and became in that moment a community of love, justice and righteousness. The sacramental banquet speaks of the end time when finally persons of every race and ethnicity, each in their inherent dignity, become one community together in what the Spanish call *convivencia*, different peoples living together in social harmony. Our eyes are opened to see the signs of the kingdom that are all around us: examples of transcendent love, of healings, of acts of grace and righteousness, in events and happenings that speak of God. The vignettes below offer examples.

As we look at the world today, the coming of the kingdom seems a very improbable possibility. Nonetheless, it is what Christ proclaimed, and it is what we pray for, a spiritual statement of a glorious endpoint. Some visionaries in the past have wondered whether they might hasten its arrival by exercising political power to bring it about, always to disastrous effect. Western intellectuals in Europe in the late nineteenth century thought that Europe's civilization had already reached such a point, that they had advanced so far that they could teach the rest of the world the secrets of their success. It was a lamentable failure. Such hubris was not to survive two world wars, the Holocaust and so many other disfiguring atrocities of the twentieth century.

Human beings cannot create perfect societies. The kingdom remains a spiritual vision. It is realizable only within the purposes of God. It is our task as the people of God, who have been enlisted to pray for this kingdom, to work with Christ that it may come. As we say each time we pray the Lord's Prayer, "Your kingdom come, your will be done on earth as in heaven".

Pentecost

Ten days after the Ascension, the fiftieth day after Easter is the feast of Pentecost. It is the day when the Church remembers receiving the gift of the Holy Spirit, of the apostles being empowered to work with Christ for the kingdom (Acts 2:1–13). We pray that the people and especially their leaders may be also so inspirited and blessed with gifts from the Holy Spirit.

John's word for the Holy Spirit is *parakletos* (John 14:16).* It means "called alongside", variously translated as "Advocate" or, in the Authorized Version of the Bible, "Comforter". The latter was a much stronger word in the seventeenth century: "com-fort", "with strength", God strengthening and empowering.

In his speech to the crowd on the first Pentecost, Peter quoted Joel's description of the Lord pouring out his spirit on all flesh (Acts 2:17–21).** Joel was writing after an appalling agricultural disaster—explored further below—and of God endowing the people with new spirit. This, Peter says, is what he and the apostles were experiencing in Jerusalem. They found themselves empowered, given new strength to work with God, to become participants in Christ within his new international body the Church to reach out in mission and prayer for the world. St Paul explains in his letter to the Romans that the Holy Spirit will be with them as they pray, and that as God knows the heart and mind of the Spirit, who "intercedes for the saints according to the will of God" (Romans 8:26–27), God will hear their prayer and respond to their needs.

In the context of this study, the saints here, the holy people of God, ourselves in other words, are the ones so endowed. We do not receive the Holy Spirit for our own personal needs alone but so that we can be enrolled as intercessors and fellow workers for the kingdom. In 1 Timothy, the writer urges us to pray "for everyone, for kings and all who are in high positions . . . " (1 Timothy 2:1–2). For a quiet life, the author adds, but then amplifies this by saying that as Christ is the one who mediates between God and humankind—the Ascension theme again—we are to pray alongside him before God. The passage picks up on Isaiah's understanding that it is too light a responsibility for the servant to pray

* See also John 14:26; 15:26 and 16:7.

** The quotation is from Joel 2:28–32.

for Israel alone, his prayer needs to be much wider, for the nations of the world (Isaiah 49:6). The same thought is repeated every day in the Evening Prayer (or Compline) canticle, the *Nunc Dimittis*, that we are to be "a light to lighten the Gentiles" (Luke 2:32).

We pray that those for whom we pray may be strengthened by the Holy Spirit. St Paul in his first letter to the Corinthians gives a list of the gifts or charisms that they have received from the Holy Spirit: wisdom, spiritual counsel, prophecy, faith, speaking in tongues, interpreting them, healing and working miracles (1 Corinthians 12:4–11) and finally—what he speaks of as the greatest gift of all—love. St Paul writes about this last gift in the chapter that follows.

The first is the gift of wisdom. Paul regularly prays at the beginning of each of his letters that the church he is writing to might be endowed with the spirit of wisdom. In his letter to the Colossians, possibly written by a close disciple, the author prays that they might be filled with the knowledge of God's will and increase "in all spiritual wisdom and understanding, . . . made strong with all the strength that comes from [God's] glorious power" (Colossians 1:9,11).

So we pray that the leaders of the nations might similarly be endowed with wisdom. When Joshua became leader after the death of Moses and was alarmed by the extent of his new responsibilities, he prayed for help. The Lord responded: "As I was with Moses, so I will be with you . . . Be strong and courageous" (Joshua 1:5–6). Perhaps this is the greatest gift we can pray for when thinking of leaders, that they should be wise and strong.

Faith is Paul's third gift—I am discussing them in a different order from Paul's list. In his letter to the Romans, Paul quotes the prophet Habakkuk. It is not known exactly when Habakkuk was writing, but he was clearly addressing some dreadful and imminent crisis. His essential message was that his people should have faith:

> Though the fig tree does not blossom,
> and no fruit is on the vines;
> though the produce of the olive fails
> and the fields yield no food; . . .
> yet I will rejoice in the Lord;
> I will exult in the God of my salvation (Habakkuk 3:17–18).

A little earlier in the book he had urged his listeners to write about this faith—or faithfulness—in such a way that any messengers whose task it was to share it would be able to encourage the people with it. When there are severe threats, he counselled, strong faith is needed. It was the only way that the people would be able to transcend the harsh conditions they were facing. Paul emphasizes this same fundamental gift. We pray that leaders may be men and women of real faith.

Faith perhaps with prudence! Ezra the priest (Ezra 8:21–23,31), when he was about to return from exile to Jerusalem, felt too embarrassed to ask King Ahasuerus for an armed escort to protect his party on the journey there, laden as they would be with the treasures they were carrying. He had told the king, perhaps rueing his presumption as he mentions the problem twice, that the Lord would protect them. His contemporary, the brusque governor Nehemiah, would not have been so rash. In this case, God honoured Ezra's witness before the king. He had taken a risk. Protection would have been provided if he had asked for it; such presumption often leads to disaster.

In the nineteenth century, several Christians decided they would refrain from putting up the recently invented lightning conductors, because, they argued, it was the Lord who would protect their churches should lightning strike.* The result was that a number of churches were destroyed. There is no wisdom in trying to frustrate God's ability to answer our prayer by refusing what the Lord has provided. We are to work with God, employ whatever sensible precautions there are, and certainly not hubristically suppose that the Lord will rescue us when we have done something stupid—though even then God often does do so if it can be done. We pray that the leaders of countries might be men and women of faith, and at the same time use their common sense.

A third gift is spiritual knowledge. Leadership is a lonely calling and wise and humble leaders look for counsel to help them discern the best ways forward in a crisis. In Ecclesiastes, the Preacher describes a small city that survived a siege because its leaders had the good sense to seek the advice of a "poor wise man" (Ecclesiastes 9:13–16). They spoilt things later by attacking their saviour, but they would have fared badly had they

---

* Peter Baelz, *Prayer and Providence* (New York: Seabury Press, 1968), p. 34.

not heeded his advice. Many leaders learn to value advisers whom they can trust, especially those who are soul-friends as well.

King David's main soul-friend was Nathan. He appears several times in the story of his reign. One occasion was after David had organized the killing of his pregnant lover's husband. Nathan confronted David by telling him a parable about a poor man whose pet lamb his boss had purloined to feed a visiting guest. Outraged, David demanded that this employer should be punished. "You are the man!" Nathan replied (2 Samuel 12:1–15). Another time Nathan acted quickly to avert a political coup. David was nearing the end of his life and who was to succeed him was far from clear. Nathan and Zadok hurriedly persuaded him to confirm his choice of Solomon and then, equally fast, organized a coronation (1 Kings 1:5–53). Perhaps his most important contribution was the counsel he gave when David thought he should build a temple. Nathan was at first impressed by David's thought, but then having slept on it, discerned that David was not the one to do it. He told David what the Lord had told him (2 Samuel 7). Nathan had no overt political power. Soul-friends do not have such power. They are there to speak spiritual words of wisdom that can of course be ignored should the ruler so decide. They often are ignored. Better if they are not. David in each of these three incidents did in fact accept Nathan's advice. He knew Nathan to be a man of God whose wisdom and discretion was exemplary. We pray that leaders may have and use their counsellors as wisely as David used his.

Prophecy, placed in Paul's list together with speaking in tongues and their interpretation, is of more general application. Paul treats the two in detail later (1 Corinthians 14:4 and verses 29–33). Many members of the Corinthian church seem to have thought of themselves as prophets with important words to share with their congregation, too many of them wanting to speak at the same time. Paul advised them to take turns and to invite no more than two or three. The call to prophesy, to listen, to discern God's purposes and then to speak of them usefully is a rare gift, requiring great courage, conviction and also an astute sense of timing. Take Jeremiah for example. He was called by God to prophesy when Nebuchadnezzar was king of Babylon and threatening Judea with invasion. Jeremiah spoke of Nebuchadnezzar as a "servant of God" (Jeremiah 25:9; 27:6) called by God to discipline his sinful nation.

Jeremiah could hardly have put it more starkly and his counsel was not well received—unless they were to repent and at the same time cooperate with Babylon, they would face disaster. His hearers abused him angrily, on one occasion throwing him into a mud-filled well where they hoped he would die. Whistle blowers, prophets who speak the truth to power, are rarely appreciated.

There is a story in the first book of Kings (Chapter 22) about two kings, Jehoshaphat of Judea and Ahab of Israel, who were proposing to go to war—at least Ahab was trying to persuade Jehoshaphat to join him in a campaign he had in mind. Jehoshaphat asked Ahab to summon the local prophets to ask them whether they thought God was on their side. Four hundred of them were assembled to do just this, and they all together told Ahab what he wanted to hear. Jehoshaphat remained uneasy: "Are you sure we are hearing from all the prophets?" he asked. "Is there not someone else we should consult?"

Ahab reluctantly called for Micaiah, whom he had imprisoned for earlier advice he had not wanted. The messenger sent to bring Micaiah told him what he was expected to say. Undaunted, Micaiah spoke sarcastically: "Of course your proposal will work!" he said. "What do you really think?" the kings asked him.

"You will fail," he said. Another of the prophets, outraged by what he was hearing, exclaimed, "How come that the spirit of the Lord has passed from me to you?"

"You will find out all too soon," Micaiah told him—which is what happened. The powers that be find it just as hard in the modern world to hear unwelcome prophecy.

Rachel Carson, writing about the ecological threat of climate change and pollution in 1962 in her seminal book *Silent Spring*, was one of the first prophets to warn the world about the dangers. There have been many others since, but even now, some 60 years later, there are many who still do not want to hear what she prophesied so long ago. We pray for the prophets and whistle blowers as they share their insights and give of their wisdom.

Two more of Paul's gifts are speaking in tongues and their interpretation. On the day of Pentecost Luke says the disciples were ecstatic when they received the Holy Spirit (Acts 2:4,8–13). The passage puts more emphasis on the apostles' newly discovered ability to communicate with and feel in communion with the different ethnic peoples who were milling around them than with the ecstasy they had experienced, but it is the latter experience which many Christians often look for. Paul here is speaking about this, the spiritual exhilaration that his converts had experienced and were hoping to have much more of. Paul thought it valuable but believed that prophecy was far more important (1 Corinthians 14:1–5).

My mother was a woman of deep prayer, but she had always longed to speak in tongues and had never been able to do so. In terms of spiritual experience, it is an important early spontaneous response—uncontrived that is—which tends to continue in churches where it is the culture that it should. Despite the absence of tongues, my mother was already full of the Holy Spirit and did not need the additional exhilaration, any more than so many other men and women of prayer do, the mystics and contemplatives among them especially! Writing in his second letter to the Corinthians, St Paul rather reluctantly tells the Corinthians about his own mystical experience (2 Corinthians 12:1–10). Teresa of Avila did so also, because she was instructed to do so by the authorities.* She gave vivid descriptions of the intense raptures she experienced, which included what sounds very much like speaking in tongues. She sometimes found it a nuisance. She and John of the Cross both emphasized that valuable though these experiences were, they were altogether secondary to the importance of living an active life of love and service.

It is not currently a popular understanding that political leaders should be persons of prayer—though there are exemplars, Tony Blair, U Thant, Dag Hammarskjöld, to name three. The secular world seems to think that if leaders pray, they must be somehow mentally unbalanced. In fact, unless persons are using prayer as an escape from reality, far from indicating disturbance it shows that they have grasped a central truth, that relationship with the infinite God, paradoxically and in contrast to the secular fear, ensures that a sound vision and values are at the heart of their thinking. We pray that our leaders should similarly be earthed in transcendent reality.

---

* Teresa of Avila, *The Life of Saint Teresa of Avila by Herself*, trans. J. M. Cohen (London: Penguin Classics, 1957), pp. 113, 137.

St Paul then speaks of healing and working miracles. This is primarily about the healing of individuals, but it is important to recognize that whenever we pray for single persons who are sick, the sickness at the same time reflects wider community distress and disturbance. Paul clearly recognized this. When he wrote to the Corinthians about a personal issue in their church, he looked at it within a wider corporate context. He was concerned not only for the personal wellbeing of the man, but much more for the impact his behaviour would have on the rest of the Church community (1 Corinthians 5). A broken relationship in one couple is a reflection of what is happening in the Church community as a whole.

When I was editing *Health and Healing* for the Churches' Council for Health and Healing, much of the journal was about the healing of individual sick persons, but we devoted one entire issue to the healing of Northern Ireland during the troubles. * Sickness in the individual person reflects the community and vice versa. When we pray for healing—and maybe also for miracles—and are thinking of individual persons, we should also be careful to keep in mind this larger issue of health within the community.

Miracles

The word for "miracles" in the Greek is *dunamis* (giving us "dynamic", even "dynamite"). It means "capable to act". Can we expect God to act, to make miracles happen today?

In exploring intercession so far, I have suggested that it is first of all rooted in thanksgiving: for our Lord's loving care for us from within the creation, that our intercession is conducted within the ongoing prayer of our ascended Lord, and that it needs always to be in association with God's will! In this section on the work of the Holy Spirit, I have further considered the different spiritual gifts that the Church receives from the Holy Spirit that the leaders of the different countries might also receive these gifts: wisdom, a readiness to accept good counsel, a solid faith in a good vision, an openness to receive the insights of prophets, a willingness to transcend division and embrace the infinite possibilities that lie within the wonders of creation, and even—who knows?—that in

* *Health and Healing* 9 (1985).

dire circumstances there might be miracles. Might we in the twenty-first century still hope that God may intervene or in some way help when we are confronted by some appalling circumstance?

It needs to be said that we do not need God to intervene because God is with us already. God does not need to change the creation, to interfere as it were from without—as envisaged in the satirical film *Bruce Almighty**—because if God were to do that it would damage the integrity of the creation. Nor is the opposite true, that God having created the universe has left it to function entirely on its own as the Deists believe. It is rather that God is always present within the universe, sustaining and upholding it from within. Rowan Williams argues in his study of Christology (the doctrine that Jesus was both human and divine) that God relates to his creation in the same way; as the divine God was within the human Christ, so the infinite is within the finite.**

This did not mean that when the apostles encountered Jesus, they immediately discerned his divinity. Hollywood films give the impression that Jesus must have been so obviously divine that anyone meeting him could be in no doubt that they were seeing God; he was a remarkable human being no doubt, but still a person, a man! It took them a very long time before they were to discern more than that, that within their finite friend and leader they were encountering the infinite divine. It was to take the Church many centuries more before they could articulate this more clearly, just how the divine might be present within the humanity of an ordinary human person. When they did, it meant that they had begun to grasp just how the infinite is encountered within the grace of the ordinary. Rowan Williams suggests that God works from within the depths of our personhood, penetrating the dark corners of our unconscious selves, to the hidden possibilities that are there, to the places where issues are reframed into fresh and creative ways forward.*** This is the way with miracles—they exhibit the infinite presence and love of God within finite human happenings. Austin Farrer describes it in his theology as "double

---

* *Bruce Almighty*, film directed by Tom Shadyac (Universal Pictures, 2003).

** Rowan Williams, *Christ, the Heart of Creation* (London: Bloomsbury/Continuum, 2018), pp. 3–5, 223–8.

*** Rowan Williams, *Meeting God in St Mark* (London: SPCK, 2014), p. 41.

agency", the reality that in Jesus Christ and in miracles generally, the divine makes the infinite known within a range of ordinary human, finite, events.

To explain this further let me give an illustration. There is a story in a recent novel by Kate Mosse, *The Burning Chambers*,* of an armed conflict in Toulouse. A devout girl, about nine years old, finds herself in the middle of a road surrounded by armed men fighting. In her terror she kneels down and, hands clasped together in prayer, pleads with God to rescue her. At that moment, the heroine of the novel, seeing her in this predicament, forgoes her own safety, leaps into the fray, scoops up the child, and carries her to safety. Both somehow escape! When the heroine was telling her friend what she had done, she told him that the little girl had said that it was God who had rescued her. Her friend replied that on the contrary it was she who had saved her. The heroine's friend and the little girl were both right. Her rescue had indeed been a finite event and the heroine had saved her; but the little girl was also right, because with her eyes of faith, she had discerned the loving act of God within what had occurred. God had heard her prayer and by a miracle she had been saved.

On any understanding the rescue speaks of love. The eye of faith adds a "more" to what happened, infinite love speaking within the natural finite incident, reconfiguring what could have been a grim accident and making of it a transcendent moment. Love does that. It reconfigures things into gracious happenings.

To give a biblical example of this double action miracle, let me return to the agricultural illustration with which I started, our Rogation prayer for the farms of our parish, and refer to the horrifying agricultural disaster which is described by Joel (Joel 1:2–12; 2:3–11). Swarms of locusts were a regular threat—they still are, especially in some parts of Africa today and, due to global warming, are becoming an increasing problem. This swarm seems to have been a particularly devastating one. The locusts devoured every single plant there was. They were like an army, Joel said, their destructive impact so extreme, it felt like the end of time, a day of

---

* Kate Mosse, *The Burning Chambers* (London: Mantle, Macmillan, 2018), pp. 233–4, 242.

the Lord. We need a miracle, he said, if we are to survive. He called on the people to cry out to God and to fast and pray (Joel 1:13–20).

Jesus, in the Gospel accounts of his instructions about prayer, speaks of a similar urgency. He tells the story of a widow who was driving a judge to distraction by her constant pleading for justice. Eventually he was so worn down he gave her what she wanted (Luke 18:1–5). In another story, he tells of a man disturbing his neighbour one night by asking to borrow some bread to feed a late-coming guest at midnight! The laws of hospitality had overcome any embarrassment he might have had in rousing his neighbour, and he got his loaf (Luke 11:5–8). This is how we are to pray, our Lord says—provided we ask in a spirit of penitence and in accordance with God's will—with just such an urgency and trust.

Back to Joel! The people similarly had responded to Joel's advice and had called upon God. The disaster was the wrath of God, Joel said, which is the biblical way of saying that the moral parameters of the creation had been violated by idolatry and sin and that this had led to the mayhem they were experiencing. The people needed to repent. This to the modern ear sounds unreal, but it is what Joel and all his contemporaries thought. And it is surely telling that prophets today, the scientists who speak about the dangers of climate change, also urge a similar change of behaviour—that is, they attribute many of our current problems to the wrong ways in which we are treating the planet and insist that we change direction. This is what the biblical word "repentance" means. Change our ways, move in a new direction. Wholesale action is required, they tell us. Equally our intercession needs to be fervent, because we also need wisdom and guidance in the face of all the problems there are, especially if we doubt we can do much about them. The planetary problems are immense. Global warming advances inexorably. We need a miracle, many miracles! "Who knows,"* Joel asks, "whether God will not turn and relent, and leave a blessing behind him" (Joel 2:14,15–17). There is always in all situations the possibility, the hope, that something gracious might come about.

Joel knew that his community's prayer would be answered in some way, whether by his community being given strength to cope with the

---

* See also 2 Samuel 12:15–23 (David's prayer for his dying son); Esther 4:14 (Mordecai challenges Esther); Jonah 3:9 (God may change his mind).

disaster or even—might it be possible?—by the locusts being driven away. Whatever was to happen, in whatever way the Lord was to act, he knew that something would.

Ruth Burrows in conversation with Mark Allen told him that she had little time for explanations about how intercessory prayer might work.* She was content to see it as a mystery. That is how Joel thought. Like Ruth Burrows he was not interested in how the locusts might be removed, simply that they should be. As a support to his prayer, he recalled an earlier occasion when God had delivered the people. It had been in 681 BC, when Judea had been delivered from the Assyrians—in fact some commentators wonder whether Joel is using the locusts as a symbol for the Assyrians. The Assyrians under Sennacherib had laid siege to Jerusalem and when the city feared that all was lost, the army had suddenly upped camp and left. The story is told in the Bible twice (Isaiah 36–37 and 2 Kings 18–19). Isaiah, a soul-friend to the king like Nathan, had told Hezekiah that this was what was going to happen (2 Kings 19:6–7), that the troops would go because there would be a crisis back in Nineveh which would make it necessary. There are other explanations, even in the Bible (2 Kings 19:35), and there has been much theorizing since. The fact remains that the city experienced rescue. It was a remarkable finite event, maybe even a chance event, but as far as the people of Jerusalem were concerned it was far more than that. It was the infinite hand of God acting for them and granting them a miracle. Joel thought that if this had happened once, why should it not happen again?

The locusts had come from the north (Joel 2:20). This was unusual, as they usually swarmed in from the south. Joel says that they were like warriors, which meant he could compare the locusts to the Assyrians. And Joel's and his people's prayers were answered. Winds arose suddenly from either direction and swept the locusts away, some into the Dead Sea to the east and the rest into the Mediterranean where they drowned. Joel observed that their demise caused a massive stink (Joel 2:20–21). Again a finite natural event—but in it Joel and the people saw a possible disaster reconfigured into what to them was a miracle.

---

* Ruth Burrows and Mark Allen, *Letters on Prayer: An Exchange on Prayer and Faith* (London: Sheed & Ward, 1999), p. 32.

In the final part of the oracle, Joel speaks of the people being endowed with a new spirit. He uses the words which I have already quoted above (Joel 2:28–32). Similarly, we pray for help in the ordinary, sometimes severe crises that we face, and who knows whether there might be a miracle? But there might not be. There is always the problem as to why some intercessory prayers and petitions are answered and so many more are not—or not as we hoped!

Different answers to intercession

Jerusalem may have been saved from Sennacherib, but the Northern Kingdom was not. At that time the Jewish people were divided into two kingdoms, the larger one in the north with its capital in Samaria, and the smaller one, Judea, to the south. Some 20 years earlier, this Northern Kingdom had been conquered by the Assyrians and the population had been dragged away into slavery and exile. One kingdom was saved, the other was not.

The problem is no different today. People puzzle as to why it is that such disasters are allowed to occur. In the past, if there was a disaster, whether political or natural, it was attributed to the wrath of God, as a punishment for sin and failure. This is the explanation that was given when Lisbon was destroyed by a massive earthquake in 1755. Almost all preachers of the time saw it as a just punishment for the sin of the city. The French intellectual and writer Voltaire saw it very differently. He described it as an appalling aberration, an immoral and cruel act which showed that either God did not care or that he did not exist. Why, so many felt, had God not intervened? Why had God not responded to the people's desperate cries for help? Despite their prayers, the city was virtually razed to the ground.* The people were not saved.

We do not really know why. Over the centuries theologians and philosophers have puzzled over the problem and while no one has advanced a fully satisfactory explanation, they have explored a number

* Edward Paice, *Wrath of God: The Great Lisbon Earthquake of 1755* (London: Quercus, 2008).

of partial ones. Let me consider three of these theological arguments which may help a little: first, that God does not impugn the integrity of the creation by intervening or altering it in some way. Second, that as Love, God is unable to act in ways that compel people to obey his purpose. Third, that genuine and full recovery from any severe crisis needs time if our personhood is to be respected.

To consider the first of these; when—as was the case with the Northern Kingdom—a powerful army attacks a smaller one, the outcome is usually defeat for the latter. It is more a mystery when this does not happen. When tectonic plates clash in a direct line with Lisbon harbour, an earthquake and a tsunami are the natural results. It is what the "wrath of God" means, that the creation runs according to its own internal logic, and grievous events follow rules of cause and effect. The inhabitants of the Northern Kingdom were probably no more sinful than the people of the Southern, nor the inhabitants of Lisbon than those of anywhere else, but they were the ones who were in line with those powerful forces. As Jesus said of the 18 killed in Siloam when a tower fell onto them (Luke 13:1–5), it was not because they were greater sinners than anyone else. Such things happen, and the way to respond, Jesus said, noting our common humanity, is to learn from them and live in a penitent manner (Luke 13:5). Every crisis is a call to penitence and renewed discipline. The human sins and wickedness certainly do contribute to the problems we face, as Amos and Hosea were all too aware and why they were continually warning the Northern Kingdom about them. But their analysis was not a complete explanation, nor does it satisfactorily explain why one group of sinners should suffer more than another. Habakkuk thought the enemy his people were facing were probably just as bad as his own people; they may indeed have been worse (Habakkuk 1:12–17). We live, as Rachel Mann argues, in a precarious world which is full of threats and danger.* While the gospel assures us that God will do everything possible to help us, God is constrained both by loyalty to the integrity of the creation and by love.

This brings us to the second argument, that God is constrained by love. Love by its very nature is unable to compel things to happen by force

* Rachel Mann, *Love's Mysteries: The Body, Grief, Precariousness and God* (Norwich: Canterbury Press, 2020).

or manipulation. As Gregory of Nyssa once said, God does not have the power to make slaves of men and women.* Let me take an illustration from psychotherapy. Such personal work always has at its heart a deep respect for relationship. Christopher McKenna, a psychotherapist and at one time vicar of the parish of St Marylebone in London and in charge of the crypt healing centre there, gave a talk to a Guntrip Trust meeting I had organized in Dunblane. Freud's greatest contribution to personal therapy, he said, was to lead a spiritual revolution into a way of listening that maintained the value and meaning of the other so that like Christ and the mystics they could come to know themselves in being loved by another. Christ knew people who came to him in distress. He listened. He did not impose his solutions upon them. He listened and related to them, respecting them as persons; only then with their permission could he heal.

St Paul, reflecting on the three theological virtues, faith, hope and love, said that of the three, love was the greatest; love is in the last resort indestructible, far stronger than death and anything that might be thrown against it, but equally and paradoxically, utterly powerless. It cannot withstand the machinations of evil. Or at least, it appears that it cannot. In fact, the way love defeats evil is to allow it to do everything it can, even if that means death and destruction. Only then does love rise again, renewed in strength. Christ was tempted at the beginning of his ministry to opt for whatever alternatives there might be for saving the world (Matthew 4:1–11; Luke 4:1–13). He rejected them all, not just because none of them would work but because they were contrary to the way of love. As the cross demonstrates, God has to accept the "limitations" that love imposes on the Trinity. Love requires the way of the cross.

This has enormous implications for our prayer. God will not ignore the human freedom of the persons and situations for which we pray. God will not impose solutions upon them. But God will be with them—as God is with us—creating new possibilities in any situation. Recipients may find this in the short term both difficult and challenging, but in the end it will

* David Bentley Hart, *Atheist Delusions: The Christian Revolution and its Fashionable Enemies* (New Haven & London: Yale University Press, 2009), p. 179.

be for the better. It may not seem like that. The people we are praying for may not want to have challenges to face. We resist hard ways. Of course we do. Love can be very demanding. But it is the way.

George Herbert in his poem "Love III" wrote:

> Love bade me welcome: yet my soul drew back
> Guilty of dust and sin.

George Herbert was first of all struggling to accept whether it was true that God did love him. Many of us find this difficult to believe. It is often a long and arduous process of learning, to come to the point of recognizing that we really are loved and can be healed. If individual persons find this difficult, communities find it even harder. Only when there is security within a just and safe environment is it possible for real change to take place. All political attempts to impose solutions by force ultimately fail. In the short term, they may look successful, but they eventually collapse, because they lack the full consent of the people. Real change has to develop slowly and steadily from within.

Which bring us to the third argument! The story of Tobit (Tobit 3–12) is an illustration of how long a healing can take. Both Tobit himself and Sarah in their separate ways and at the same time prayed that they might be relieved of their pain by being allowed to die. At that very moment, the story goes, "the prayers of both of them were heard in the glorious presence of God" (Tobit 3:16). The angel Raphael was dispatched to deal with the crisis. It was to take some nine chapters of description before Raphael was actually able to bring about their healing. Our prayers are heard and acted upon, but it often takes a long time before a solution can be delivered; sometimes a very long time and sometimes not at all.

Let me take an illustration from Oliver Sacks's remarkable study *Awakenings.* His book is a description of what happened when patients in his New York neurological ward began to emerge from the sleeping sickness illness—*encephalitis lethargica*—that had developed among some of those who had been afflicted by the Spanish flu pandemic that killed so many after the First World War. A number who had initially recovered began to develop distressing aftereffects. Many of them relapsed into coma, a coma which was to last for years. This was because the disease had deprived their brains of dopamine, and in the mid-war years there was no known way of treating this. Towards the end of the 1960s, a new treatment, L-Dopa, was discovered. When it was given to patients, the effect was astonishing. They suddenly "awoke"—hence the title of the book. One of them, who had been comatose for 20 years, suddenly leapt out of bed and in joyful triumph paraded up and down the ward exclaiming with delight.* Her nurses were dumbfounded. All Sacks' patients were "awakened", but only a few of them actually recovered. After varying periods of time, they encountered what Sacks calls "tribulations", hidden problems of one sort and another that only became apparent once the initial excitement of awakening had subsided. All of them faced alarming upheavals in their thinking and new and dispiriting challenges which they found very hard to cope with. They would eventually come to an "accommodation", as Sacks puts it, which varied with each patient. Some recovered almost completely. Others made the best they could of things. Others again were quite unable to process the possibilities and quietly slipped back into illness. Towards the end of the book Sacks comments on this. He suggests that for those who did not recover, their healing had become "incompossible".** In other words, they might have been able to recover if there had been just one problem—in their relationships, their inner beings—but it became impossible when there were so many more. Embracing recovery was too much for them. Much as we might wish our problems to be zapped away, as if removed by divine diktat, it is rare that they actually can be without causing far more problems in the process. Trying to solve a problem too early does more damage than it resolves. Persons, because they are persons, need respect. All this is very suggestive about much of the prayer we offer for persons and situations. Sometimes what we pray for simply cannot be resolved immediately. Sometimes it cannot be solved at all. If it could be, the freedom and humanity of the people and situations we are praying for would be compromised. We are not robots, automatons which can be programmed to respond correctly. We are persons, who respond to love. As Oliver Sacks says at the very

---

* Oliver W. Sacks, *Awakenings* (London: Pelican Books, 1976), p. 127.

** Sacks, *Awakenings*, p. 310.

end of his book, healing someone, making them whole, is in the final analysis an achievement of Love.*

If this is true of persons, it is equally true of countries. The factors which prevent the growth and development of a corporate entity like a whole country can be intractable. Recovery from disaster, as we can see from history, is very hard, but it does happen—perhaps not back to what the situation was before, but into something new and creative. Jeremiah when he wrote to the exiles after the destruction of Jerusalem told them that they must live full lives where they were now living and be encouraged by his prophecy that in 70 years they would return to their own land (Jeremiah 29). There is nothing in the Bible to say what happened to the Israelites who were dispersed to Assyria other than that they were moved into what is now northern Syria (2 Kings 17:6), but we know that the Babylonian exiles, as Jeremiah counselled them to expect, did return. And in the long experience of exile, they had made something immensely creative out of what had happened to them. They had forged a new understanding of their faith. Some returned to Jerusalem and started again, others stayed where they were, others went elsewhere. Over the centuries the Jewish diaspora has made incalculable contributions to the wellbeing of the rest of the world, often at immense cost to themselves. They have often conferred a blessing wherever they have settled.

The destruction of Lisbon was so severe that many at the time thought the city should be abandoned, as so many other cities throughout history have been. Had it not been for Sebastião Carvalho (later the Marquês de Pombal), it might indeed have been. As David Ferguson says, commenting on those who saw the earthquake as a divine punishment, it was surely better to see God's will being done in what Pombal and others did in shoring up the defences and attending to the wounded than in the earthquake itself.** Pombal's statue presides over the grand Avenida da Liberdade that leads into central Lisbon and bears witness to this truth.

This still leaves us with many questions, not least questions as to whether life does need to be quite so difficult. We might think especially

* Sacks, *Awakenings*, p. 327.

** David Ferguson, *The Providence of God: A Polyphonic Approach* (Cambridge: Cambridge University Press, 2018), p. 330.

of those sleeping sickness sufferers who fell ill once again, or of peoples like the Palestinians whose problems seem to go on for ever. Like the psalmists they might well plead with God that God should do something about it:

> Rise up! Why sleep, O Lord? * Awake, and do not reject us for ever
> Why do you hide your face * and forget our grief and oppression?
> Our soul is bowed down to the dust * our belly cleaves to the earth.
> Rise up, O Lord, to help us * and redeem us for the sake of your steadfast love (Psalm 44:24–27, Common Worship Psalter).

It is then not surprising that people often speak of God as not answering their prayer. Pete Greig, the Surrey Independent Church pastor, has written about this in his book *God on Mute*, which has the subtitle *Engaging the Silence of Unanswered Prayer*. I am not sure whether he himself thinks that prayer goes unanswered or whether he is addressing what many so often believe. In fact, he gives clear and wide-ranging arguments as to why so much of our prayer does appear to be unanswered. The book is bravely built around the tragic illness of his wife Sammy, who suddenly became sick with a brain tumour. He gives ample evidence of the many ways God responded to their urgent prayer. He begins with his own immediate response, then speaks of the actions of the ambulance crew, the doctors, nurses, hospital, and all the many others who came to their help–and up to a point successfully. She recovered but was left with difficult problems to contend with. Much later, on an occasion when Sammy had recovered from one of the intermittent attacks she suffered from, Greig comments that this was the very first time they had seen an actual physical effect as a result of their prayer.* Maybe his emphasis here is on what they both saw as a first sign of direct action by our Lord, but given his testimony throughout the book, their prayers I would have thought had been answered again and again many times already. Many of us do think that God is mute, even the psalmists rail against God for being asleep, but–to continue Greig's title metaphor–it is not so much that

* Pete Greig, *God on Mute: Engaging the Silence of Unanswered Prayer* (Colorado Springs, CO: David C. Cook, 2020), p. 174.

God is mute, it is more that our audio equipment is inferior. We cannot underestimate the sense of abandonment that many have, especially in the later years of life—as Christ himself experienced on the cross—but the reality is that God is with us however little we feel or experience in bad times. In fact, the reality is that God always answers our prayer.

On a personal note, throughout our married life, my wife Joy and I also prayed for her healing from a debilitating mental illness. She was not healed of it, but our eyes were constantly opened to the many ways that our Lord was in fact both answering our prayer and accompanying us through the hard times. We found our lives opened up to futures we had not in any way envisaged. In fact, we often don't know what we should pray for, as St Paul teaches when writing to the Romans (Romans 8:26). It is probably important that we don't. If we did, we might become blind to the gracious responses that we do in fact receive. It is a matter of our eyes being opened, our ears unstopped. Many of Jesus's healings were to do with precisely this, with opening the eyes of the blind so that they could see and the ears of the deaf so they could hear.

There are two main ways in which our prayers are always answered. First, by Christ's promise that he will always be with us (Matthew 28:20); second, by God giving us grace and the Holy Spirit to strengthen us for the way.

The writer to the Hebrews was deeply conscious of this when he wrote about Jesus's experience of praying for deliverance in the garden of Gethsemane. The writer says that:

> Jesus offered up prayers and supplications with loud cries and tears to the one who was able to save him from death, and he was heard because of his reverent submission (Hebrews 5:7).

An agonizing prayer! But, the author notes, he was heard! There was no possibility that Jesus could be saved from the way of the cross. Yet he was heard, and God was with him in the person of the angel agonizing with him. The first answer to all of our prayer is this promise, that God in Christ will hear us and he will be with us—always!

Moses too prayed earnestly for this, that God's presence might be with him. He was the leader of his band of desert wanderers and was constantly harassed by their behaviour. He told God that if help was not forthcoming, it would be beyond his strength to continue:

> [The Lord] said, "My presence will go with you, and I will give you rest." And [Moses] said to him, "If your presence will not go, do not carry us up from here . . . " The Lord said to Moses, "I will do the very thing that you have asked, for you have found favour in my sight, and I know you by name." (Exodus 33:14–15,17)

God strengthens us with the Holy Spirit to live through whatever or wherever our vocation requires us to go. At the end of the Lukan parables about intercession, referred to above, Jesus assures his listeners that if they ask for something, provided that what they ask for is in line with God's will, he will hear their prayer. The important thing is that we are heard, that God remains with us, and that God gives us the Holy Spirit to strengthen us for the way (Luke 11:13). There is no greater answer to prayer than that.

In reading so far, you first accompanied our parish of Ovingham when we were giving thanks at our Eucharist and interceding for the farms one Rogation Sunday. You were then with us celebrating the Ascension, reflecting on its twofold themes of Christ's rule and his intercession for us at the right hand of God: then at Pentecost, where we were thinking of being empowered by the Holy Spirit and of the different gifts identified by St Paul which we were being given. Our prayers were also that such gifts might endow the leaders of the world whoever and wherever they were. Let me rehearse the gifts once more: wisdom, the humility to accept good counsel, invigorating faith, courage to reflect creatively on the insights of prophets, vision to find fresh ways of overcoming society's ills—with a willingness to receive ideas which might improve our corporate living—and readiness to be open to the possibility of change. Sometimes the Lord will grant us a miracle. Most of the time, because of the several reasons explored above and more, much of what we pray for will not happen as we might have hoped—or not as immediately as we had hoped. Nonetheless, Christ accompanies us as ascended Lord whatever our situation, holding the world and each of us in his love before God. Despite our doubts and fears, the Lord responds, Christ accompanies us and God strengthens us by giving us the Holy Spirit.

Preparing the petitions

Using the vignettes

How we pray our intercessions is a telling indicator of what we as a Church are really concerned about. Are we hiding away from the needs of the world, escaping into a safe and more comfortable haven? Or are we instead obeying God's call and in following Christ along the way of the cross, praying with him for the world that God loves?

When we come to prepare for an intercession in the Eucharist—which is the first concern of this book, though the principles also apply to any personal intercessions—there are two aspects to the task: knowing what we should pray for and the actual prayers we use to accompany these petitions. This book is about the first of these, preparing the petitions. For the prayers there are templates already provided. *Common Worship* offers several alternatives and there are further suggestions in the books listed in the bibliography. It is important to note that these templates are not all that long (about 200 words, see the introduction) and that any petitions we prepare should not be too much longer. We must resist the temptation to use too many words or, worse, preach a mini sermon.

Intercession, as I have been exploring, is fundamentally the work of the ascended Lord. The Christ represents his concerns and love for the world before the Father. Our intercessions are then our sharing in this love and concern, that God's will may be done and the kingdom come. It is an exercise of cooperation with a loving God who longs to heal and strengthen us. Our intercessions are our response to Christ's original proclamation, that the kingdom of God is near (Mark 1:15). We pray the Lord's Prayer petition—"Your kingdom come, your will be done". We may well expand this by using terms like justice and peace and the Common Good as synonyms; essentially we are still praying for the kingdom in a general way. We can also expand our prayer by offering specific petitions.

—

Walter Brueggemann in his reflections on the prophetic imagination speaks of the kingdom of God as an alternative to what he calls the "totalist" world of those in power, those who are content to have the fundamental ordering of things remain as they are.* There is a constant tension between the world as it is now and the world as it will be when the kingdom has fully come. Meanwhile, it stands as a visionary expression of an almost unimaginable future that will only finally come as a gift from God. When we pray for specific concerns, we are looking to expand our understanding of what the kingdom of God is.

Jesus himself was aware how difficult it was for his disciples to understand his teaching about the kingdom. He did it mainly by healing the sick and by telling stories. These opened their eyes and ears to a beginning of understanding. The healings were powerful events which brought the hugeness and reality of the kingdom as an end point of history into manageable focus. If we apply this to our prayer, by focusing on some specific concern, we are also able to envisage the possibility of seeing things happen that illustrate the kingdom. It is what journalists do when writing about an international situation. They focus on one family for example, or a small incident, to help the reader grasp what is otherwise too large and complex. Let me give some examples to illustrate this: the first when we do not know what to pray for, the second, when we perhaps do.

Dorothy Day (Week 26) once commented after visiting a convent of nuns during the Vietnam War, that given the depth of their corporate relationship with God, she wished they had at least formed some intention, even if they did not know precisely what they should pray for.** They probably knew little about Vietnam. Still, they would have known about the effects of war, that atrocities occur. They might well have known too of the Buddhist and Catholic presence there, very probably

---

* Walter Brueggemann, *The Prophetic Imagination*, 40th anniversary edn (Minneapolis, MN: Fortress Press, 2018).

** Dorothy Day, *The Duty of Delight: The Diaries of Dorothy Day*, ed. Robert Ellsberg (Milwaukee, WI: Marquette University Press, 2008), p. 383.

the latter, and prayed for these communities. It so happened that during the Vietnam War, the Buddhist monk Thich Nhat Hanh was in the States. He was one of those who persuaded Martin Luther King (Week 33) to preach his important Riverside sermon against the war; a real concern for the kingdom.* A petition referring to persons, Christians and Buddhists already working for peace in Vietnam makes for a good intention.

A second example is from the Greece, Turkey and Cyprus vignette (Week 42). I spent some of my National Service in Cyprus and for that reason pray about the island often. There is peace between Greece and Turkey at the moment, but the tension between the two peoples goes back centuries and finds contemporary expression in Cyprus. Because of it, the island has been divided into two for the past 50 years, the Turkish and Greek communities being kept well apart by a barrier maintained by the United Nations. We might indeed want to pray in a general way for a solution to this problem, but we could add to the prayer if we were to pray for something specific. The reality now is that half the community would like the division to remain permanent while the other half would like it to end. Effecting either course is a political decision.

During the Second World War, the Archbishop of Canterbury William Temple used when praying for peace to ask that God's will should be done. In contrast the Archbishop of York Cyril Garbett had no qualms about confronting God directly with the demand that God give victory to the Allies. Very much in the spirit of some of the psalmists! We do have these situations when we feel sure of where God's will lies and pray accordingly—especially in our personal prayer. In the Second World War, it seemed pretty clear, as it was when Russia invaded Ukraine in 2022, but in most situations opinion is divided. This is certainly true in a congregation. Our petitions have to be sensitive to that.

In the Cypriot context, I personally pray that the island might become one once more—as Hayriye says (quoted below), it is a small island—but in the corporate situation, given the difference of opinion, it may be wiser to present the dilemma as it is. It was like this during our EU referendum;

---

* "A Time to Break Silence", in James M. Washington (ed.), *A Testament of Hope: The Essential Writings of Martin Luther King, Jr.* (London: Harper & Row, 1986), pp. 231–4.

the intercessions were not the place to tell the congregation how they should vote, whatever we might have thought personally. We need to reach through to the deeper spiritual issues, to that point when UN forces are no longer needed and Greek and Turkish Cypriots have learnt to appreciate and value each other. Those are the spiritual challenges whatever political decision is eventually made, the coming together of the two communities. As I describe in the vignette, in Nicosia there is a Home of Cooperation dedicated precisely to this vision of the two peoples becoming one. This is an initiative we can always pray for. It adds a reality to the prayer because it is where the Holy Spirit is already at work and, in so praying, we are supporting those already striving on the front line. If we don't have this kind of information, there is the internet to help us. Others may know of Cypriots in the community—to add a local reference. Another may have read Elif Shafak's novel *The Island of Missing Trees* and could glean ideas from that.* Using such knowledge in a careful way adds a dash of salt to the petitions we are presenting.

Intercession is a spiritual exercise which addresses the fundamentals of life. We are called to cooperate with God, aligning ourselves with Christ's prayer, that God's will may be done. The prayer penetrates to the roots of needs, to the depths of their unconscious, that God might awaken the hearts of their personhood towards the good. The spiritual gifts, explored in the previous chapter, are particular things we might ask for: that leaders may be wise; that they may have the humility to accept good advice; that they may be faithful to their vocation to lead; that they may be courageous in the face of the task before them, open to the insights of the prophets in their country, and anyone with vision, as to the wisest course ahead. They may also hope for a miracle, though I suspect congregations might jib at hearing this put into words. Perhaps above all, that those for whom we pray may be aware of the presence of God within them, in whatever way they might understand that. In the present climate, where false news and propaganda is such a problem, we might also pray for an end to false witness (Exodus 20:16) and that truth might prevail, remembering also those brave people who strive for truth at great personal cost to themselves.

* Elif Shafak, *The Island of Missing Trees* (London: Viking Penguin, 2021).

It is important not to be discouraged. Just because what we ask for is not immediately answered in the way we hoped does not mean it is never going to be. There may be things we need to do, we may need to wait, be open to surprise, or it may indeed be that our prayer has already been answered and we failed to notice it. We are to trust! Cooperate with and wait upon God!

As a coda to all this, if we look at Eucharistic intercession generally, we cannot fail to notice that intercessors tend to offer general intentions when they pray for the world and specific ones when they pray for the sick. Sick persons are usually prayed for by name. Rarely do we hear prayers for wider health concerns, for those who lead departments of health for example, or for the National Health Service as a whole. It is good to pray for the sick by name, but it is good also to pray for health generally. Equally, when we pray for peace in the world, it is good to add specific concerns.

—

The vignettes are also designed to help in two other ways: to build our intercessions round a particular country or region, or alternatively to build them on an appropriate theme. I must remind the reader to refer back to what I said about the vignettes in the introduction: they are not lists of what we are to pray for, or even descriptions of countries and their problems—apart from the short accounts in the information box, which explain where the countries are, the population of each in July 2022 rounded up to the nearest half million (under a million to the nearest 100), their main religious affiliations and some brief historical notes—but are personal associations with different parts of the world.* They are mine so some of them are personal. Inevitably if you were to make your own, they would be different. Sometimes the vignettes will seem relevant, at other times they won't—situations change! Where the

* United Nations, World population by country, <https://worldpopulationreview.com>, accessed 4 September 2022. For up-to-date figures refer to this website, which is constantly updated. The religious affiliation figures, where they are included, are from the same source.

vignettes do stimulate your powers of association then they will have done what they are meant to do.

To take the first approach, when I came to think about the Caucasus region (Week 28) the only association I could think of was that I had once worked with an Azerbaijani, Russian-speaking interpreter. Others may have read Nino Haratischvili's novel *The Eighth Life*, been on holiday there, or perhaps have Armenian or Georgian relatives.* We don't have refugees from the Caucasus in Newcastle as far as I know, but there must have been many who were devastated by the wars in Chechnya, the Russian incursions into the Georgian provinces of South Ossetia and Abkhazia, and the more recent quarrel over the Nagorno Karabakh Armenian enclave in Azerbaijan. We could remember the internal refugees who have suffered in these and similar conflicts. This in its turn might encourage us to pray for a greater understanding between the different peoples and ethnicities who live there, one of the major themes of this book. We might then be moved—in the opening section of the Eucharist intercession—to pray for the Georgian Orthodox Church, the Armenian Apostolic Church or the Azerbaijani *Ummah*; when thinking of the last, this might open up further possibilities of prayer for dialogue, that there should be a growing understanding between the different great faiths—another major theme of the book. We could then refer to our own country's attitude toward refugees who seek asylum here; Kurds and Iranians from just south of the Caucasus for example are numerous in the Northeast. These are suggestions. They cannot all be prayed for. We have to be selective. A link to the local community is valuable though and why in most of the vignettes I have pointed to some connection to the Northeast where there is one. And here it is good to be specific, to mention a particular agency that is working for example with refugees, in our case the West End Refugee Service, or perhaps the local branch of "Freedom from Torture". Best to mention only one of these and leave the others for a later date!

Turning to the theme approach, the theme index shows where each of these is to be found. They are obviously not tied to a particular region. Say

---

* Nino Haratischvili, *The Eighth Life (for Brilka)*, trans. Charlotte Collins and Ruth Martin (London: Scribe Publications, 2014).

we turn to the Iran vignette (Week 39), where the theme is the spiritual journey, the *Sufi* one in particular. A day or two before I was writing this, we had a baptism in our church of a young Iranian woman and her daughter. We have a wonderful ethnic mix in our congregation, as is now more generally the case in the Northeast—with a large number of Iranians among them—and a theme like this opens the possibility of praying not only for the spiritual journey of the two of them, but also for ongoing dialogue between Christianity and Islam. Referring back to the Caucasus vignette and its discussion of the counselling of asylum seekers, there are further ideas to be gleaned from that. We do not have to say too much, just enough to focus the prayer. We then hold them in the presence of God. Sometimes in silence, especially if a situation is beyond words. Each vignette ends with a simple prayer, the first part of which is virtually the same each time. The second is built around the theme.

Praying like that provides an alternative to praying the News. We have to be a little wary of doing this anyway. The News tends to concentrate on crises. Sometimes the Church does so too. Take the EU referendum again. We prayed hard about this when the poll was actually upon us, very little if at all in the lead up. Of course we have to hold crises in prayer, but better if we pray also about them before they reach catastrophic proportions. Who knows? Our prayer might contribute to a better outcome.

And let us be brief. We do not have to say too much. As our Lord says, prayer does not require a multitude of words (Matthew 6:7). No need to fear that we might leave something out. When we pray for the one, we pray for the many. Equally, when we pray generally, we pray for the specific.

In the space where I pray at home, the cross on the *prie-dieu* was one that used to be in my father's chapel. Before that it had been in the chapel of the Anglican spiritual director Reginald Somerset-Ward, who wrote his books under the pseudonym "the Author of the Way". Written on the pedestal are the words: "Remember with thanksgiving E. S., whose gifts as teacher and intercessor were offered to God in this Church." E. S., so my father told me, prayed for one concern alone. Just as E. S. was praying for the one, she was also praying for the many.

As we look round the world at this time—at any time—there are so many problems: to name a few current ones, the division of Cyprus into two sectors, the same in Korea, the problematic relationship of Taiwan with China, the incursions of Russia into its neighbours, the tension between India and Pakistan (and China) over Kashmir, the debacle in Afghanistan, the Middle East divisions between Jew and Arab, between Sunni and Shia at the time of writing, crushing the Yemen and elsewhere, the tensions in the Sudan and South Sudan and so many more troubles in Africa; and if to these we add the rise of populism and extreme politicians of the far right and extreme left, the problems are immense. Above all, there is the challenge of climate change. Every church in its prayer has a contribution to make.

In using this book, I think a church might gain by using the weekly cycle over a year as a spiritual exercise. Other churches might want to select a particular week, perhaps on a monthly basis, or because a particular part of the world is important to a member of the congregation. For the elderly with more time on their hands for prayer, a widening intercession is a major contribution they can make.

Ovingham is a small village in Northumberland. It is hardly the centre of the universe except for those who live there, and even they recognize that it is in a fairly distant part of England. The position is not very different from that of a young girl in Nazareth when the Lord called her to become the mother of the Christ. Where we happen to live is of little importance. Wherever it is, this is where we are to pray and live out our faith however small our contribution might seem to be. As our Lord explained in his parable of the mustard seed (Matthew 13:31–32; Mark 4:30–32; Luke 13:18–19), it is amazing what can grow from a tiny seed. Who knows what our prayer might contribute?

1

China 1

Week after Advent Sunday

Population: 1 billion, 426 million in July 2022. Communism is the current ideology governing the State. Confucianism (named after the founding sage K'ung Ch'iu) and Daoism (Lao Tzu) are the traditional underlying philosophies that inform the Chinese vision. There is a long Buddhist history, a growing Christian community and a large Muslim presence. The Anglican Church in China (Chung Hua Sheng Kung Hui) no longer exists, though there are still a few churches. See Week 24 for Hong Kong and Taiwan.

Morning prayer in Urumqi

Hans Küng, in his magisterial studies of the great monotheistic faiths, states:

> No peace among the nations
> without peace among the religions.
> No peace among the religions
> without dialogue between the religions.
> No dialogue between the religions
> without investigation of the foundations of the religions.*

* Hans Küng, *Judaism: The Religious Situation of Our Time*, trans. John Bowden (London: SCM Press, 1992), Frontispiece.

Add to this Stephen O'Shea's understanding of *convivencia*,* the Spanish word which carries the meaning of social harmony better than its English equivalent, "conviviality"—as Ivan Illich noted in using the English word in his writing, conviviality tends to imply public house banter; Illich hoped its Spanish meaning of autonomous persons who are creative and interdependent in their relationships would prevail when they read him about it. *Convivencia*, he said, is about ethics and value within community.** O'Shea similarly uses it of the capacity of peoples of different faiths to exist, mingle and live together in harmony—so a fundamental word for this book. It describes how people of different faiths and understandings might live in harmony with each other—an issue of enormous importance in Urumqi.

Urumqi is the capital of Xinjiang in the far northwest of China. Xinjiang has been part of China since 1894 and, straddling the Silk Road as it does, it has for centuries been the link and border province between east and west. The three main faiths of the constantly invaded region have been Buddhism, Islam and now Communism. Islam is the dominant faith of the Central Asian Uighur people whose home it is. Urumqi is a city of 2 million people, small by Chinese standards, but vast by ours. Its position has become increasingly important to the government, concerned as it is to develop its relations with other parts of the world beyond its western frontier.

Two months before my arrival in October 2009, there had been a serious riot in the city. A number had been killed, mainly Han Chinese, but Uighurs as well. In recent years, central government in Beijing has been encouraging Han immigration to the region, especially to Urumqi, as part of its policy of making the regime more Chinese. With the rise of Wahhabism, the strict Muslim teaching attributed to Ibn Abd al-Wahhab (1703–92), and the development of the ISIS caliphate in parts of the Middle East, they feared growing trouble from the Uighur peoples, who are largely Muslim. They thought a hostile indigenous people would seriously hamper their purpose. Since these 2009 riots, and trouble

* Stephen O'Shea, *Sea of Faith: Islam and Christianity in the Medieval Mediterranean World* (London: Profile Books, 2006), p. 6.

** Ivan Illich, *Tools for Conviviality* (London: Calder & Boyars, 1973), p. 11.

before, the government started to implement a much harsher policy towards the Uighur population, not so much to try and persuade them as to force them to comply.* Thousands have been interned into what are called "Vocational Training Centres", with the underlying aim of compelling the people to abandon their Islamic faith—because it is equated with terrorism—and embrace instead the Communist vision. Observers reckoned that by 2020 the centres were housing up to a million of the Uighur people and that they were less schools of vocation than centres of aggressive evangelism—to use another theological word to match the government's use of "vocation". Vocational training is properly defined in its secular usage as a way of identifying and equipping people with particular skills for jobs; it can in no way be used to describe the intimidation of a people into some pre-determined ideological groove. Nor is it in any way congruent with the Confucian vision of the Golden Rule—"In everything do to others as you would have them do to you" (Matthew 7:12; Luke 6:31)—which counsels kindness and concern for the other. Some think the Golden Rule was first summarized by Confucius as the right way of grasping the *li*, which is the "code of practice" or principles of appropriate behaviour marked by courtesy, kindness and deep respect, the standard of behaviour expected of every Chinese citizen. As it is, it is hard to imagine that the Chinese government policy of the last decade will succeed in its endeavour. It might be superficially effective in the short term, but not in the long. Indeed, it is far more likely to have the opposite effect, of enhancing the Uighur people in their Muslim faith.

Things were not so bad in 2009. I was staying at the Peacock Hotel in the centre of the city. A little way from the hotel, at a crossroads on the way to the nearby Renmin Park, there was a command post, a small detachment of armed soldiers standing in readiness. An American friend told me he found this a comforting presence. I cannot say I did. This was the only sign I saw of the earlier troubles.

It is my custom when abroad to say Morning Prayer in a park, if there is one. In England and Europe generally, going to such a park is a quiet

---

* Ian Evans, *Stop the 21st Century Holocaust: The Plight of the Uyghur in Modern China* (Middletown: DE, 2019).

experience. What company there is comes from the wildlife, birds flying among the greenery and pecking at my feet, squirrels darting about. Such a park is a *carmel* in Hebrew, a garden of peace in which persons can pray and perhaps experience a glimpse of heavenly things. Not quite like that in Urumqi. I walked there with my prayer book to find that most of Urumqi had gathered there before me. In the green space immediately beyond the gate, there was a small corps of men engaged in drill, a little further in another group were being led in the balletic movements of T'ai chi, and yet another were doing Aikido. I thought some kind of harangue was developing to my right, until it was received with applause and then song—perhaps a choir practice going well. Further into the park there was a covered walkway, a bit like a Swiss bridge, zigzagging in the Chinese fashion, each corner occupied by a single person or group taken up with a craft or exercise; someone singing, a few engaging in conversation, everyone doing something. Eventually I found a quiet bench. I was joined there by another old gentleman, a Muslim no doubt, the two of us sitting together, an oasis of quiet amidst the hubbub. It was our gentle contribution to the morning's cacophony of praise. It included my own sotto voce singing of the Benedictus: that as "children" of God on our different paths and called to prepare God's way we might know the tender compassion of God, the dawn from on high, breaking upon us–and I pray, especially upon the Uighur people.

Let us pray for the people and leaders of China, for the peoples of different faiths called to live together, and especially for ethnic minorities, the Uighur people of Xinjiang in particular, that we may all align our purposes with the Way towards Heaven.

2

Brazil

Week after Advent 2

Brazil's population is 215.5 million. The majority are Christian, about 65 per cent Roman Catholics according to official figures, 22 per cent Protestants. Some witnesses think that the latter, largely Pentecostal, will soon equal or outnumber the Roman Catholics. The Episcopal Anglican Church of Brazil is made up of nine dioceses. From the sixteenth century, the country was ruled by Portugal, becoming independent in 1822 and a Presidential Republic in 1889. A military junta ruled from 1964 until 1985 when democracy returned. The Amazon Rainforest, described by one commentator as "the lungs of the world", is currently subject to constant depredation.

Blessed are you who are poor, for yours is the kingdom of God

In the late 1970s and early 80s, when I was Priest in Charge of Ryhope (in Sunderland), two of my colleagues and I used to meet on a monthly basis for prayer and support. In time, we formed a group called SPINE (Spirituality in the North East) and from 1982, for three years, came together for prayer on Holy Island during the week of prayer for Christian unity. This led us to organize another project, this time a prayer pilgrimage through the poorer parts of Newcastle and Gateshead. We took the theme of the desert in the city ending up in what was then the gaunt ruin of St Mary's Church in Gateshead. The church still stands high on the banks of the Tyne next to the Tyne Bridge. At that time, it presented a sorry sight. It had almost burnt down a year or so before. An African priest who accompanied us on the day commented, "It is not the custom in my country to leave a dead body lying in the street". We had taken Hélder Câmara's book *The Desert is Fertile* as our inspiration for the day.*

Hélder Câmara at the time was nearing the end of his ministry as Archbishop of Olinda and Recife in Brazil. He had been the bishop there since 1964, had been a strong voice in Vatican II, and by this stage had become internationally known for his writings on Liberation Theology and its application to the needs of the poor. Locally he was known as the Bishop of the Slums. When he was first ordained bishop, he was sent as an auxiliary to the diocese of Rio de Janeiro. It was there, among the *favelas* of Rio, that he began to appreciate both the dignity and the needs of the poor. In 1959, he opened a bank in the cathedral. It was an early precursor of the micro-credit movement which Muhammad Yunus was to start in Bangladesh some 20 years later (see Week 43). The idea was to make loans so that the poor could free themselves from the slavery of destitution.

One day in Recife, Bishop Hélder was presiding over a special Mass. In one of the prayers addressed to Mary, he used the West African term for her name, "Mariama". He used it to honour the people in the congregation whose ancestors had come to Brazil from West Africa so many years before as slaves. He was aware how many there were in the wider community who opposed his concern for the poor, and he addressed this opposition in his sermon: "Mariama, they will say, Mariama, that it is politics, that it's subversion, that it's Communism. It is not," he said. "It is the Gospel of Christ, Mariama."** His concern for the poor was palpable. He was concerned not only to meet their needs; he sought also to honour and value their grace in knowing how to live the simple life.

Hélder Câmara was born in Fortaleza, a city to the north of the two adjoining cities of Recife and Olinda, which are in the northeast of Brazil. It is one of the poorer parts of the country, the region to which many of the slaves transported by Portugal were first brought. There are far too many

---

* Hélder Câmara, *The Desert is Fertile*, trans. Dinah Livingstone (London: Sheed & Ward Ltd, 1974).

** Margaret Hebblethwaite, "Liberating Mary", *The Tablet*, 12 December 2020, p. 7.

of their successors still trying to scratch a decent living there, struggling in impoverished circumstances to survive. Bishop Câmara once told a group of European Union MPs that if he had been an archbishop in Europe, his pastoral policy might have been different, but in Recife it had to be about the rights and needs of the poor.

The Brazilian writer Clarice Lispector, when she first arrived in Brazil, also came to the northeast. She and her Jewish parents lived in Alagoas, to the south of Recife near to Maceiô. They had fled from Ukraine, victims of the devastating famine of the 1920s there. In her last novella, *Hour of the Star*, she dedicated the book to her own early experience of poverty, describing her heroine, Macabéa—also from Alagoas—as also desperately poor.* Macabéa is excessively thin, not an attractive woman, and she judged herself to be both incompetent and thoroughly out of date. She did not really know who she was, Lispector writes. She held on to the fantasy that one day she might become a film star. She reflected that people ought to be happy, so she determined that she indeed would be. There is a real sense in the novel that in her simplicity she did find a way to be so. She is "befriended" by an aggressive young man called Olimpico, also from the northeast. He treats her badly and then leaves her for her best friend. The male narrator asks himself why it is that he should write about such a girl when her poverty could surely be of no appeal or interest. He reflects that it is perhaps because he saw within her a sense of the holy. At the end of the book, Macabéa has a serious road accident. As she is lying in the road, slowly dying, she reflects that to die like this felt like a summation of all that life had been like for her, a truth of what she had gone through. As people gathered around her, she understood that now at last she had become a star, that she was who she was. She had found the life of God that was within her.** She had experienced resurrection in the silence at the end of her poverty-stricken way!

The northeast of England, rather like the northeast of Brazil—whose people, like the Geordies, speak with a lilt to their voice—is a poorer part of our country. Since our pilgrimage reflecting on this very point,

---

* Clarice Lispector, *Hour of the Star*, trans. Benjamin Moser (London: Penguin Classics, 2014).

** Lispector, *Hour of the Star*, pp. 14 and 74.

St Mary's Gateshead has been restored and brought back to life. Not as a church, though it still looks very much like one and therefore still speaks of the presence of God. After restoration, it first became an antique store—the clock face still records the antique dealer's name—and now at the time of writing it is the Gateshead Tourist and Information Centre. The Sage Concert Hall stands opposite. I attended a conference there on the health of the city, especially of poor people affected by mental health issues. The church that was so ruined had become a restored place concerned for the needs of Gateshead/Newcastle and for its poor. Elsewhere in Gateshead and in Newcastle Cathedral, visible just across the river, the Church's spiritual and prayerful concern continues. As Hélder Câmara observed, the desert remains fertile.

Let us pray for the people and leaders of Brazil, and especially for all who live in material poverty, those enslaved by torment but maintaining the dignity of their being, that we may live graciously, simply and share together the goods of our world.

3

Denmark (Greenland and Faroes), Iceland, Norway and Sweden

Week after Advent 3

Denmark's population is just under 6 million, and its autonomous regions are Greenland (56,500) and the Faroe Islands (53,100). Iceland's population is 373,000, Norway's 5.5 million, Sweden's 10.5 million. Seventy per cent and more are Lutheran, and since the Porvoo agreement of 1992 the Lutheran churches of Sweden, Norway and Denmark have been in communion with the Anglican churches in Europe. As a result, Newcastle diocese for example has links with the diocese of Møre in Norway. In the medieval period, the Scandinavian nations were ruled as one. There have been variations since: Iceland for example, always self-ruling, separated from Denmark in 1944, Norway from Sweden in 1905. All are kingdoms apart from Iceland. Sweden and Denmark are in the European Union with their own currencies; Iceland and Norway are not.

Diplomacy and reconciliation

It was 18 September 1961. I was standing in Stockton-on-Tees High Street looking at a placard; "Hammarskjöld dead", it said. I was profoundly shocked. Dag Hammarskjöld at the time was Secretary General of the United Nations and had been trying to bring some kind of solution to the crisis in the Congo following its sudden independence in 1960. With Pope John XXIII in the Vatican, the two of them had seemed to be offering fresh visions of hope to our world, the one in effect as a secular pope working for peace, the other the spiritual visionary who in 1963 was to publish his encyclical *Pacem in Terris.** Hammarskjöld died in a plane crash in Ndola in what was then Northern Rhodesia (Zambia) just outside the Congo pedicle, not far from Elizabethville (Lubumbashi). Every so often there has been speculation as to whether his plane was shot down. At the time most observers thought it was an accident. A library in nearby Kitwe—the Mindolo Ecumenical Centre—stands as a memorial to him.

Thirteen years later, Joy and I were in Sweden. We had sailed from Newcastle by the ferry that used to ply its way to Oslo, and from there went by train to Stockholm. Joy's aunt, Tante Ulla, had been born in nearby Uppsala, as had Hammarskjöld, and they had not only been in the same school, but in the same class. I did not get the impression she was all that struck by the young Dag, thinking him far too shy and unattractive. I was at the time writing a book, which was to have a large section about Hammarskjöld, and to help me she arranged with a friend, Ulf Zandren, a Swedish priest, that Joy and I should meet some of Hammarskjöld's friends.** Per Lind, a colleague of his in New York and later an ambassador, and Karl Ragnar Gierow, then Secretary to the Swedish Academy, were two that we met. Both told us how surprised they had been when *Markings*, the book of Hammarskjöld's spiritual jottings, was published after his death. Lind was concerned that the book might turn people away from his creative innovations in diplomacy. I had the impression that Gierow was moved by the book. He had reservations about a prominent Swede admitting to having such a faith but shared with us his view that Hammarskjöld had been the ideal person for the UN task.

Hammarskjöld was appointed Secretary General in early 1953, the second in the post after his Norwegian predecessor Trygve Lie. He gave his first year to sorting out administrative matters, and then, at the end of 1954, was ready for the challenge suddenly presented to him. Eleven

---

* Pope John XXIII, *Pacem in Terris, Peace on Earth* (London: Catholic Truth Society, 1963).

** David Goodacre, *Four Ways One Goal* (Newcastle: Leighton Co. Services, 2006).

United States airmen had been captured during the Korean War.* They had all just been sentenced by China to long terms of imprisonment. The Americans had tried to have them released but had made no progress. Perhaps, President Eisenhower thought, the United Nations would be able to do better. Hammarskjöld saw it as a significant opportunity. He decided that the best way to tackle it would be to go to China and talk with the leaders there. This was very soon after the Communist takeover when relations between China and the United States were at a low ebb. On 10 December, he asked China if the leaders would receive him. He wrote in *Markings,* quoting from the *Book of Common Prayer*, "God *spake* once, and twice I have also heard the same, that power belongeth unto God: and that thou, Lord, art merciful: for thou rewardest every man according to his work" (Psalm 62:11–12). A week later, the Chinese prime minister replied. In the interests of peace, he said, he would be prepared to meet him and discuss "pertinent" questions. A few days later, Hammarskjöld had a private meeting with China's ambassador in Sweden to determine whether talking about the airmen would be understood to be "pertinent". It was, he was told. He was moved to write in *Markings*, "To have faith—not to hesitate!", and on 30 December as he set off for China, quoting again from the Psalms, he wrote: "If I take the wings of the morning and remain in the uttermost parts of the sea: even there also shall thy hand lead me" (Psalm 139:9–10a).**

He was impressed by Chou En Lai. The diplomacy was not immediately successful, but six months later, on 29 July 1955—Hammarskjöld's fiftieth birthday—the Chinese released the airmen. They said he should see it as a birthday present. He was embarrassed, delighted by their release, alarmed by the focus that it placed on himself, and concerned that while he himself and his role as Secretary General were indeed the same person, it was the United Nations that should be taking the credit. He wrote in *Markings*, "God sometimes allows us to take the credit—for His work", but then "watches our capers on the stage with an ironic smile".***

---

* Brian Urquhart, *Hammarskjöld* (London: Bodley Head, 1972), pp. 96–103.

** Dag Hammarskjöld, *Markings*, trans. W. H. Auden, Leif Sjöberg (London: Faber, 1964), p. 94.

*** Hammarskjöld, *Markings*, p. 98.

Later that November on a weekend away walking in the snow-covered northern mountains of Sweden, in the silence he reflected on what had happened—and on the art of diplomacy. He described it in *Markings*, identifying four rules for engaging in the search for peace and concord: firstly, that before anything could be done, he must identify within himself any personal inclinations he might have about the matter so that he could listen well and understand what motivates the other; secondly, that he should see the "face" of the other as more important than his own; thirdly, to recognize that if he were to be in any way pleading a personal cause he would fail; and fourth, that if there was to be a lasting solution he must seek to see the other objectively while at the same time understanding his own position subjectively.* His colleagues thought he had gleaned these ideas from his meetings with and readings of Martin Buber.** Buber had taught that when people doubt the integrity of any persons they were meeting they create a dangerous atmosphere of distrust. Added to these four observations, Hammarskjöld thought it essential that he should like and value the first-hand experience of the other and approach with the intention of learning a new language.

The purpose of diplomacy, he thought, was to tease out the truth—and with "uncompromising honesty" to avoid at all costs the pitfall of reaching a decision just because it might be popular. Instead, he said, the task was "to reach the bedrock of decency" that would be there even beneath the deepest layers of evil. If then any final decisions made might seem to lack what he called "diplomatic 'finesse'", then so be it. The important thing was to achieve the objective.

Let us pray for the people and leaders of Scandinavia,
for all they contribute to the peace of the world. And let
us pray for all who act as ambassadors and diplomats
and work for peace and concord between nations.

---

* Hammarskjöld, *Markings*, pp. 102–3.

** Aubrey Hodes, *Encounter with Martin Buber* (London: Penguin, 1973), pp. 153–71.

4

Israel, Palestine, Jordan, Lebanon, Syria, Iraq and Kuwait

(The Fertile Crescent)

Week after Advent 4 (Christmas Day)

These countries together form a crescent running from the countries beside the Mediterranean to the Persian Gulf, an arch as it were over the Syrian Desert. The western part, sometimes all of it, is referred to as "The Levant". The overall population is 96.5 million. Iraq has 42 million. (This includes the Kurdish autonomous region. There are 30 million plus those who live in Turkey, Iran and Syria, each speaking their own version of the Kurdish language.) Five million Syrians went into exile during the civil war, reducing the population considerably. In 2022, it was back up to 19 million. Jordan is 10 million, Israel 9 million, Palestine (Gaza and the West Bank) 5.6 million, Lebanon is 6.5 million and Kuwait 4.5 million.

Israel is 80 per cent Jewish. The rest are Muslim with Christian minorities especially in Lebanon (a third of the population), Iraq and Syria (now much reduced to between 1 and 2 per cent). As Middle Eastern Jews have moved into Israel, so many Christians have emigrated, some to Lebanon and Jordan (6 per cent Christian), others to the west. The Anglican Church has a separate province, Jerusalem and the Middle East. Until 1918, the whole area was part of the Ottoman Empire; the different countries became independent during the 1930s and 40s. The region has suffered constant turbulence since.

Breaking down the walls of division

The parish of St Mary's Ovingham stretches four miles to the north, to the hamlet of Harlow Hill which straddles Hadrian's Wall. The Vallum is visible, and there are a few stone remnants to the east at Rudchester and Heddon on the Wall, but nothing now at Harlow Hill. It is all under the Military Road, built to counter the Jacobite rebellion of 1745. Earlier, and after the battle of Flodden (1513), further northeastern defences against the Scots were set up in Berwick. These were built to the very latest designs by Italian engineers.

Building such barriers is always a temptation to anxious rulers trying to contain perceived threats; the wall dividing Mexico from the United States is a current example, and the 444-mile wall protecting Israel from the West Bank is another. The latter was built in 2000 to put a stop to the rash of suicide bombing that had developed. It worked to an extent at the beginning. Since then, it has caused more problems than it has solved.

An earlier trauma only eight years into Israel's history was the Suez crisis of 1956. In that debacle, Israel together with the British and the French concocted a covert plan to regain control of the Suez Canal which had just been nationalized by Egypt. It lasted a very short time. The United States and the United Nations both acted quickly to end the war—initially by creating as it were a virtual wall, an armistice between the main antagonists monitored by a UN Emergency Force sited between the two countries. It was the first time this had been done. It was an idea of the Canadian politician Lester Pearson to give space and time until the politicians could find a permanent solution.* The idea has been deployed many times since, not least in nearby Cyprus.

Another wall, the one that divided Berlin in two, was eventually pulled down in 1989, after it had been in place for 28 years. The Israeli/Palestine conflict dates from Israel's independence in 1948. The new wall dividing the two is already 21 years old with no sign yet of it being taken down. Is there a way forward?

During the 1980s, I was the editor of the Churches' Council for Health and Healing's journal, *Health and Healing*. The ninth issue at Easter 1985

* Brian Urquhart, *Hammarskjöld* (London: Bodley Head, 1972), pp. 175–6.

was given to the question of community healing in Northern Ireland. It included stories of the Corrymeela Centre, of a project in Rostrevor, and of several others which had been developed in Belfast and Derry. We were fully aware that none of these were actually going to solve the problems in the short term, but each were steps in the right direction. As politicians make clear, without the support of the wider community, trying to solve a problem is almost impossible. So writing about the projects, however small, which were engaged in the struggle was important. Similar ventures in the Holy Land are the West-Eastern Divan Orchestra, the Tantur Ecumenical Institute for Theological Studies in Jerusalem, the Yitzhak Frankenthal's Parents' Circle Initiative—a body that seeks to bring together bereaved parents of both sides—and Fr Bruno Hussar's "Oasis of Peace" Foundation in Nablus. Each of these is an enacted prayer for peace, initiatives preparing the ground for the political negotiations that will eventually have to take place (see Week 3).

Every so often as a parish priest I would be called upon to mediate in some boundary quarrel: a parishioner in dispute with a neighbour, a couple in terminal deadlock, an upset in the congregation. The task was to mediate, not to tell one party how badly they were behaving or to side with the other I thought was behaving better, but to listen to both. It would have exacerbated the problem if I had done anything else. It is not all that different on the international stage. Binary problems, in which two countries hold rigid positions from which they refuse to budge, are not going to be resolved easily.

In Pope Francis's more accessible exposition of his encyclical *Fratelli tutti*, his book with Austen Ivereigh entitled *Let us Dream*, he draws a distinction between "contradiction" and "contraposition".* By the first he meant two opposites which cannot be reconciled; by the second two contrary positions that can. In "contraposition", he identified the possibility that if a mediator is to listen carefully, and discern accurately what is happening, without in any way trying to force the pace, there will come a particular moment when out of the struggle and tension something new will emerge. He described this as "overflow": like a

* Pope Francis, a conversation with Austen Ivereigh, *Let us Dream: The Path to a Better Future* (London: Simon & Schuster, 2020), pp. 78–9.

river bursting its banks and water flowing everywhere, ideas will come to mind, engulfing in their impact. The outcome would lead beyond compromise to new ways forward.

One might very well wonder where the stone that used to make up Hadrian's Wall actually went. The replica at Vindolanda, well to the west of Harlow Hill, shows how high it used to be, and it was 60 miles long—a massive quantity of dressed stone! Happily, a good part of it is now to be found in the Saxon churches and towers of the Tyne Valley. Every time I walked up to our church in Ovingham, I would appreciate the stone of Hadrian's Wall recycled into our tower. It is what happens to redundant dividing walls. It was the same in Berwick. When in 1603 James VI of Scotland crossed the Tweed to become James I of England, he had to use the ferry—an unpleasant experience he found, so he had a bridge built. It is still there! Instead of a barrier the Berwick defensive walls now constitute a delightful walk. In some years' time, sections of the West Bank Barrier may also have to be recycled, perhaps into a new mosque or a synagogue, maybe even a church.

Let us pray for the people and leaders of the Fertile Crescent (or Levant, or Middle East), so many of whom have suffered and died in years of conflict. Be with those who work for reconciliation and peace between peoples, for the different faith communities, that in the overflow of grace and the work of the Holy Spirit new possibilities for the future may be discerned.

5

France, Netherlands, Belgium, Luxembourg

Christmas Week

France's population is 65.5 million. The country includes Corsica and several places elsewhere: French Guiana in South America, the island of Réunion in the Indian Ocean, New Caledonia and Tahiti etc. in the Pacific. Monaco is a small principality near the Italian border. The Netherlands' population is 17 million (it also includes islands in the West Indies: Bonaire, Sint Eustachius and Saba), Belgium 11.5 million and Luxembourg 643,500.

The Roman Catholic Church is the largest in all four countries: roughly France 50 per cent or more (said to be one of the least religious countries in the world), Netherlands 25 per cent, Belgium 50 per cent and Luxembourg 65 per cent. The first two are about 5 per cent Muslim. The Church of England's diocese in Europe maintains chaplaincies in the countries. In 1958, France became a new republic, for the fifth time. In the early nineteenth century, the Netherlands, Belgium and Luxembourg were one country; Belgium seceded in 1830, Luxembourg a little later. The Netherlands, Belgium and Luxembourg are constitutional monarchies, Luxembourg a Grand Duchy. All are founder members of what was to become the European Union, Brussels being its main capital with Luxembourg City, Strasbourg and Frankfurt (in Germany) the other capitals.

Contemplation of the birth of Christ

As my grandchildren, Ruth, then 14, and the twins, 13, were about to go into Hall 2 of the Sage in Gateshead, an usher cautioned them, "You do realize that this concert lasts for two and a quarter hours—and that there is no interval." "We do," they replied. "We have been warned." I had issued whip-like instructions to the family telling them that they were expected in Newcastle to hear Steven Osborne play Messiaen's *Vingt Regards sur l'enfant Jésus.** It had taken me some effort to persuade the Sage to invite him to come, and there were many who assured me that the audience would be small, especially in a place as far away from London as Newcastle. They all came, loyally travelling from their homes in the south for a December evening of musical contemplation.

Olivier Messiaen had composed the 20 contemplations in 1944. His gifted student Yvonne Loriod was the first to perform them in public. In writing the third of his meditations, "*L'échange*" (The Exchange), he had been influenced by the Belgian spiritual writer Dom Columba Marmion, who in his *Christ in His Mysteries* had meditated on the mystery of the Word of God becoming Jesus Christ, in particular the moment of exchange, when divinity became clothed in humanity. Messiaen, following Marmion, quotes the opening words of the Christmas midnight prayer which is said at the offertory. In the Latin, the exchange is referred to as *sacrosancta commercia*, which Messiaen translates as *terrible échange*, the awe-inspiring wonder that God should take on our humanity.** In a sermon which St Basil of Caesarea preached one Christmas, he said of Christ's birth that while "He did not relinquish his own nature . . . yet

* Olivier Messiaen, *Vingt Regards sur l'enfant Jésus*, Steven Osborne (Hyperion, CDA67351/2, 2002).

** Edward Forman, "L'Harmonie de l'Univers' Maurice Toesca and the genesis of '*Vingt Regards sur l'Enfant-Jesus*'", in Christopher Dingle and Nigel Simeone (eds), *Olivier Messiaen: Music, Art and Literature* (Aldershot: Ashgate Publishing, 2007), p. 17.

the Word became flesh. Earth received him from heaven, yet heaven was not deserted by him who holds the universe in being."*

Messiaen's mother was the poet Cécile Sauvage. After she had conceived, she began to write a series of 20 poems reflecting on her experience of becoming a first-time mother: *L'âme en bourgeon* (the burgeoning soul). There are lines in the tenth of the poems where she writes of praying for her unborn child:

> Et moi, je chercherai dans mon âme plus haute
> Ce qui tend ton jeune âge et tes regards pensifs.
> (I'll seek, with my highest soul, for what will make
> Your young years and your gaze, contemplative).**

His mother was probably more Wordsworthian than orthodox Christian in her faith, essentially someone who responded to the beauty and wonder of nature. She, nonetheless, had Olivier baptized on Christmas Day in 1908, in the church of St Didier in Avignon. There is a plaque to record the moment. When I was there one midday and looking around especially at the font, the church bells began to ring: the *Angelus*, the daily carillon of praise to celebrate the birth of Christ. In Messiaen's tenth contemplation, he explores the glory of joy, *l'esprit de joie*, his own joy that he was one who had been baptized into Christ.

The Messiaen family had relations in the Aube region of France, near to Troyes. An aunt lived in Fuligny, and there is a family tomb at the nearby *L'église de la Chaise*. It was here that the young Messiaen first began to note the singing and music of the birds. When I was there, it was extraordinarily quiet, the two villages empty in the way French villages so often seem to be, so still indeed that bird song was easy to hear. The music of birds is in several of the contemplations. In the fourteenth, for the contemplation of Christ by the angels a blackbird sings to the shepherds

---

* Basil the Great, "A homily by St Basil the Great", in Stephen Mark Holmes (ed.), *Celebrating Sundays: Reflections from the Early Church on the Sunday Gospels* (Norwich: Canterbury Press, 2012), p. 28.

** Cécile Sauvage, "L'Ame en bourgeon", trans. Philip Weller, in Dingle and Simeone, *Olivier Messiaen: Music, Art and Literature*, pp. 224–5.

of the glory of God at Christ's birth. An earlier contemplation, number eight, has the songs of a nightingale and a garden warbler—with a skylark carolling its ascent, soaring into the heights before suddenly dropping to its nest. There is a bird-song background to the fifth contemplation too, the Son of God meditating on the mystery of his being the Son.

For much of his life, Messiaen lived in Paris. He was the organist at the huge *L'église de la Sainte-Trinité* in the middle of the city. I went to Mass there in the autumn of 2007, joining a mixed congregation of young and old as we were ushered into the worship by Messiaen's music. After the death of his first wife Claire, he married his pianist friend and collaborator Yvonne Loriod who, as I mentioned above, first performed the *Vingt Regards.* The two of them had a holiday cottage to the south of Grenoble, by the Lac de Laffrey. The cottage is fairly hidden, nestling in the trees, close to the lake. On the road above is a room where Loriod used to practise. Messiaen is now buried in the grounds of the nearby *L'église de St Theoffrey.* His tomb stone, shaped like a sea bird, has a brief score of music engraved on it together with his name and dates, 1908–1992—nothing more! It marks the completion of his spiritual journey which had begun in Avignon at his baptism into Christ and ended here not too far away in the hills. Back in the car, I listened to *Eclairs sur L'au-Delà* (Lights upon eternity), his meditation on the resurrection life after death. The piece has birds again singing in the tree of life.

Returning to that moment in the Christmas Midnight Mass, the prayer at the offertory speaks of the mystery of the infinite divine Word becoming the finite human Jesus. The priest says—and I quote from the 1998 Roman Missal, which is easier to understand than the one in the current 2010 edition—"Accept our offerings, Lord God, on this festive night, that through this holy exchange (*sacrosancta commercia*) we may become like Christ, in whom our nature is united to your Godhead."*

Let us pray this Christmas for the people and leaders of France, the Netherlands, Belgium and Luxembourg and for all of us as we celebrate the mysteries of Christ's birth, of the Word who became flesh, that we, who are human and baptized, might become one with Him and divine.

---

* See the Roman Missal (London: Catholic Truth Society, 2010) for the current translation.

6

North India

Epiphany Week

The population of India is 1.4 billion, the second largest population in the world but expected by 2023 to overtake China. Roughly 80 per cent are Hindu, 13 per cent are Muslim, and 2 per cent Christian. Sikhs make up 2 per cent, Buddhists and Jains between 0.5 per cent and 1 per cent each. The Anglican Church joined with other churches in 1970 to form the Church of North India. In 2014, for the first time the country was ruled by a predominantly Hindu movement led by Narendra Modi, the Bharatiya Janata Party. The party had three central aims: to replace the mosque in Ayodhya with a Hindu temple, to establish a Universal Civil Code for Hindus and to revoke Kashmir's autonomy—which was done in August 2019. Kashmir, population 12 million (two thirds Muslim overall, but almost 100 per cent in the Kashmir Valley itself), is divided: China rules the Aksai region, an enclave to the west of Tibet; Pakistan and India rule the rest. They signed the Simla agreement in 1972, which set a "line of control" between the region's north to be ruled by Pakistan and the south by India. India's Kashmir is now divided into Jammu/Kashmir and Ladakh.

Understanding mission

Sonauli, a village at the foot of the Himalayas, lies at the entrance to India from Pokhara in Nepal. We took the bus from there to Gorakhpur—and then another to Varanasi, a journey which took the entire day, largely because of the several breakdowns and delays we suffered on the way. Our host, when we reached Varanasi in the dark at a much later hour than we had intended, was to tell us, "India's situation is always hopeless, but never serious".

Roger and Pat Hooker had been missionaries in India since 1965 and in Varanasi from 1972. Our visit was in 1975. Roger and I had been ordained together in June 1960, and we had both started as curates in different parishes in Stockton-on-Tees. He was a brilliant scholar, notable during our post-ordination training for the amazing number of books he had managed to read between each of our sessions. In Varanasi, Roger was learning Sanskrit at the university. I think I learnt more about mission in the few days we spent there—and later in reading Roger's books—than from anyone else.

When they first arrived in India, Roger soon came to realize that the Hindu assumption was that if Indians had become Christian, it was because they had been bribed, or compelled in some way. It was, after all, a fact that the Anglican Church had always had the British army to back its mission. So when people asked him why he was in Varanasi, he would explain that he was there to study Sanskrit. He had to acknowledge to himself that he was also actually there as a missionary, indeed employed as such, but he tried to carry its baggage as lightly as he could. He explains in his book *Journey into Varanasi* that he had had to relearn the meaning of the word "mission".* He decided he must try to model his understanding of it by studying how Christ himself had sought to exercise his ministry—as God's incarnate Word, the mystery of whose coming we are once again celebrating this Christmas.

What he came to understand about mission among a people of different faiths was that he and Pat should live simply as a presence among the people of Varanasi. They knew they carried no power or authority; they were certainly not there to criticize the faith of the people they were with, nor to claim that their own faith, their Christianity, was actually better than theirs. They were there as guests. They started by both learning Hindi. They saw it as a courtesy to their hosts that they should.

---

* Roger Hooker, *Journey into Varanasi* (London: Church Missionary Society, 1978). See also Roger Hooker with C. A. Lamb, *Love the Stranger* (London: SPCK, 1978), and Roger Hooker, *Voices of Varanasi* (London: Church Missionary Society, 1979).

Roger then set out in addition to learn Sanskrit, the ancient language of the Vedas and Upanishads, and to do so by sitting at the feet of the Hindu pundits at the Benares University. The two of them saw their task as one of waiting upon God and rejoicing in valuing the company of their various Varanasi friends.

Roger took Joy and me on visits to several places in the city. One of these was an ashram being run by some Roman Catholic priests. The priests were trying to learn how to worship in a more Indian style, feeling their way into the culture and, like Roger, studying the Hindu scriptures. In the light of their meditations, they reflected on what their mission might be. Their chapel was a blaze of colour, and the aumbry behind the altar was shaped to look like a Hindu shrine with icons of Mary and Jesus on its door. Since the Spring Festival had been only a few days before, there was a floral display of myrtle. Marigolds, symbols of detachment, were laid out in dishes. The carpet in the main chapel was an Indian iconographic depiction of wisdom, a symbol of Mary in Christian iconography. Like Roger, these priests understood that they had to become artists as much as missionaries if their mission was to be true.

In a pamphlet produced by the Roman Catholic bishops of England and Wales in 2010, *Meeting God in Friend and Stranger*, the writers emphasize the fundamental importance of such dialogue between the faiths.* Indeed, they argue, it is part of the Church's evangelism and mission. In the opening essay of this book, I referred to King Oswald's recruitment of Aidan from Iona to come and preach the gospel to the people of the Northeast. The first person sent from Iona had been unsuccessful, and in his report back to the community had said some pretty harsh things about the stupidity of the people he had encountered. Aidan, a much gentler soul, was more successful. He had of course King Oswald with him to back him up, but then in the seventh century, if the local thane gave a lead their people had to follow. Some in the Indian community had similarly feared that they were expected to follow the lead of their British rulers and, in that light, Roger had had to think out his fresh approach. It led him to adopt a humbler style, one that gave

* Catholic Bishops' Conference of England and Wales, *Meeting God in Friend & Stranger* (London: Catholic Truth Society, 2010).

space to the Holy Spirit to act. It showed him how to follow Christ as a missionary there. It is the same for us here in England. We live in a secular society. We certainly cannot compel or manipulate people into following Christ. Nor can we use friendship as a cover to groom someone into it. We are rather, as Roger taught, to live out the faith and model a mission like that of Christ himself, who as incarnate Word came among us as a totally vulnerable babe in arms.

In the twenty-first century, when the call of God is that people of all faiths should learn how to live together, the challenge of mission is much more that we learn how to live and work together, praying in Christ with the Holy Spirit that God's ultimate purpose—the bringing of all humankind into a oneness within the kingdom of God—may come.

Let us pray for the people and leaders of India, giving thanks
for their deep faith, for the colour and beauty of their culture
and worship, and give us wisdom to engage in dialogue,
that we may discern the Common Good for us all.

7

Canada

Week after Epiphany 1 (The Baptism of Christ)

Canada has a population of 38.5 million, the majority living along the 5,255-mile border with the United States. In terms of landmass, the country is the second largest in the world. About 70 per cent are Christian: half are Roman Catholic, a quarter Protestant and the rest claim to be without religion. The Anglican Church of Canada (about 5 per cent) has two provinces, Rupert's Land, and Yukon and British Columbia. Canada has been fully independent since 1931, Britain's "Canada Act" of 1982 severing the remaining legal dependence of Canada on the UK; the British monarch remains the Constitutional Head of State. Quebec has sought independence in two referenda, 1980 and 1995. The latter was close.

The call to be a politician

Writing of his stint as leader of the opposition in the Canadian parliament, Michael Ignatieff described politics as "the noblest and most vexatious of all human activities".* He served as an active politician for five years, from 2006 until he and the Liberal Party lost the 2011 election and he his Toronto seat. In his retrospective memoir, he reflected on what had happened, writing it also as a plea to any young person to be prepared to heed the call and embrace the life of a politician.

Before all this, Michael Ignatieff had been a professor at Harvard. In 2004, three men in black–his description of the delegation that came to

* Michael Ignatieff, *Fire and Ashes: Success and Failure in Politics* (Cambridge, MA: Harvard University Press, 2013), p. 172.

see him—asked him if he would come back to his home country and take over the leadership of the Liberal Party. The Liberals were at the time in power, but as his visitors told him, in such dire straits they would lose the coming election. Ignatieff and his wife Zsuzsanna Zsohar decided to accept their invitation.

Michael Ignatieff's grandparents were from Ukraine. They had moved to Canada at the time of the Communist takeover in 1917 and had settled near Quebec. During the war, their son George married Alison, a fellow Canadian, while they were both working in London at Canada House. As a diplomat, George worked closely with his friend Lester Pearson, who was in later years to become Canada's prime minister. They both shared a concern for international affairs. Years later it was Lester Pearson who had the idea of setting up a United Nations Force to keep the peace between Israel and Egypt during the Suez Crisis of 1956 (see Week 4). Being with powerful political leaders and giving public service was at the heart of the young Michael's upbringing.

In Canada, constituencies are called ridings. In 2006, Ignatieff stood for the Etobicoke-Lakeshore riding in Toronto, which he won. As he had been warned, the Liberals did lose the election. The leader of the party resigned, and as he had been recruited as a possible leader, he stood in the election of his successor; perhaps fortunately, he lost. He had long been a lecturer on politics, but working at the coal face, as it were, was a new experience. Already, in standing for the post his training had begun. He soon began to acquire much more knowledge about the current needs of the country as he travelled round the vastness of Canada and met the different branches and members of the party. A politician needs to know his country, Ignatieff explains in his book. He has to become as the French have it "*un homme de terrain*", someone who knows what makes the people tick, what their values are. One of the major issues in Canadian politics at the time—and still very much is—was the tension between the different ethnic groups and in particular the tension between French-speaking Quebeckers and the English-speaking rest. He found that he had learnt, on the hoof as it were, what were the minutiae and practicalities of the politician's life.

There was another election late in 2008. The Liberal Party lost this one too, and once again the leader resigned. Ignatieff put his name forward and this time, he won. From the outset, the Conservative Party argued that because Ignatieff had worked for so many years abroad he was not really a Canadian but merely a visitor. How could he, they argued, act as a proper leader and represent a country from which he was in effect apart. The accusation was unfair, but it had enough truth in it to damage him. He might be a Canadian, but he had indeed worked abroad for many years. Both his party and he found it difficult to counter the slur, especially as the Conservatives had far more money to pay for their adverts—which they placed everywhere. Ignatieff reflected that a politician has to be able to tell the electorate that he was truly one of them, that he was indeed deeply concerned for their wellbeing and that as a dedicated compatriot, he was prepared to give everything for the good of the people. But he knew he needed to acquire "standing", as he put it; a standing that went beyond the inevitable partisanship which all politicians have to observe—the responsibility to vote loyally with the party whatever their personal views—while at the same time retaining integrity as a politician with a vision for the improvement of the country. When the next election came in 2011, not only did his party lose, he also lost his seat. He was devastated; but I suspect, though he does not say this, that what he had been able to do for his party during the five years he was leader ultimately did have a significant impact. He had been asked to refresh the party, and he had done that. His calling in the end was not to become a successful prime minister, as he had thought and hoped, but it was to contribute new ideas and refresh the party. The Liberals won the election in 2015 and were still in power in 2021.

In his book, Ignatieff shares his vision of what it is to be engaged in such a high calling, the vocation to serve as a politician. In his final chapter, "the calling", he renews his plea to the young. He uses the words from Reinhold Niebuhr's prayer as a summary of the political task; to try to change what can be changed, to preserve what needs to be preserved, and to have the wit to discern the difference. His own vocation had come via the three men in black. He certainly saw his call as a vocation, and uses further theological insights to speak about it, not because he saw it as a response to God—western politicians currently feel they cannot possibly do that and survive—but rather because for him it was indeed a spiritual and visionary awakening, a call to serve. On the final page, he uses an Epiphany image: "think of politics", he says to the young, "as a calling that inspires us onward, ever onward, like a guiding star."* If nothing else, it suggests that, whether we have a secular or a religious understanding, we need to heed the call.

Let us pray for the people and leaders of Canada and for all called to serve as politicians, that they may be persons of faith and vision, that they may hone their vision of what a well-ordered society might be as they encounter and listen to the people they represent, together serving and seeking the Common Good.

* Ignatieff, *Fire and Ashes*, p. 183.

8

Italy, The Vatican, San Marino, Malta

Week after Epiphany 2

Italy's population is 60.5 million, Malta's 444,000. Almost everyone is Roman Catholic. The Anglican Church maintains a Centre in Rome (Palazzo Doria Pamphilj, Piazza del Collegio Romano 2). After the *Risorgimento* (reunification) in 1870, Italy became a monarchy—and then in 1945 a republic. San Marino is a small enclave to the south of Venice where Garibaldi once took refuge. Vatican City remained independent after 1870 and was formally recognized as a state by the Lateran Treaty of 1929. Malta, given the George Cross in 1942 in honour of its bravery during the Second World War (still on the national flag), became independent from Britain in 1974. Italy, a founder member of the European Union, hosted the signing of the Treaty of Rome in 1957. Malta joined the EU in 2004.

Surprises of grace

The Roman Catholic Church featured little in my thinking or experience before I was ordained. It was a very different matter when I moved to the Northeast. Here Anglican parishes are often coterminous with Catholic ones. This was certainly the case when I was priest in charge of Ryhope and equally when serving as a curate in Stockton-on-Tees. It was easy to tell who was Catholic in the latter. They would studiously avoid looking at me should we meet each other in the street. It was dispiriting. But then things suddenly changed. In the 1961 Week of Prayer for Christian Unity, at the invitation of the priest, we attended Mass in our local Catholic church. Our decision was not popular with some, especially some critics writing from Northern Ireland, but the effect on our ecumenical relations was startling.

This had all come about because a couple of years before, the Patriarch of Venice, Angelo Roncalli, had been elected pope. It is hard now to recall just how dramatic a change this was. It affected me so much I was led to study Pope John XXIII's life and indeed included it later in my book *Four Ways, One Goal.* Angelo Roncalli was born to a farming family in Sotto il Monte, a village as its name implies beneath the foothills of the Alps, to the north of Bergamo in northern Italy. He was the eldest son of a large family with two older sisters. He trained for the ministry in Bergamo and returned there after further study in Rome and ordination in 1904 as chaplain to the bishop. The cathedral and also the college is in the upper part of Bergamo, high above the plain below. When I was last there, I was on my way to Bulgaria from the Milan airport in Bergamo, to see where Fr Roncalli had worked when he had been appointed Apostolic Visitor to the country from 1925. There is a statue of him outside the Catholic church in the middle of Sofia. From Sofia ten years later he became the Apostolic Delegate in Turkey, and then at the end of the war, and to his surprise, he was appointed the Nuncio to France. In 1953 he moved to become the Patriarch of Venice. On 28 October 1958, he was elected pope.

Loris Capovilla, later the Archbishop of Loreto and his chaplain and companion of many years, says that Pope John had the idea of convening a council as early as two days after his election. He had shared his thoughts with Fr Loris. Don Loris replied that he thought this far too much, that he would be wiser to use his undoubted gift for fatherliness and forgo at his age doing something so extraordinarily difficult. Pope John said he would reflect and pray about what he had said. Was the idea indeed from God or merely a personal conceit? A few days later he told Don Loris that he was not at all concerned about having a good reputation; "only when the ego has been trampled underfoot", he said, "can one be fully and truly free".* Two or three months later, in January 1959, he presented his idea to his Secretary of State, Cardinal Tardini. According to his diary, Tardini responded by saying that he thought it

* Peter Hebblethwaite, *John XXIII: Pope of the Council* (London: Geoffrey Chapman, 1984), p. 308.

a "splendid initiative". Pope John, in his, wrote, "I thanked the Lord for my idea which now received its first seal of approval here below."* A few days later, on 25 January—the feast of the Conversion of St Paul—he met with an assembly of cardinals at St Paul's-without-the-Walls for the final observance of that year's Week of Prayer for Church Unity. Unlike many Roman Christians of the time, Pope John always observed the week. In announcing the council at such a service, he wanted to symbolize both St Paul's concern for the worldwide Church and that it should also be ecumenical. He spoke for half an hour; basically, he began by appealing to their conservative instincts and then at the end told them what he had in mind. "Trembling with emotion," he said, "and yet with humble resolution, we put before you the proposal of . . . an ecumenical council for the universal Church." It would, he said, also include "a friendly and renewed invitation to our brothers of the separated Christian Churches to share with us in this banquet of grace and brotherhood". His words were received in total silence. Pope John writing about this later chose to interpret this as "a devout and impressive silence", but at the time he was very disappointed to see just how lacking in enthusiasm they were.**

When speaking of discernments like this, Pope John would describe them as "surprises", surprises of grace. Towards the end of his life, he wrote in his journal of two graces he had received: the first, that he had accepted his election as pope; the second, that he had received the idea of the council. He did not mean by using the word "surprise" that the grace had come upon him suddenly. It clearly had not. It was more that as he reflected on each one, he recognized them as singular, grace-filled moments when he had known himself addressed by the Holy Spirit.

His concern was that the Church should renew its mission to the world. His encyclical, *Pacem in terries*, was the first encyclical to be addressed not only to the Catholic Church but to all "people of good will". He wanted to reach out to all the four corners of the world. In Piero della Francesca's great San Sepolcro painting of the Resurrection, Christ is depicted standing boldly above the empty tomb, triumphant in his victory. The fresco is not in the parish church but—a "surprise"—on

---

* Hebblethwaite, *John XXIII: Pope of the Council*, p. 315.

** Hebblethwaite, *John XXIII: Pope of the Council*, pp. 321, 322.

the wall immediately behind the local mayor's chair in the town council debating chamber—what was the local council building! It speaks to the town, named for Holy Saturday, of the purpose of local politics: working for Easter resurrection in the community. Like the encyclical it calls for the Church to align herself with the risen and ascended Christ as he intercedes for the world, that the kingdom might come.

Let us pray for the people and leaders of Italy, the Vatican and Malta—and for the vocation of the Church to discern what spiritual ways there are that make for peace and justice on earth, that cooperating with Christ, and strengthened and guided by the Holy Spirit, God's kingdom may come.

9

Mexico, Guatemala, Belize, Honduras, El Salvador, Nicaragua, Costa Rica, Panama, Central America

Week after Epiphany 3

Mexico's population is 131.5 million. The other seven countries, in the order above, stretch along the 1,000-mile isthmus that divides Mexico from Colombia. Guatemala, with Belize in its northeast corner, is followed by Honduras and the much smaller El Salvador, Honduras in the north, El Salvador on the Pacific to the south. Nicaragua is next, then Costa Rica and finally Panama with the Canal. Their populations together add a further 52 million. Most are Christian and Catholic. The Anglican Church has two provinces, the Church of Mexico and the Church of Central America. Honduras is part of Province IX of the United States Episcopal Church. Spanish is the language of all except Belize (English). In recent decades, migrants–from Honduras, Guatemala and Mexico in particular–have been leaving regularly for the United States in attempts to escape the drug cartels, violence and poverty. The USA border wall was intended to stop this.

Present your hearts (bodies) as a living sacrifice

Mexico City has some stunning architecture. Examples are the excitingly designed stations on the Metro, the trains swishing through them on their rubber wheels. The University on Insurgentes Sur is another. In 1500, it was very different. The city was then called Tenochtitlan. It was on an island in the middle of a large lake in the centre of which stood the Zocala, a pyramid, huge like the nearby Pyramid of the Sun at Teotihuacan.

There is no pyramid there now, nor much of a lake. The only remnant of the lake is at Xochilmilco where local people gather for picnics at weekends–as we did on our final day there.

It was on the top of this pyramid in Tenochtitlan that sacrifices used to take place. Uitzilopochtil was a harsh and demanding god. The Mexica, the *Nahuatl* name for the Aztecs, believed that unless they made daily sacrifices of blood from the hearts of living people the god would not maintain the stability of their world. Life was difficult enough already. They did not want to make it worse by laxity in their worship. The ceremonies of sacrifice were silent, numinous affairs, terrifying though they were for the victims. By the time the Conquistadores arrived, the sacrifices, although still continuing, had become less about placating their god and much more about terrorizing their vassals who provided the victims for the sacrifices. The Spaniards may have been used to political cruelty in their homeland, but they were horrified by this.

This giving of the heart and soul to God in sacrifice is a feature of all religion. The account of Abraham going in obedience to God to the mountain of Moriah to sacrifice his son Isaac (Genesis 22:1–18) is an early example. The act satisfies the primitive urge, the desperate need to placate the hostility of a possibly malevolent God. The Old Testament offers a different interpretation. Human sacrifice may happen, but God insists that Abraham must not do it.

Many years after the conquest of Mexico, Christian writers argued that the king of the Mexica, Montezuma, had not fought hard enough to withstand the Spanish. They claimed his reason was because he thought that Cortes was a reincarnation of the god Quetzalcoatl returning to his people; there was a Nahua myth that he would. Camilla Townsend, a scholar writing from the Mexica perspective, doubts this.* Montezuma, she says, had a good intelligence service and had judged, given the advanced weaponry and horses the Spanish possessed, that his army would lose. He tried to deflect them from their purpose. When that failed, he tried for a peaceful settlement. For their part, the Conquistadores had three aims: they wanted to incorporate this New World into Spain,

* Camilla Townsend, *Fifth Sun: A New History of the Aztecs* (New York: Oxford University Press, 2019).

to find gold and to convert the newly conquered to Christianity. They certainly prevailed militarily, and they found gold. Their third aim they tackled differently.

Fernando Cervantes describes the success of this third aim as "one of the most remarkable episodes in the history of Christianity".* Spanish Catholicism in the sixteenth century may have been harsh with the Inquisition and its *autos-da-fé*, but it also had a gentler and profound faith. It was the Mendicant orders, the Franciscans and Dominicans, who came as missionaries. They had heeded the teaching of the Dutch theologian Erasmus and the advice of Pope Gregory to Abbot Mellitus recorded by Bede: that missionaries should seek to preserve what was good from the past, and at the same time look for gentle ways of converting them to the true God.** In the Mexican situation, a new understanding of sacrifice was required; Jesus, they taught, had already given his heart to God in the crucifixion, rendering any further sacrifice of human hearts unnecessary. Pleading our Lord's sacrifice was enough. As an example of preserving the old, the missionaries repurposed the *cuauhxicalli*—the receptacle used previously for receiving the sacrificed hearts—as the font in the new cathedral they built on the site of the Tenochtitlan pyramid.

Twelve years after the conquest, in 1531—so the legend written some 124 years later says—a middle-aged Mexican Christian called Juan Diego was passing the Tepeyac Hill on his way to the Franciscan Mission. Before the conquest, there had been a shrine to the goddess Tonantzun on the hill. It was here that he had a vision of the Virgin Mary. She told him to build a chapel in the place where they were standing. Juan went to ask the bishop for permission to do that, with no success. A few days later, Juan saw the Virgin again. He told her to find someone else. If she would not, he said, he would need to present some proof to the bishop. She would do that, she said, and arranged to meet again. By this time, Juan had become so alarmed he decided to miss their next meeting and went off to visit his sick uncle instead. When Mary found where he had got to, she

* Fernando Cervantes, *Conquistadores: A New History* (London: Allen Lane, 2020), p. 203.

** Bede, *A History of the English Church and People*, trans. Leo Sherley-Price (London: Penguin Classics, 1955), p. 86.

expostulated, "What is this? Am I not your mother? Now", she continued, "go up the Tepeyac Hill. Gather the flowers you will find there and take them to the bishop." It was not the season for such flowers, but he went, found them and once more went to see the bishop. When he opened his cloak, the flowers fell out, and there on his tunic was also a picture of the Virgin. Juan's chapel was built. Later it was replaced by a basilica. It has now been rebuilt again: the basilica of Our Lady of Guadalupe.

There has been much debate as to whether all these surprising events actually took place, especially as there is a similar story associated with a shrine at nearby Tlaxcalla. Camilla Townsend comments that whether it was true or not, it was what the people wanted to believe. Cervantes argues that such oral testimony and its regular enactment in liturgy is testimony enough to the real impact that Christianity had made upon the people. The Guadalupe story marks the moment when the Mexica people accepted the faith as their own. Juan Diego—canonized in 2002—had freely offered his heart to the Lord.

When we went to Guadalupe, we had to push our way through the crowds attending the several masses, each one a remembering of Christ's sacrifice, that the hearts of the people might be sprinkled clean (Hebrews 10:22).

Let us pray for the people and leaders of Mexico and the several countries of Central America, that with pure hearts they may offer themselves anew to the Lord.

10

The Arabian Peninsula: Saudi Arabia, Yemen, Oman, United Arab Emirates, Qatar and Bahrain

Week of Candlemas, Epiphany 4, 5 before Lent

The overall population of the Arabian Peninsula is 87 million; the two largest countries in terms of population are Saudi Arabia with 36 million (largest in land size too) and its south-western neighbour Yemen with 31 million. Oman occupies the eastern side of the peninsula, east of Yemen and south of the Arab Emirates. The Emirates are along the strip of land beside the Gulf which separates the Peninsula from Iran. Qatar is next, a horn of land reaching out into the Gulf. The island of Bahrain is immediately to the west of Qatar. Saudi Arabia is Sunni Muslim, where the city of Mecca is, where the most sacred Ka'bah stands. Yemen is roughly half Shia, half Sunni; in recent years it has suffered a civil war between its government backed by Sunni Saudi Arabia and Houthi rebels (Shia) supported by Iran.

Early encounters with Islam

In November 1955, a battalion of the King's Own Yorkshire Light Infantry embarked on the *SS Dilwara* to sail from Mombasa to Aden. Both Kenya and Aden were at the time British colonies. The ship rounded Cape Guardafui in Somalia, the eastern-most point of Africa, and arrived in the immense Aden harbour about three days later. The harbour is dominated by the rock of the extinct volcano which stands guard over the entrance. It presides over the peninsula on which Aden lies. I was just over halfway through my National Service. We were to camp in tents beside the RAF base, which was then at Khormaksar. The base is now Yemen's international airport.

For those of us born in the 1930s, two years' National Service constituted our generation's "gap years". I was 19. I had been accepted for training for the Anglican ministry at the beginning of 1955, and was now preparing as best I could for that to begin in September of the following year. Like anyone in their late teens, the three things most important to me were my faith, what my role in life was going to be, and a clear hope that somehow I might meet some girls. The first two were decided–almost–but having been at a boys-only school and now in the army, the third was proving elusive.

In Aden, there was a purpose-built garrison chapel. On the first Sunday there, my diary tells me what interested me most about the service. "There is a very attractive girl who attends Holy Communion", I wrote. "She really adds quite a bit of spice to the day." Later that same day, I saw her again at the swimming baths: "Quite made my day!", I wrote. A fellow ordinand was similarly entranced. Pat, we were soon to learn, was in fact only 14, and–further intelligence–about to leave for England with her RAF family. A brief fantasy! It was to be another two years before I would meet Joy. I can remember little about my Aden days, but I do remember Pat.

To return to the other important things on my mind, faith was not too much of an issue. I might have been living in an Islamic country, but apart from hearing the muezzin cry, I was only thinking about my own faith. It has been different since. The other question, my vocation, was much more of a concern. Was I really sure that my decision to become a priest had been right? Did I really have a vocation? Was I offering myself simply because it was what my father did? Where was God in all this? It was almost a year before I was to understand that I did indeed have a vocation, but in the months in between and indeed in the opening weeks at King's, London, it had become a spiritual crisis; important now that I look back on it, but at the time a frightening struggle, a time of inner searching and testing.

Aden was a different posting from Kenya where we had been before. Our cohort had joined the first battalion of the KOYLI in Naro Moru where we were stationed. I knew nothing then of the atrocities imposed on the Kenyan peoples during the Mau Mau crisis of 1952–60, it was just good to be there enjoying the beauty of the country near Nanyuki and the towering presence of Mount Kenya on the horizon.

Aden was to remain under British rule until 1967. It became part of Yemen in 1990. One Sunday, a group of us from the chapel ventured beyond Aden itself into the interior and through the desert-like country to Lahej. I can remember walking past the bazaar shops and being shocked—so my diary tells me—by the filth of the street and the displays of unprotected meat sweating in the heat. Going to Lahej was the nearest we came to visiting Yemen proper. Saudi Arabia and Mecca were many miles to the north. Many years later, Shazad Hussain, the project director of the York Mosque, came to speak to an inter-faith conference I had organized in Chester-le-Street and told us a story about the early years of Islam. His story was from the Hadith—one of a collection of the sayings of Muhammad—of Gabriel. The Prophet Muhammad was sitting with Umar and his friends when they were joined by a man with jet black hair, dressed in a brilliant white robe. He had evidently been travelling, but there was no trace of it on his clothes. He sat down close to Muhammad, and they began to talk: "Muhammad," the visitor said. "What is Islam?"

"Islam," the Prophet replied, "requires us to worship Allah, and no one else." And he went on, "I, the messenger of Allah, have been given a message to tell the people to pray, to give to charity, and to fast at Ramadan. I am also to urge them to perform the Hajj—the pilgrimage to Mecca—if they can."

His questioner replied, "You have told the truth."

After talking together for a while their visitor left. Muhammad turned to Umar and asked, "Do you know who my questioner was?"

Umar replied, "Allah and his messenger are the only ones who know that."

Muhammad said, "He was Gabriel, who came to us to teach you about the Way."

In the five pillars, Islam sets a high standard of spiritual formation: they are to worship God alone, to acknowledge Muhammad as his prophet (*Shahadah*), to pray five times a day (*Salat*), to give the charity tax (*Zakat*), to fast during Ramadan (*Sawn*) and if possible, make the

Hajj, the pilgrimage to Mecca. They constitute the necessary disciplines of the spiritual life. Basically, each of the Abrahamic faiths observe the same ones. In my teens and in the way one thinks about such things as a teenager, I did try to give some thought to such rules: prayer to the one God was already essential. My parents were persons of prayer, and each day they used to go to the chapel we had in our home to say Morning and Evening Prayer. As children, when we went to bed, our mother used to take us into the chapel and tell us Bible stories, which as a gifted raconteur she told with verve. Prayer with fasting and almsgiving are the notable duties listed by St Matthew (Matthew 6:1–18). Fasting beyond some limited Lenten rule was as far as I had got to at this time; giving was marginally better, though I was to learn much more about this from Joy and her family who were models of generosity. Spiritual exercise—pilgrimages, retreats, quiet days—were to become important in the days ahead. Foundations had been laid.

In the course of our Chester-le-Street conference, Shazad told us how he had once had to cope with a right-wing demonstration outside his mosque. He and his colleagues decided to invite the group to come into the mosque. It was clear to Shazad when they talked with them that most of them had no idea why they were there. Being so welcomed by this Muslim *Ummah* (Islamic community gathered together) was disarming.

Let us pray for Saudi Arabia, Yemen and the countries of the Arabian Peninsula, that learning from the five pillars of the Islamic Ummah, peoples of all faiths and none may develop the basic and necessary disciplines of the spiritual life.

NB. For weeks after fourth and third Sundays before Lent go to Weeks 47 and 48.

11

The Indian Ocean: Madagascar, the Seychelles, Comoros and Maldive Islands, Mauritius

Week after Second Sunday before Lent, Trinity 22

Madagascar is 1300 miles to the east of Mozambique in Africa, the fourth largest island in the world. The Comoros Islands are to its immediate north, the Seychelles a further 1100 miles to the north (on the same latitude as Tanzania). The Maldives are to the east, southwest of the far south of India. Mauritius is 700 miles east of Madagascar, with its partner island, Rodrigues, about 400 miles to its northeast. Réunion (an island of France) is 150 miles southwest of Mauritius. The Chagos Archipelago is a further 1300 miles to the east of Mauritius. Madagascar's population is 29 million, the Comoros Islands (apart from Mayotte, which is also French) 908,000, the Seychelles 100,000, Mauritius with Rodrigues, 1.5 million and the Maldives, 541,000.

Madagascar and the Seychelles are Christian, Mauritius is half Hindu half Christian, the Comoros and Maldives are Muslim. The Anglican Church has the province of the Indian Ocean. The Maldives have suffered much political instability. A recent ruling of the International Court urged the UK to return the islands of the Chagos Archipelago, which includes Diego Garcia, to Mauritius.

Blessed are you who are poor, for yours is the kingdom of God

Walking from Newcastle Central Station to the cathedral before the pandemic, there was usually someone begging just outside the *porte-cochère*. There was another person outside the Station Hotel and a third beside the Mining Institute. They were there even when it was raining or very cold, huddling for warmth under their flimsy blankets, sometimes accompanied by a dog. Every city in the United Kingdom in 2020 had its quota of people begging, a distressing symptom of the growing poverty among so many in our land. It was brought to the public mind by the 2020 Marmot report—a review of the Health Foundation's 2010 report on the health of the country in a fair society—which, when published, showed that poverty in the Northeast was worse than anywhere else in the country. Is being poor in England as bad as being poor in Madagascar? Madagascar may be warmer, but poverty is bad wherever it is, and it is one of the poorer countries of the world. It is even one of the few remaining countries where bubonic plague remains endemic. Every year between September and April a number fall ill with this very contagious pneumonic disease. I only know this because my granddaughter Lucy, who is a biologist, is studying the problem for her PhD at Aberdeen University.

Towards the end of the 1990s, Madagascar, so Paul Collier says in his *The Bottom Billion*, was on the cusp of breaking away from its deep-seated poverty.* Under America's "Africa Growth and Opportunities Act", 300,000 jobs had been created, and things in the country were fast improving. Then in 2001 there was an election. Didier Ratsirikara, who had been leading the country for most of the years since the country's independence, had just lost an election, which he refused to accept. Even after the courts had ruled that the result was valid, he still refused to accept it! In the troubles that followed, Ratsirikara moved his government to the coast; there he effectively blocked the main port and forced it to remain closed for eight months. The effect was devastating. At the end of

* Paul Collier, *The Bottom Billion: Why the Poorest Countries are Failing and What Can Be Done About it* (Oxford: Oxford University Press, 2008).

the blockade two thirds of the newly created jobs had gone. A manager of an American company in the country told Collier that he could not understand how a leader could so deliberately set out to wreck his own country.* This was of course before the events in the United States of 6 January 2021.

Our Lord makes the point that the poor will always be with us (Matthew 26:11). Given such actions by some leaders, it is hard to see how this is ever going to be reversed or at least ameliorated. Collier argues that there is still much that can be done. There is still hope. He identifies four problems that afflict poor countries and prevent them from developing: they are usually landlocked and are also usually surrounded by badly ruled neighbours; they depend on one particularly valuable commodity; they often experience conflict; finally, they are almost always badly governed. The first and the second are obviously not the case with Madagascar—though the departing president's decision to block the main port did landlock it for a critical time—nor is the third. The main cause is the fourth. It is always the poor who suffer most when there is hardship in a country; because this is always so, their needs are paramount. The gospel makes this abundantly clear: "Blessed are you who are poor, for yours is the kingdom of God" (Luke 6:20), and Luke here does mean the materially poor.

Paul Collier makes the additional point that, quite apart from the rich countries' spiritual and moral responsibility to do something about all this, they will damage themselves if they don't. They need to make fair agreements with poorer countries. Collier argues that there are several ways they can help themselves; first in putting an emphasis on education. Education makes a critical difference, he argues. Only when a country has a sufficient number of well-educated people is there any chance of it breaking free from the poverty cycle. Then, the country needs to be awake to the *kairos* moment when it occurs. *Kairos* here is one of the Greek words for time. It refers to time as a singular moment, a grace-filled opportunity, a surprise perhaps, when things can be changed. Such a moment came in Madagascar and could have led to great things had not the president opted to rebel against his people. He crushed the possibility.

---

* Collier, *The Bottom Billion*, pp. 83–4.

If a country takes an opportunity when it occurs, then a new dawn is possible and necessary steps towards addressing poverty can be taken. What these are, Collier says, are readily available; his team has prepared a sort of DIY kit, a manual of know-how gleaned from countries which have been poor in the past. It is possible, he suggests, but it takes grace and wisdom for it to happen.

Let us pray for the people and leaders of Madagascar and the islands of the Indian Ocean and for all who are poor in the world, especially those ill-served by their leaders.

12

Nigeria

Week of Ash Wednesday

Nigeria's population is 217 million—the largest population of a country in Africa and one of the countries where the population is predicted to go on increasing. It is by far the largest of the West African countries on the southern Atlantic coast. The north is largely Muslim, almost 50 per cent, the south predominantly Christian, around 45 per cent. A quarter of the latter are Catholic. The Anglican Church of Nigeria has ten provinces. There are 250 ethnic groups speaking as many as 500 languages; the three main groupings are the Hausa-Fulani in the north, the Yoruba in the west, and the Igbo in the east. Independence from the UK came on 1 October 1960. Biafra, an Igbo region, tried for independence between 1967 and 1970. After years of military dictatorship, Nigeria became a democracy in 1999. Recently *Boko Haram* and similar organizations have terrorized the north. Ongoing corruption remains a problem. The oil industry is vast.

Fostering understanding and friendship

"Shola! Shola!" the crowd roared as the Newcastle United forward headed for goal. St James' Park is near the centre of the city so everyone shopping around Earl Grey's monument would know that a goal had been scored. On this occasion, two of my grandchildren, their dad and I were sitting in the loftier reaches of the stadium watching the game. Shola Ameobi's father is the pastor of a Nigerian congregation in the Spital Tongues area of Newcastle. Ever since Andy Cole played for Newcastle, local attitudes towards its Black players—and towards Black people in general—have greatly improved. Geordies value anyone who can play well for Newcastle; and Mackems, for Sunderland.

The Pentecostal congregation in Spital Tongues is by no means the only Black church in Tyneside. There is another Nigerian one and several more ethnic churches scattered around the city (see Week 51). Some Nigerians have come to our country willingly; a number of women have come because they have been trafficked here.

In the course of my work, I met several of them, almost all of them here in Newcastle because they had been moved from London under the government's dispersal scheme for asylum seekers, which began in the late 1990s. Moving to a new place is difficult for anyone, and when you move to somewhere so radically different from anything you have ever known before it is seriously challenging. When, further, you have been traumatized by abuse in the coming it becomes utterly daunting. Some of the women were orphans who had come from the poorer parts of Nigeria, trafficked in their teens; one I recall was very beautiful, and as a result particularly vulnerable. In Africa generally when a child becomes orphaned, they are the responsibility of a near relative, who is often tempted to treat her as a lesser Cinderella-like member of the family who can be made to do the chores. Since she is also another mouth to feed, if a trafficker appears in the village, it is a way of getting rid of her. There are others who encourage a daughter to go to England in the hope that they will prosper and earn enough to send money back to their family.

When trafficked women arrive in England, their passports are taken away from them. They are usually housed somewhere in London, are effectively treated as slaves, and many are then groomed to become prostitutes. Any thought of escape, they are told, will bring retribution on their families back home. In 2015 the Modern Slavery Act was passed here in England. There is still a long way to go before its effects will have an impact on the plight of these women.

The same tragic story is repeated in a different way in Nigeria itself. *Boko Haram* means "Western Education is forbidden", and is a shorter form of the group's official title, which is "The People Committed to the

Propagation of the Prophet's Teaching and Jihad".* The militia claims an Islamic faith and over the past 20 years has wreaked havoc, taking girls and more recently boys into slavery, and forcing the Christians among them to become Muslim. In recent years, the problem has become worse. The Catholic bishop of Sokoto writing recently blamed its activities on the various interventions of the west against Islam—for example the killing of Osama Bin Laden—and that its aim is to rejuvenate faith and eventually install a new ISIS (Islamic State of Iraq and Syria) type of government.** In 2014 a cell of *Boko Haram* kidnapped 240 Christian girls from a school in Dapchi. More recently they have attacked one in Chibok where they took 276 more. There have been many more attacks since. The Dapchi girls, apart from one, Leah Sharibu, who refused to renounce her Christian faith, have since been released. Many at the time of writing are still missing. Girls again being forced into sexual slavery!

Boko Haram like ISIS is an Islamic heresy, reminiscent of the Iranian and Syrian eleventh-century Shiite movement called the assassins—from which the word "assassin" comes.*** Like these first "assassins", *Boko Haram* tries to drive its purpose by violence and arms. Not too far away from northern Nigeria, in the forests of the Central African Republic and Uganda, there is another active terrorist group, this time led by a Christian heretic, Joseph Kony. His outfit is called the "Lord's Resistance Army", and like his *Boko Haram* counterparts, his intention is also to force people to accept his interpretation of the Ten Commandments and establish his own idea of dictatorship. It is estimated that over the years more than 10,000 boys and girls have been captured and forced to become camp followers or soldiers by these people. Kony's army is now much reduced, but in 2020 it was still harassing peoples in Central Africa.

One of the problems which secular western society finds difficult to comprehend is that indifference and hostility to religion does do

---

* Christina Lamb, *Our Bodies Their Battlefield: What War Does to Women* (London: William Collins, 2020), pp. 41–68.

** Matthew Hassan Kukah and Sam Chuilo, "When poverty and ignorance kill", *The Tablet*, 7 March 2020, p. 4.

*** Hans Küng, *Islam, Past, Present & Future*, tr. John Bowden (Oxford: One World Publications, 2007), p. 353.

extensive damage. This is one reason why *Boko Haram* is so alarmed by western education. They think it is designed to crush their faith. When people despair that their faith will be taken seriously, they all too easily look for security in some form of fundamentalism or worse, an extreme form of religion; *Boko Haram* is an example of this latter, making Christians and Muslims unable to live creatively together in harmony and *convivencia*. It is a problem that typifies our age: frightened peoples revert to identity positions—fastening onto a faith or an ethnicity—to define who they are, in the hope that together they may survive. It is a destructive path. In contrast, St Paul made it a cardinal point of his mission to teach the Church that peoples who were in Christ, whatever their gender or race, whether they were Jews or Gentiles, were now brothers and sisters together (Galatians 3:26–29). This Christ-like insight is something that now needs to reach far beyond the Church. It is a lesson for the whole world. As the ecumenical movement informed the twentieth century, so now in this century, as a vital step towards this kingdom insight, the people of the great faiths, Christians and Muslims in particular, need to work for mutual understanding between their faiths. The work has begun and needs to continue, fostering dialogue, friendship and understanding between them, the children of Sarah and Hagar together knowing they are engaged in one common endeavour (Galatians 4:21–31).

Let us pray for the people and leaders of Nigeria—and especially the women, girls and boys, who have been abducted and abused there and abused here in the United Kingdom. Bring Christians and Muslims into deeper understanding of each other and of their faiths and help them to work together for the Common Good.

13

Germany, Austria, Switzerland, Liechtenstein

Week after Lent 1

The population of Germany is 84 million, of Austria and Switzerland, 9 million each. As with Europe generally, the population figures are stable and projected to go down. German is the common language apart from the French- and Italian-speaking cantons of Switzerland. Liechtenstein, on the border with Austria, aligns with Switzerland.

Austria is predominantly Roman Catholic; the rest are fairly equally Catholic and Protestant (Lutheran, Reformed or Calvinist). Anglicans are part of the Diocese in Europe, which is in communion with the Old Catholic Churches in these countries. The first half of the twentieth century was dominated by the two world wars, Switzerland remaining neutral throughout. Germany was divided from 1945 until 1990, the Berlin Wall coming down in 1989. West Germany with Benelux, France and Italy formed what is now the European Union. Austria joined in 1995, Switzerland remains outside. Each country is a democracy.

Learning to love those who had been enemies

My late wife Joy was five months old at the beginning of the 1939 war with Germany. I was three years old. Three weeks before the war began, her parents took her to Switzerland to meet the Swiss branch of her family, her mother's family and her grandparents from both sides. They all came from Morges, a small town beside *Lac Léman* which is near to Lausanne in Canton Vaud. Neither of us remembered very much about the war.

My family was in Bradford and had equipped our dining room with a Morrison Shelter—for those houses which lacked a cellar or big enough garden Morrison Shelters were available, in case we were bombed—a large metal affair with sharp corners, under which for mysterious reasons beyond my understanding we were sometimes taken to sleep. In fact there were few bombs in Bradford. There were many more where Joy was living, especially when her family moved to Banstead in 1943. The doodlebugs—the flying bombs—started to bombard the south in the summer of 1944. They had a powerful effect on Joy's dreams. I remember the end of hostilities and the bonfire that we had at our school, but little more; except that as I grew up, I came to realize the effect the war had had on my thinking about Germany—that Germany was the enemy. It was to take me a long time to put this right.

Very soon after I was ordained, a friend and I went to Hamburg. We stayed with a family in a beautiful village on the Elbe. Our host told us about his experience of being a soldier in the war, and I shared mine about my years as a National Serviceman. It was the beginning of a change of heart. Then in the 1970s, there were the *Heimat* films on television about the people of a village in the Ruhr before, during and after the war.* This gave me a much more positive view of Germany. Many years later my spiritual director was German, a sister of the Dominican community based in Roding, near Schwandorf close to the Czech border. Renate's kindness over the 15 years she guided me was to complete the transition from distaste to real love and appreciation. Coming away from Roding once I was on my way to Switzerland to celebrate my eightieth birthday. We were to meet there for a family celebration. Come the birthday morning, I was in Munich, staying in a hotel. When I came down for breakfast, the staff showed me to a table decorated with streamers, flowers and a bottle of Prosecco. I was so touched. My hosts must have noted the date in my passport.

---

* *Heimat*, films directed by Edgar Reitz (Germany, 1984). The story of a family in the Hunsrück region of Germany, 11 episodes, 15½ hours, broadcast by BBC 2, 1986.

Renate was keen that I should read about Edith Stein, the great Jewish German philosopher who in 1921 had become a Catholic.* Renate told me of the time when Edith and her sister had ventured into a Frankfurt church and had seen a woman there, praying. The woman had come into the church with her shopping for a brief moment of prayer. Synagogues were not like that, open for prayer to anyone who might wish to come in and pray. Both women were struck by the naturalness of what they were seeing, this woman taking a moment to be with God.** Not long after this, Edith Stein became a Christian. She later joined a Carmelite community and became known in religion as Teresa Benedicta of the Cross. The book I read was her study of St John of the Cross. "The soul," Stein says, "united with Christ lives out of his life—however, only in surrender to the Crucified when she has travelled the entire way of the cross with him."*** This was to become her personal way. When the Nazis came to power, her community moved her to Holland for her protection. Once the Netherlands were invaded, her safety was gone. She was interned. Later she was transferred to Auschwitz and there—on 9 August 1942—she was murdered. She was canonized as a martyr and confessor in 1998.

There were others who had the courage to oppose the Nazi regime. Sophie Scholl was a member of a Protestant family.**** She had initially thought the Nazi regime a good development, only to become more and more disillusioned as the atrocities increased. She, her brother Hans and a friend, Christoph Probst, formed "The White Rose", a non-violent resistance group which campaigned secretly for some six months against the war. On 18 February 1943, she and her friends were leafleting

---

* Edith Stein, OCD, *The Science of the Cross*, trans. Josephine Koeppel, OCD (Washington DC: ICS Pubs, Inst. Carmelite Studies, Vol VI, Collected Works, 2002).

** A recent biography gives a different story, that she read a biography of Teresa of Avila. See Peter Tyler, *The Living Philosophy of Edith Stein* (London: Bloomsbury, 2022).

*** Stein, *The Science of the Cross*, p. 20.

**** *Sophie Scholl: The final days*, film directed by Marc Rothemund, written by Fred Breinersdorfer (Germany, 2005).

Munich University when Sophie was seen by a janitor. He summoned the Gestapo, and they were arrested. They were summarily tried, and four days later guillotined. Their story, like that of Edith Stein, was one of outstanding courage as they trod their perilous way. The science of the cross, as Edith Stein had written, is about God's power showing itself in just such powerlessness in the face of evil. Their witness and their rejection of hatred brought life to others.

Jesus said, "I say to you, Love your enemies and pray for those who persecute you, so that you may be children of your Father in heaven" (Matthew 5:44–45).

Let us pray for the people and leaders of Germany, Austria and Switzerland and for all who tread the way of the cross in the struggle against tyranny and oppression. Teach us to learn the ways that make for peace.

14

Egypt, Sudan and South Sudan

Week after Lent 2

Egypt has a population of 106 million, which is expected to go on increasing. Sudan is 46 million and South Sudan 11.5 million. Egypt and Sudan are largely Muslim, 5 per cent of Egypt are members of the indigenous Coptic Orthodox Church, which is subject to persecution; 21 Copts were murdered by *Daesh* (the term preferred by Muslims because it dissociates the terrorist group from Islam: it means "one who crushes something under foot") in February 2015. South Sudan is largely Christian, divided fairly equally between the Roman Catholic and Anglican churches. The new Anglican province of Alexandria covers Egypt. Sudan and South Sudan each has its own province. Egypt and Sudan were one country when Britain ruled, but they separated when they became independent in 1956. South Sudan (see below) became independent from Sudan in 2011. Each of the countries has suffered political unrest; the genocide in Darfur (to the west of Sudan) lasted from 2003 to 2008 and there are still occasions of unrest at the time of writing.

Working for peace in South Sudan

During Holy Week in 2019, the two leaders of South Sudan, President Salva Kür Mayardit and the former rebel leader Dr Riek Machar, were invited to the Vatican to "reflect and pray" with Pope Francis and the Archbishop of Canterbury, Justin Welby. Mr Kür is Roman Catholic, Dr Machar Presbyterian. They were there to pray for a resolution of the many problems their country had suffered since independence. At the end of the retreat, on Maundy Thursday, Pope Francis knelt down in front of the two leaders and kissed their feet—an enacted prayer that the leaders might uphold the peace agreement they had recently made. Peace did hold up, but sporadic atrocities were to continue and many threats remained.

War between the north and south of Sudan began almost immediately after the 1956 independence of the united country. The first war was to last until 1972. Ten years later, in 1983, a second war broke out, this time because the then President of Sudan, President Numeiry, had decided to revoke—or simply ignore—the Addis Ababa agreement which had brought the first war to an end. His intention was to impose Islamic Sharia law on the whole country. This time war was to continue for a further 20 years. At last, in 2005 a comprehensive peace agreement was agreed and signed. South Sudan was granted autonomy with the promise that in six years there would be a referendum as to whether they should opt for independence or not. When 2011 arrived, the country voted almost unanimously for independence. It was a thrilling moment for the people, and it is all vividly described by Peter Martell in his history of the country.* Tragedy was to follow soon after. Two years later, war broke out once again; this time a civil war orchestrated by the two leaders battling for pre-eminence. This was the war that came to an end of sorts in 2018.

When the first war began in 1955, Paride Taban was a 19-year-old South Sudanese man training to become a Catholic priest. At the same time and at the same age, I was doing my National Service. It was in May of the same year, as a young soldier, I passed through Sudan on the way to Kenya—in fact the elderly plane in which we were flying landed at Khartoum. During the first war Fr Taban honed his skills as a priest and pastor. In 1983, he was ordained bishop and appointed to the diocese of Torit, a town southeast of Juba, the capital, on the southern edge of the country. Throughout this second war he suffered with his people. For a time, he was in prison. Later he played an important part in preparing the ground for the Comprehensive Peace Agreement which was signed in 2005; the one referred to above. Once that agreement had been achieved, he resigned his bishopric so that he could work for new ways to ensure

* Peter Martell, *First Raise a Flag: How South Sudan Won the War but Lost the Peace* (London: Hurst and Company, 2018).

peace. He moved from Torit to an even remoter part of the country, to the village of Kuron in Kapoeta East Province. At first, he lived in a tent. It was the beginning of his idea of building a community of peace. He purposely chose a poor region of the country. He saw this as the best way of addressing the challenge facing a country where almost everyone was starving, and where tribal rivalries made everything so much worse.*

Fr Taban's idea came initially from an early experience he had had as a child being brought up in the logging town of Katire. Katire was then a small community where religious differences were not an issue. If there was no Roman Catholic service in Katire in one week, he would that Sunday go to a Protestant or Anglican service. If there was no Christian worship anywhere, he and his friends would go to the mosque. Katire was a place where people had learnt to live in harmony with each other in *convivencia*. Now he wanted to replicate this in a new community.

Another influence was a visit he had made in 1993 to the Oasis of Peace Community in Israel (see Week 4). Yet another inspiration was the theology of his training, that in the Trinity there was already a model of corporate oneness: Father, Son and Holy Spirit in harmony as One. So Bishop Taban called his new community "The Holy Trinity Peace Village".

Starting in this very small way from his tent in Kuron, he set out to show that the Good News of Christ was real by providing—eventually—secure homes, educational facilities and a clinic promoting practical health and healing for the people who joined him. He determined that the setting should be peaceful. People of different tribes and religion were to mingle together. By 2020, 15 years later, a new secondary school was about to be built with funding obtained from the European Union. Fr Taban quotes a verse from Jeremiah, "I know the plans I have for you, says the Lord, plans for your welfare and not for harm, to give you a future with hope" (29:11). The community now has people within it from many of the different tribes, Nuer and Dinka especially; people of faith and of no faith, all of them living and working together in cooperative harmony.

---

* Emmanuel Katongole, *The Sacrifice of Africa: A Political Theology for Africa* (Cambridge: William B. Eerdmans Pub. Co., 2011), pp. 135–47.

One of them said of it, that he felt renewed, because he had found himself treated as a human being.

The problems of South Sudan are immense. In addition to so much war, the country now has to cope with floods and in 2020 storms of locusts (see opening essay), both thought to be the results of global warming. Bishop Taban's vision is a powerful earnest of the future that will eventually come to be true of the whole country.

Let us pray for the people and leaders of Egypt, Sudan and South Sudan, especially for those who light flames of hope in all three countries.

15

The Southern Cone of South America: Argentina, Chile, Paraguay, Uruguay

Week after Lent 3

Argentina has a population of 46 million, Chile (with Easter Island) 19 million, Paraguay 7.5 million and Uruguay 3.5 million–76 million in all. Chile is on the western side of the Andes mountains, Argentina on the east. Paraguay has a border with Bolivia, and each are between Argentina and Brazil. Uruguay is on the coast, across the *Rio de la Plata* from Buenos Aires, the capital of Argentina, and it too has a border with Brazil. The majority faith is Catholic with a growing Pentecostal Church, especially in Argentina. The Anglican Church has two dioceses in Argentina, one in each of the other countries. Anglicans in the Falkland Islands etc. are cared for from England by the Bishop of Dover. The southern tip of Argentina is the jumping off point for Antarctica. Politically, each of the countries has been subject to times of military rule; in Argentina a military junta was in power from 1976 until 1983, and in Chile from 1973 (see below). In recent years, Argentina, Uruguay and Paraguay have become members of the Mercosur trading bloc–with Brazil. Chile is an associate.

Vocation: caring for the wounded

Sheila Cassidy was born in Lincolnshire in 1937. Once the war was over, when she was about 12, her family moved to Sydney in Australia where she was educated at a convent school. She was very devout–and as can happen sometimes, despite not being called to the religious life, she developed a fear that she might be. In a talk she gave in St Paul's

Cathedral many years later, she referred to this fear as "vocationitis",* a scrupulously obsessional conviction that she had to become a nun, even though in her heart she knew she wanted to become a doctor. She studied medicine at the Catholic University in Sydney, and when her family returned to England, finished her training at Somerville College in Oxford. Once qualified, she shared a flat with a fellow doctor, Consuela, who was from Chile. When Consuela returned to her country, Dr Cassidy decided that she would herself go there too to join her. It was 1970. Tragically, her friend by this time had become an alcoholic; cirrhosis of the liver followed, and a year or so later she died. Despite the loss, Cassidy decided she would remain in Chile.

On 11 September 1973, General Augusto Pinochet and his fellow army officers, with support from the United States and the rich of the country, overthrew Salvador Allende's Socialist government. Pinochet, like all military governors, could not brook opposition. He saw it as insubordination that needed to be controlled by discipline and punishment.

Meanwhile Dr Cassidy felt she had really found her vocation. Dorothy Day used to say that you know your vocation by the joy it brings you,** and this was how she felt: a sense that she could now abandon herself to God and go wherever she was led. She was in touch with several people who were opposed to Pinochet's new regime and one of them, a Jesuit priest friend, asked her on one occasion to attend a man who was on the run from the police. She went to see him at the priest's house. There were no immediate repercussions, but a year later, on 1 November 1975, the Secret Police came to her home. The DINA, as Pinochet's Gestapo was called, took her into custody. She was taken to their torture house, the Villa Grimaldi on the outskirts of Santiago. There she was brutally treated. She was later to describe what they did to her in newspaper

---

* Suffering: Sheila Cassidy and Frances Young speak at St Paul's Cathedral (2010), <http://www.youtube.com/watch?v=kzmd65jWwmc>.

** Liz Dodd, interview with Kate Hennessy, "Planted for the Future", *The Tablet*, 28 March 2020, p. 13.

articles and in her book;* it was unspeakable! A Chile report later put the figure of those tortured at 40,000; a further 2,300 were executed. Many simply "disappeared". The British Government, with the help of an Argentinian diplomat, managed to organize her release and two months after she had been arrested, she was flown back to England. The day was 31 December 1975.

Recovery from the mainly psychological effects was to take a long time—and in one sense, since such trauma never fully leaves a person, it has remained a part of her being. She had been asked by her fellow Chile prison inmates to tell the world about their suffering. That she did so in fact made a huge impact on the country, but it was at a cost; a necessary one, no doubt, since she had felt herself commissioned, but it also had the effect of distancing her trauma. It also, of course, gave her time to begin processing it. In my own work as a counsellor with seriously abused persons, I had to learn to be wary of pressing too quickly for the story; the psychological and spiritual wounds are so intense. They are a massive violation and insult to the being, and in order to cope persons have to anaesthetize themselves for a time until they have recovered enough to begin the process of owning and comprehending it all. Eventually—partly because she had spoken and written about it—her own numbness began to wear off, enough for her to be able to start. She had to address not only the physical torture but also the inner terror she had experienced throughout.

Shortly after her Chile experience, she decided she should once more test whether she really did have a vocation to the religious life. She entered a Carmelite monastery. It did not go well, and to her embarrassment she was asked to leave. Not long afterwards she met the Abbess of Stanbrook, who asked her what she was now doing. After she had explained, the two of them stood in silence. Then the abbess said, "Why don't you just be Sheila?"**

---

* Sheila Cassidy, *Audacity to Believe* (London: Darton, Longman & Todd, 1977).

** Sheila Cassidy, *Made for Laughter* (London: Darton, Longman & Todd, 2006), p. 129.

A number of years later, in July 1983, I was at a conference organized by the Churches' Council for Health and Healing, and Dr Cassidy was giving the keynote speech. I was struck by the fact that throughout it she hugged a teddy bear to herself. In one sense, it spoke of her acceptance of herself as Sheila, as the abbess had advised. In another, it spoke of her trauma. Holding the teddy bear had to do with the therapy she had received.

A manic working pattern when she became medical director of the Plymouth Hospital for the dying had helped distance her depression and post-traumatic stress for a time—until she sought help in counselling. In the course of the work, she learnt the value of having a teddy bear to comfort her. It became a companion, a presence to embrace her. I thought when she was speaking to us that she must be using it as a transitional object; in the Winnicottian sense, as a symbol representing the absent mother (see Psalm 131),* and indeed she describes it as such in her biography.** It was remarkable that she was able to so share her vulnerability with us. It spoke of her Chile wounded-ness but also of childhood hurts that trauma so readily hooks into. She has used her ease with her own bear to encourage the many hurt souls she has cared for to have bears of their own. Dr Cassidy is now retired, living quietly with her Chow dogs, contemplating the beauty of the sea from the windows of her home.

Let us pray for the people and leaders of the countries of the Southern Cone, for those who were killed, made to "disappear" or traumatized when the countries were ruled by the military—and may each country know the gifts of justice and lasting peace.

* D. W. Winnicott, *Playing and Reality* (London: Routledge Classics, 2005), pp. 132–4.

** Cassidy, *Made for Laughter*, p. 178.

16

North and South Korea

Week after Lent 4

North Korea's borders are with Russia in the east (11 miles long) and with China (880 miles). North and South Korea are divided by a de-militarized zone at the thirty-eighth parallel; each country has roughly half the peninsula. North Korea's population is 26 million, South Korea's 51.5 million. North Korea is officially an atheist state with a few secret Buddhists and Christians. In South Korea, about 45 per cent claim to be unattached to a faith; of the rest a quarter are Christian, rather more Protestant than Catholic, and a number are Buddhist. The Anglican Church of Korea (*Daehan Seong Georg Hoe*) has three dioceses. In 1950, North Korea invaded the South. The war ended with an armistice in July 1953, maintaining the division of the country into two. North Korea is a Communist state with a Supreme Leader, by 2022 the third of the Kim Dynasty. It has an enormous army and an arsenal of weapons. South Korea is a Democratic Republic.

Preparing for retirement

Shortly after retiring in 2001, I went to St Beuno's, the Jesuit house which lies to the south of St Asaph in North Wales. I was to be there for three months, a solitary Anglican among a group of 30 Roman Catholics—priests, religious, lay—studying Apostolic Spirituality. In the midst of the course, we were led on a 30-day Ignatian retreat. In the next room was Fr Thomas Timpte, a German monk of the St Ottilien Congregation of Missionary Benedictines based at Waegwan Abbey in South Korea.

His community had first arrived in Korea in 1909. In 1920, they had moved to Tokwon near Wonsan in what is now North Korea. By 1949, they were a community of some 60 monks, 25 of them Korean. Twenty Benedictine sisters, also from Germany, had their convent nearby. In May of that year, the Secret Police arrived and arrested both communities. They were imprisoned in Pyongyang. The Korean monks were executed; the others were sent to a penal labour camp in the mountains near Ganggye. Thirty-two of them with six more associated Korean priests died there from the hard labour and harsh conditions for which North Korea is so tragically noted. Those German monks who survived were eventually sent home by the Trans-Siberian Railway. They were in a desperate state when they arrived in Germany. Their abbot Boniface Sauer, together with Fr Benedict Kim and their companions, are being considered for beatification, a process which began in May 2007.

Some of the Korean monks and nuns had managed to flee to the south before all these things happened, and they started new communities there, the sisters in Daegu, the brothers in Waegwan—both places in the southeast of the country. In 1952, some of the German survivors from the Tokwon community returned to Korea and joined the community at Waegwan. In 1964, their house became the St Maurus and Placidus Abbey. Fr Thomas had joined them in 1962. The abbey is now one of the largest Benedictine monasteries in the world. It has 120 monks, almost all of them Korean.

The Anglican Church owes an immense debt to the Benedictine rule.* Our divine office, Morning and Evening Prayer in the *Book of Common Prayer*, which all Anglican priests are required to say, is based on it—though not, it has to be said, during an Ignatian thirty-day retreat, which calls for a different mode of prayer. Our retreat ended on a Friday. Our guides insisted that we take a short break before we resumed our studies and, gratefully, Fr Thomas and I set off for Holyhead. His plan was to visit Dublin and Ireland; mine was to explore Anglesey. I remember, as we waited for his ferry and were walking through Holyhead, his delight in recognizing the Chinese characters that emblazoned the various restaurants there and that he could translate them for me.

---

* Benedict of Nursia, ed. Abbot Justin McCann OSB, *The Rule of St Benedict (in Latin and English)* (London: Burns & Oates, 1952).

The Ignatian retreat had been an extended spiritual exercise, a long conversation with the Lord; five hours of meditative prayer each day and a long period of time to discern in what ways the Holy Spirit might be directing us in the future. I had retired from full-time ministry a couple of months before. Joy had died in 1998, and now that I was alone and with a new stage of ministry ahead, it was important to discern what the Lord required of me in my retirement ministry. I imagine it was much the same for Fr Thomas.

The retreat did all that I had hoped for, both practically and spiritually–practically in showing me what shape my retirement ministry might take, spiritually in discerning new ways in which to respond prayerfully. The daily office was to remain fundamental. The Rule of St Benedict of Nursia has 12 detailed chapters on how the office is to be said. The word "office" is a shortening of the Latin, *opus facere Dei* (to do the work of God). Benedict prescribes the daily adoration and worship which is to be offered to God. The two Anglican offices of Morning and Evening Prayer were adapted by Thomas Cranmer from the sixteenth-century sevenfold Catholic Office, which in its turn had been drawn from early Christian usage and in particular the teaching of St Benedict. Cranmer redesigned the offices so they could be said by both lay and ordained Christians. The provision of psalms was much gentler. While the Rule required a weekly recitation of the entire psalter, the Anglican Church spread it over a month. *Common Worship*, the new Anglican provision, reduces it even more, scattering psalms over a rather longer period. The important point was that by praying the office, Anglican Christians were to be led to centre their prayer on the majesty and the wonder and the beauty of God.

A gift of retirement is that it allows more time for prayer–in its threefold form of Office, Eucharist and Personal Devotion. In the last decade of our married life, Joy and I had used to say the offices together. Now in the prayer space of a new home which for the most part had become a hermitage, my solitariness was to be centred within this wider Church's prayer to the Father, becoming one with the local Church community by joining in eucharistic fellowship in Christ together, by offering silent meditation and contemplation in the stillness of the home to become strengthened and empowered by the Holy Spirit—the whole an ongoing meeting with the Mystery.

The Rule of St Benedict balances this life of prayer with its two further concerns for ongoing study and practical work. This last was where the Ignatian retreat was so helpful, designed as it was to enable Ignatius's first followers in his Society of Jesus, Francis Xavier in particular, to discern their way—in Francis's case to become an apostle to the Far East. The whole experience was not unlike being psychoanalysed and as an exercise in discernment truly remarkable. For me, two of the outcomes were that I work with asylum seekers in Newcastle and second, as a concern for the unity of the Church, especially the Anglican with the Catholic, become a friend of the Anglican Centre in Rome; there were to be more projects ahead.

After our break and the rest of the course, Fr Thomas—now retired and living away from the community—returned to Waegwan to join once more with his community's prayer, amongst which one concern would have been that the two halves of the Korean Peninsula might eventually become one in love and friendship.

Let us pray for the people and rulers of both North and South Korea, that they and we may be so rooted and grounded in prayer that in peace and justice we may come to value and love each other, coming together to the glory of God.

17

East Africa: Kenya, Uganda, Tanzania

Week after Lent 5

Uganda and Kenya are immediately to the south of South Sudan, Ethiopia and Somalia, with Tanzania to their south. The island of Zanzibar is 70 miles to the northeast of Dar es Salaam, the coastal city of Tanzania. Uganda's population is 48.5 million, Kenya's 56.5 and Tanzania's 63.5 million; Tanzania's population is expected to go on increasing. Kenya and Uganda are each largely Christian with a significant Muslim minority. In Tanzania, this is reversed, the Muslim community being slightly larger than the Christian. Within the Anglican Church, each country is a separate province. Uganda and Kenya were British colonies, Tanganyika was German until after the First World War, when Britain took over the rule. Independence came to each country in the early 1960s. Tanganyika and the island of Zanzibar united in 1964 to become Tanzania. Since independence, Uganda has had a chequered political life, Kenya a rather better one, while Tanzania has been the most settled.

Intimate friendship

The three countries are gathered around Lake Victoria. In 2003, I was staying in Fort Portal, leading a week's study on pastoral care. The dean of the cathedral had a brother (a cousin in fact, but brother in the African sense), and he arranged for me to cross Lake Victoria by ferry to Mwansa in Tanzania. Unfortunately, the boat I was to go on was delayed for a day, so I went back to the guest house in Kampala and took the opportunity to visit the cathedral.

It was 5 May 2003, the Monday after the third Sunday in Easter. I walked up to Namirende Cathedral for Evensong. There seemed to be something going on, an organ playing and somewhere not too far away a brass ensemble, but apart from these everything else was quiet and shut—until I spied an almost hidden door that was open. I slipped inside, rather nervously found a pew and in the silence savoured the moment, of being one in prayer with the Ugandan Church. This was where the early martyrs, James Hannington and his fellow missionaries, had been killed in 1885. More recently, in 1977, there had also been the murder of Uganda's Archbishop Janani Luwum by President Amin.

I was writing this piece just as a new archbishop—Stanley Ntagali—was being installed in the same cathedral. Archbishop Justin Welby was there as head of the Anglican Communion to share fellowship with a Ugandan Church which at the time had become part of a largely Evangelical grouping, the Global Anglican Future Conference (GAFCON), whose main concern among others was its opposition to homosexuality. An American bishop was the preacher at the service and drew attention to this "sin", which he deplored. To great applause he said, "As for me and my house, we will serve the Lord".*

It is surprising looking back over a 60-year ministry that when I was ordained in 1960 practice as a homosexual was a criminal offence. At the time, there were thousands who were sentenced to prison or prevailed upon to take drugs to alter their orientation—which it doesn't. Things though were changing fast. In 1957, the Wolfenden Report was published with the support of a number of religious leaders.** It argued that homosexuality should cease to be a criminal offence. Ten years later the law was changed by the Sexual Offences Act. It was an important moment, a cultural shift which was in fact part of a much wider international change in understanding.

At the beginning of my ministry, insofar as I thought about it at all, I had simply accepted the traditional view. A pivotal moment that altered

* Madeleine Davies, "Welby too supportive of gays, says Uganda", *Church Times*, 6 March 2020, p. 13.

** The Wolfenden Report, *The Report of the Departmental Committee on Homosexual Offences and Prostitution* (London: HMSO, September 4, 1957).

this happened when I was in New York during the 1980s. It was at the beginning of the AIDS outbreak, and during a visit to the St Patrick's Cathedral on Fifth Avenue, in the chapel there that was dedicated to those who had died of AIDS, a young man was praying, evidently in deep mourning, praying for his lover.

In my counselling work, a number, many of them clergy, Evangelical as well as Catholic, told me that they were gay and that in order to survive in ministry they had had to pretend that they were not. It was safer, they said, to have casual relationships than live with a single partner. It was clear that the Church had to act. Talking with young people generally and my grandchildren in particular, it was clear that to their generation being gay was of no consequence. They were bemused to think that to some people it was.

African society on this matter is different. As we have learnt from gay African asylum seekers here in Newcastle, one of the reasons why they have sought refuge in our country is to escape severe punishment, or even death. The difference between our societies inevitably leads to mutual misunderstandings, particularly within the churches. The presence of Archbishop Welby representing the Church of England at the cathedral was therefore important.

GAFCON would of course tell us that it is we in the English Church who are wrong, and that the Bible is clearly against homosexuality. Our Church is most certainly opposed to any form of sexual abuse (Genesis 19:5–11), urges faithfulness in marriage, and witnesses that relationships should mirror the love of God. It has had more difficulty with intimate friendship between persons of the same sex. Perhaps we should turn more to the relationship between David and Jonathan (1 Samuel 20), to David's lament when Jonathan died–when he described his love as surpassing his love for women (2 Samuel 1:25b–26).*

St Aelred of Hexham would have agreed. Aelred (1109–67) was the son of a married priest on the staff at Hexham Abbey and was probably himself gay. He joined the Cistercian community at Rievaulx, not far from Whitby, and later became its abbot. He wrote about his love for his

---

* Aelred of Rievaulx, *Spiritual Friendship*, trans. Mary Eugene Laker (Kalamazoo, MI: Cistercian Publications, 1977), pp. 85, 115–16.

fellow monks, modelling his understanding of friendship on Cicero's *De Amicitia*.* You become a friend, Aelred taught, not because you expect to gain anything from him, but because you value him for himself; you want only the best for him. By this stage, Aelred was not afraid to encourage affection between his monks. He even allowed them to hold hands, which in a twelfth-century context was unusual. In a religious community today, it would be equally so. But friendship is fundamental for all persons if they are to be truly human.

There is a moment in the story of David and Jonathan when they were both afraid that Saul would kill David. Saul asked Jonathan why David was not at dinner, and after Jonathan had explained, angrily accused them of being sexually involved (1 Samuel 20:30). Saul was being prurient. I remember once when I was telling my counselling supervisor about some client's sexual problems, his asking whether I was enjoying the sex. I was offended, but in that instance he was right. I had been roused by what the client had shared with me. It is usually the quality of the relationship we should be interested in, not the sex which may or may not be a part of it. Sexual concerns are important to the couple and to God, but not to the rest of us.

A long-established church tends to be conservative. It reflects the general accepted attitudes of its culture as the norm, probably not its faith tradition. Africa and the west are different and face different issues. The Church in Uganda is strong, a Church of the martyrs, and I personally experienced great kindness and consideration there. May our two churches remain in union with each other, each of us seeking to serve the Lord.

Let us pray for the people and leaders of Uganda, Kenya and Tanzania, that by their example of faith and service, they and we may grow together in understanding and unity. May we give thanks for and remember all who suffer rejection because of their sexual orientation.

---

* Aelred of Rievaulx, *Spiritual Friendship*, pp. 21–2.

18

Mozambique, Malawi, Zambia, Zimbabwe, Angola

Holy Week

Usually described as Central Africa, the five countries are well to the south of the Equator in the southern half of the continent. Angola is on the Atlantic coast, Mozambique beside the Indian Ocean with the three other countries in between. Zambia and Malawi are side by side below Tanzania, and Zimbabwe is south of them on the other side of the Zambezi River. Angola's population is 35 million, Mozambique 33 million, Zambia 19.5 million, Malawi 20 million and Zimbabwe 15.5 million. Each country is largely Christian, more Protestant than Catholic, with significant minorities of Muslims (Mozambique 18 per cent and Malawi 25 per cent).

The Anglican Province of Central Africa serves the three central countries and Botswana. Angola and Mozambique have a diocese each and are now grouped together in a new province. These two countries were both Portuguese colonies; Malawi, Zambia and Zimbabwe were British. In 1953, these three were formed into one country, the Central African Federation–which ended in 1960. Soon after, in 1963, Zambia and Malawi became independent. Zambia has been the most settled politically, Malawi rather less so. In 1964, Southern Rhodesia unilaterally declared itself independent and remained so until 1980 when it became properly independent as Zimbabwe. Economic difficulties since have led to an enormous exodus from the country. Angola's civil war lasted from 1975 until 2002. Mozambique fared better but has suffered recently from flooding and Islamic militant incursions in the northern province of Cabo Delgado.

Holy Week and Easter in Zambia

The Tazara railway which runs from Dar es Salaam to Kapiri Mposhi in Zambia passes through Mbeya and Kasama on the way. After I had crossed Lake Victoria, referred to in last week's vignette, and had reached Mpanza, it took a week or so to reach Mbeya in the far south of the country, on the border with Zambia. The train journey into Zambia took most of an afternoon and evening.

This 2003 visit was my first to Kasama. It was where Joy and her friend Elizabeth had taught for two years between 1962 and 1964, Elizabeth as Head of Miller Girls' School, Joy as her deputy. They were both just 23, a year out of college and in their second year of service in what was then Northern Rhodesia. For Joy, these two years in Kasama were to define her life. She loved being there—the girls, the challenges, the privilege of teaching at such an important time. The colonial era was drawing to its close. Sylvia Usher, a friend of ours who had worked for Christian Aid, told me that she saw Joy and her friends as Christians who understood, worked for and welcomed this coming end. It was at a cost to her, both physical and mental, but it was a price she was willing to pay. She denied herself and walked the way of the cross there.

Miller Girls' had become Ituna High School with 900 pupils by 2003. It was very much larger than it had been in 1963 and struggling because it was too poorly funded. The Head told me that only staff salaries were paid by the government, everything else had to be raised by the community of Kasama itself. The result was that they had virtually nothing: a lab empty of scientific equipment, a computer room with no computers, a library with no more than a dozen books, toilets that did not work, and buildings in dire need of repair. Parents had rallied as much as they could, but they too had limited resources. The school was operating on an impossibly tight budget. Back in 1963, the girls had been excited that their country was about to become independent. They knew it as a time of real hope. Joy felt the same.

Nine years after this visit, in 2012, I was once again in Kasama, this time to inspect a project that was being funded by the Zambia Society Trust. Joy had been a founding member and later a vice-president. After she died, I joined the trust in her stead, and since the trust was funding an Orphans and Vulnerable Children project—founded by the Roman Catholic cathedral in Kasama—I was there to see how it was going. The local committee took me to a village where there were 50 orphans, all of whom had lost their parents to AIDS. A young villager had prepared a speech, which my surprised host translated from his Bemba for me. The village wanted, he said, to expand their work; they needed money for education and to buy bicycles. This latter, he said, so that they could deliver the produce they were growing for the benefit of the orphans to the nearby markets. The speech was a highlight of my inspection. Our small trust responded as best we could. We paid for some bicycles certainly.

That evening, I invited this Catholic Kasama committee and members of the local Anglican congregation to join me for supper. The hotel made the dinner memorable, and both groups shared the vision they had for their community, a sign of their continuing hope in the midst of so much continuing despair. It was a vision I hoped we would be able to support.

All this took place a couple of days before Palm Sunday. It was now Wednesday in Holy Week, and I left for Lusaka on the 3 p.m. bus; that is, 3 p.m. was the scheduled time for departure. In fact, following the African custom of waiting until everyone travelling had actually arrived, we left at 8 p.m.—with 535 miles to go. There was one spare seat beside me, empty until Mpika, and then occupied by a silent mother and her infant, the three of us squashed together in an over-full bus for the rest of the journey to Lusaka, where we arrived at 6 a.m. It was Maundy Thursday. Straight to a hotel to catch a couple of hours sleep before the Maundy Thursday Chrism Mass. A snatched breakfast, fast to the cathedral of the Holy Cross (Anglican, but also the city's national centre for prayer and reconciliation), almost on time. Late but not too late! During the service, along with the priests from Lusaka diocese with their bishop, David Ngoya, we gathered round the altar and together renewed our ordination vows.

I was staying with Joy's and my goddaughter, Pauline Allen. Next day we were again at the cathedral for the Good Friday Stations of the Cross. The service began at a large cross on the green sward which surrounds the cathedral. This was the first station, a further 21 more to come, with a sermon and short liturgy at each one. It was a marathon! The young people's talks were the best of the many sermons.

Easter Day and we were at the cathedral once more—the hymns sung in English were each a dirge; those in the local language alive and joyful. That afternoon, Pauline invited Rosemary Mumba—Joy's and Elizabeth's head girl at Miller Girls' in Kasama—the widow of a former bishop of Lusaka, and Rosemary's son-in-law Patrick to join us for an Easter meal. As we shared our meal, my hostess and her guests spoke of their Easter lives: Pauline about her productive smallholding, Patrick about his project to help people damaged by AIDS, Rosemary her experiment with new techniques in farming to encourage new ideas in her community. New signs of resurrection hope on a Zambian Easter Day.

Let us pray for the people and leaders of Angola, Mozambique, Zambia, Malawi and Zimbabwe, that all who, denying themselves, take up their cross this Holy Week find themselves transformed as they contemplate the crucified and risen Lord.

19

United States of America 1

Easter Week

The United States population is 335 million; 75 per cent are Christian, a quarter of them Catholic. There are a growing number claiming to be atheist. The Episcopal Church (Anglican) is made up of nine provinces (for Province IX see Week 26). For most of the twentieth century, and indeed into the twenty-first, the United States has been the dominant country in the world, in general responsible for a *Pax Americana*. The USA favours the political right and is viscerally opposed to countries attracted to socialism or communism. In the late 2010s, it was constructing a wall along its southern border.

Campaigning for righteousness—small victories

Writing in 1932 the American theologian Reinhold Niebuhr argued that the Black Communities of the southern States might be able to liberate themselves if they could find a leader with the necessary skills.* Such a leader would need to adapt Gandhi's *satyagraha* principles and apply them to their situation. Niebuhr considered that the Black Christian Community had the spiritual strength to do this, if they could find such a person. In 1955, they did.

Martin Luther King was in his late twenties when he was called to lead. He was the minister of the church next door to the Alabama capitol, at the top of Dexter Avenue in Montgomery. He had been there a year when

---

* Reinhold Niebuhr, *Moral Man and Immoral Society* (London: SCM Press, 1932, 1963), pp. 252–4.

Rosa Parks, the local secretary of the main Black Americans Association, was arrested for sitting in a seat on a bus reserved for white passengers alone. It was December 1955. Her action triggered the Montgomery boycott and marked the beginning of the Human Rights Movement. Dr King was not the first choice for the leadership. He was as surprised as everyone else that he was the one chosen.

A major reason why Martin and Coretta King had moved to Montgomery was so that they could stand with their southern American compatriots in their fight against oppression. While studying for his doctorate, Dr King had come to understand Gandhi's concept of *satyagraha*—the harnessing of a community's spiritual disciplines to attain some political purpose, in India's case independence from British rule. *Sat* in Sanskrit means "truth", *agraha* "firmness"! Its aim was to convict oppressive authorities of their wrong-doing and shame them into amending their ways. In Dr King's adoption of Gandhi's thinking he linked it further with Jesus's Sermon on the Mount (Matthew 5–7). This led him to recognize, as he told a group of students a couple of years later, that "every person who believes in non-violent resistance believes somehow that the universe in some form is on the side of justice".* He said further that a community has to learn how to love those who oppose them if they are to create a real and just community. Of the whites, he observed, "their soul is greatly scarred. They need the love of the Negro . . . to remove (their) tensions, insecurities and fears".** Thirdly, he said, violence has to be avoided; violence always breeds violence, doing as much damage to the perpetrators as it does to its victims. "The aftermath of violence," he said, "is bitterness."*** Following these three principles, and after the success of the Montgomery boycott, he and his colleagues formed the Southern Christian Leadership Conference (SCLC) to advance their cause. It was to be an immense task, and in the years ahead the progress they made was depressingly slow. Many in fact claimed that

---

* Martin Luther King, Jr, *A Testament of Hope: The Essential Writings of Martin Luther King, Jr.*, ed. James M. Washington (London: Harper & Row, 1986), p. 38.

** King, *A Testament of Hope*, p. 19.

*** King, *A Testament of Hope*, p. 12.

SCLC and Dr King had failed—mainly because they did not achieve the total success that they were fighting for. Dr King for his part was realistic about this; he knew, as all political activists have to learn, that great endeavours take a long time. He had the necessary political gift of being able to accept any small advance as a victory; no doubt a small one, but a step in the right direction. Even the most limited victory is still a victory.

Almost ten years after this boycott, SCLC planned a campaign to register the disenfranchised Black community of Selma, in Alabama.* The State of Alabama had laid down that any Black person applying to be on the electoral register must take a number of elaborate tests to prove their eligibility. The result was that very few had done so. SCLC started its campaign on 2 January 1965. They marched with a select group from the Brown Chapel to the Selma courthouse a few blocks away. There they were met by a hefty body of the opposition and had to withdraw. Two months later they planned a much larger march, a long walk of about 40 miles along Highway 80 to Montgomery. Dr King could not be with them on the first day of this march, 7 March. They crossed the Pettus Bridge which straddles the Alabama River and once again found themselves opposed by a phalanx of storm troopers. The troopers charged into them wielding weapons and clubs. They had to retreat fast. For their next march, Dr King was with them. To avoid a bloodbath, they determined to march only as far as the troops if they were there, and that they would then turn back. All went as planned, and they did indeed have to turn back, Dr King being strongly criticized for doing so. A fortnight later, this time with the permission of the courts, they set out one final time; this was a much larger march of 3,000, again proceeding over the bridge. Some 300 of them went on further, all the way to Montgomery. There they were joined by a further 25,000, the whole crowd marching up Dexter Avenue, past Dr King's former charge, and up to the imposing State Capitol. Dr King, in his address, told the marchers of his dream, that one day their country would become a society able to live with its conscience. "How long will it take?" he asked; "It will not be long,"

---

* David J. Garrow, *Bearing the Cross: Martin Luther King, Jr and the Southern Christian Leadership Conference* (London: Jonathan Cape, 1988), pp. 356–430.

he asserted. He repeated the question, "How long?" He paused. "Not long!"* he said to thunderous applause. SCLC had been careful to limit what it might be able to achieve. Its purpose was to get people onto the electoral register; and this it did—the government then responding by passing a new Voting Rights Act that had the effect of overturning the old Alabama rules.

Many years later, my family and I were visiting this part of America and went to Selma and Montgomery. "Terrible to have them marching around for four months," the white custodian of a museum told us. On one side of the road to the Pettus Bridge in Selma, there is an estate of grand villas where the white community lives; on the other side are the barrack-like lines of the much smaller homes of the Black community. A memorial to Dr King stands just outside the A.M.E. Brown Chapel. We walked over the bridge and then drove along the highway to Montgomery, finally arriving like the march at the capitol.

In the same year that Martin Luther King was assassinated, he came to Newcastle to receive an honorary degree from the university, Newcastle being the only British university to honour him in this way.** It was a brief visit, but the city has basked in the glory ever since. The film of his speech has been used as a centrepiece of several conferences since.

Let us pray for the people and leaders of the United States of America, giving thanks for Martin Luther King and the Black Community, whose lives matter—and we pray for social harmony and the grace to appreciate and value all who contribute to the life of their country.

---

* King, *A Testament of Hope*, pp. 227–30.

** Brian Ward, *Martin Luther King in Newcastle upon Tyne* (Newcastle: Tyne Bridge Publishing, City Library, 2017).

2 0

Pakistan and Afghanistan

Week after Easter 2

Both Pakistan and Afghanistan have borders with Iran to the west, the Central Asian nations to the north, and Pakistan has a troubled border with India (see below). When Pakistan was formed in 1947, it included East Pakistan, now Bangladesh. A war in 1971 led to their separation (see Week 43). Pakistan's current population is 230 million and expected to continue rising; Afghanistan's is 41 million. Both countries are Muslim with small Christian communities; the Anglican Church is united with other churches to form the Church of Pakistan.

The border in the Himalaya mountainous region of Kashmir is disputed between Pakistan and India. Since the July 1972 Simla agreement, a "line of control" marks the boundary between the two countries, Kashmir being divided between them (see Week 6). To the east of Kashmir there is also the Aksai region, which is claimed by China. Afghanistan has been in almost constant turmoil since the 1979 Soviet Union invasion. After 9/11 in 2001, the Taliban rulers were ousted, the western nations maintaining a peace until 2021 when the Taliban resumed power.

Demanding respect for God and his prophet

Naboth had a vineyard next door to King Ahab's palace (1 Kings 21:1–16). Ahab thought it would make an excellent vegetable garden so he approached Naboth to ask him if he would part with it. Ahab said he would give him a much better one in exchange or he could simply buy it from him. Naboth did not wish to exchange or to sell. The vineyard, he told Ahab, had been in his family for generations and he wished to keep it that way. Ahab was upset; in fact, so upset that he went home, took to his bed and sulked under the bed clothes. When he did not appear for dinner, his formidable wife—the redoubtable Tyrian princess Jezebel—came to see where he had got to.

"What is causing all this?" she demanded. "Why have you not come down to eat?"

Ahab miserably mumbled his story. "Ahab!" Jezebel expostulated. "Are you not the king? Can you not do what you want? Come down at once and eat. I will deal with the vineyard problem for you." Jezebel, as a prophetess of Baal, had no moral scruples about what she needed to do.

That afternoon, she wrote to the various officials of Naboth's community. "Proclaim a fast," she said, "and make certain that Naboth is made to sit somewhere prominent. Recruit two rogues and tell them that they are to charge Naboth with blasphemy against God and the King. You will know what to do. Tell me when it is sorted."

A few days later the message came back. "Naboth is dead."

Up she went to tell a delighted Ahab that the vineyard was now his; straightaway he went and purloined the vineyard. At times, a blasphemy law is a useful tool if there are people one wants rid of.

Pakistan inherited a blasphemy law from the British. It was strengthened in the 1980s when the military were in power and it was still on the statute books some years later when a Christian woman, Asia Bibi, was arrested for blasphemy. Until then almost all who had been convicted under the law had been Muslim, many of them members of a minority Muslim community, considered by the orthodox to be heretics—like Christians sometimes who consider alternative Christian groups to be unacceptable. It has to be said that at the time of Asia Bibi's arrest no one had actually been executed under the act. Still, all too many had been abused and more than 60 killed in the community because of it. What eventually brought the problem to international attention was this arrest and conviction in 2010 of Asia Bibi. Since then, two politicians have been murdered, many more have been abused, and the hatred of minorities in Pakistan has become greater. This was not the idea behind the act; it was supposed to be about respecting the faith of others. Sadly this is the kind of effect such legislation has.

It all started when Asia Bibi (Assiya Noreen) and her fellow villagers had been harvesting berries. A quarrel developed as to the spiritual cleanliness of the water they were drinking. It sounds like the kind of parish problem that could have been handled pastorally by the local imam and quickly resolved. Instead he reported it to the police. A minor problem then began to escalate into an international incident. Asia Bibi was convicted; she was sentenced to death and in the meantime put in prison. She was to be there for eight years. Her conviction was eventually overturned by the appeal court in 2019. Since then, she has been allowed to move away with her family to Canada.*

Islam is exceptionally sensitive about anyone suspected of abusing the Prophet, the reason for passing the act. Islam in Pakistan largely follows the strict Barelvi understanding of Islam, which stems from the even stricter Hanafi school of jurisprudence. This was a tenth-century reform led by Ibn Hanbal which was then extended in the fourteenth century by the austere scholar Ibn Taymiyyah (1263–1328), who was a mystic but not a *Sufi*. In fact, he was strongly opposed to Sufism. Ibn Taymiyyah was born at the time of the Mongol incursions from the east and the Crusades from the west—a pincer movement that held Islam within a deadly embrace during the thirteenth century—and he urged Islam to look to its roots, to the Quran, to a strict interpretation of Shariah law. He was austere in his dislike of innovation and of music and dancing. Much later this school of learning was taken up by another preacher, Ibn Abd al-Wahhab (1703–92—referred to in Week 1), who became attached to the Saud family—later the rulers of Saudi Arabia. Saudi support for Wahhabism stems from their relationship with him. It continues the puritanical strain of Islam, and with the oil riches that Saudi Arabia has accrued its Wahhabism has become a major "export", especially to Pakistan. Indeed it also contributes to the Taliban ideology in Afghanistan. A number of Wahhabi madrassas have been opened in Pakistan. The Barelvi are not actually opposed to Sufism, which has always been a part of Pakistani Islam, but they are adamant that the blasphemy law should be upheld.

---

* Malala Yousafzai, *I am Malala: The girl who stood up for education and was shot by the Taliban*, with Christine Lamb (London: Weidenfeld & Nicolson, 2013, 2014), pp. 173–4.

They rightly want respect for the Prophet, as indeed many Christians would like the western secular world to show more respect for Jesus, but a blasphemy law is not the way to ensure it. No advance, in fact, on what was happening back in ninth-century-BC Samaria.

Not long after Ahab had acquired his vineyard he was confronted by an angry Elijah (1 Kings 21:17–29). Elijah had been instructed by the Lord, he told Ahab, to meet him in Naboth's former vineyard. "Have you killed and also taken possession?" Elijah asked him.

"O my enemy," a chastened Ahab replied, "have you found me?"

"I have found you," Elijah said, "because you have sold yourself to do evil—an evil that will not only destroy you but your whole house with you." Evil actions do eventually redound upon their perpetrators.

Let us pray for the people and leaders of Afghanistan and Pakistan, and for love and understanding between the people of different faiths and ethnicities, that all of us may learn how to respect and value each other.

21

Countries Bordering Russia: Finland, Estonia, Latvia, Lithuania, Belarus, Ukraine, Moldova

Week after Easter 3

Each of the countries that lie to the west of Russia has at some time been dominated or ruled by Russia; some still are. Finland and the three Baltic States are beside the Baltic Sea. Belarus, or White Russia, has a northern border with Latvia and Lithuania and a southern one with Ukraine. Ukraine reaches to the Black Sea. Moldova is a much smaller country in Ukraine's southwest, close to the Black Sea but not on it, and next to Romania. Overall the population of these eastern European countries is small, and in Ukraine's case diminishing: they are Finland 5.5 million, Estonia 1.5 million, Latvia 2 million, Lithuania 2.5 million, Belarus 9.5 million, Ukraine 43 million and Moldova 4 million. Ukraine and Moldova are Orthodox in faith, Ukraine with various branches of Orthodoxy. Forty per cent of both Belarus and Estonia are atheist, but more profess to be Christian, the majority of them Orthodox. Since the Porvoo Common Statement of 1992 (signed in Porvoo Cathedral in Finland), the Lutheran Churches of Finland, Estonia and Latvia have been in communion with the Anglican Churches of England, Wales, Scotland and Ireland. Finland became independent from Russia in 1917. The Baltic States were invaded by the Soviet Union in 1940, independence coming after 1989. Belarus has retained a number of features from its Soviet past. In 2014, Russia claimed the Crimea from Ukraine, and in 2022 invaded the whole country, claiming that it had always been part of Russia. The Crimea is already linked to the Taman Peninsula in Russia by an 11.8-mile bridge. Moldova was also a part of the Soviet Union.

Welcoming migrants

At the end of the Second World War, and the appropriation of much of eastern Europe by the Soviet Union, there was a massive exodus of peoples to the west, especially from the Baltic States. A number were to move to the north of England—and some to our home in Coniston Cold, the small village and parish where my father had just become the vicar.

Such migratory movements of peoples between countries is a constant of world history. After the Second World War, it was an early sign of what by the 2020s was to become massive new movements of peoples, some 5 million exiles from the war in Syria for example and more from other countries, Zimbabwe in particular. At the time of writing, there are some 10,000 plus Syrians and 200,000 Zimbabweans living in Britain. There are millions more in other countries. Despite massive governmental efforts to prevent people coming to their country and harsh conditions when they succeed, for the most part migrants remain.*

No country finds it easy to accept new peoples. Inhabitants fear they will lose their jobs, that migrants will marry their womenfolk, that their women will marry their men and that customs and culture will be overwhelmed. There are some genuine fears, sometimes justified in the short term, but most native populations react with hostility, inventing reasons why they do not want them to come. The newcomers for their part feel equally anxious, fearing that they will become disoriented by living within a different culture and further afraid that they will lose their own.

It was very similar in biblical times. The story of the exiles returning to Judea from Babylon is a story of immigration. What happened is vividly described in the books of Ezra and Nehemiah, the two leaders of the returning exiles. They reacted with horror when they found that some of the returnees had married women from the receiving community. They decreed that anyone living with a foreign wife should separate from her forthwith (Ezra 9 and 10; Nehemiah 13:1–3, 23–31). They feared for

---

* Randall Hansen, "Migration to Europe since 1945: Its History and its Lessons", *The Political Quarterly* special issue (2003), pp. 25–38.

their faith, that the newcomers would be seriously compromised by their close association with peoples they reckoned as alien and unbelievers.

This was one view. Another is in the book of Ruth. This was probably written at about the same time as the above events. Ruth was a foreigner, an alien from the neighbouring state of Moab, who had come to Judea with her mother-in-law Naomi when they had both become widows.

My mother, who was also called Ruth, used to love telling us this story. We had moved to Coniston Cold in Upper Airedale from Bradford in 1945 and were living in a rambling old farmhouse with extensive outhouses that had been enlarged in the nineteenth century to become the vicarage. It was cold beyond words. There was no electricity—in fact, there was to be none until 1958! It did not matter to us children, but our urban mother, catering on a miniscule budget on post-war rations, found it challenging. To help the finances, she took in paying guests. The first were displaced persons from eastern Europe.

Naomi had tried to persuade her two daughters-in-law, Ruth and Orpah, when they left Moab with her, to return there and to their Moabite god, Chemosh. She, for her part, would return to Judea. Orpah said she would, but Ruth refused. "Do not press me to leave you," she told Naomi. ". . . Where you go, I will go; where you lodge, I will lodge; your people shall be my people, and your God my God. Where you die, I will die . . . May the Lord do thus and so to me and more as well, if even death parts me from you" (Ruth 1:14–17). Whenever I hear the words, I hear my mother relating them to us. She was always so moved. As Boaz was to say to Ruth when she came to glean in his fields, "May you have a full reward from the Lord, the God of Israel, under whose wings you have come for refuge" (Ruth 2:12).

Initially, the allied authorities at the end of the war tried to repatriate the many east Europeans who had fled into Germany. It was only when they realized that it was impossible that they adopted a different policy. The refugees were decreed "displaced persons", and 24,000 of them, men, women and children, came to England. A number came to Skipton and worked in the cotton mills. Three of the families came to live with us. George and Regina Caks (pronounced Charks) were some who came. George had been a pastry chef in Riga, and when rations allowed, would bake us wonderful creations. The family eventually left for a new life in

Canada. Another was from Estonia, a third from Hungary; one of these stayed in a sort of "school" room that we had in the back garden. "It is very damp," Mother explained when she showed them round. "I'm not even sure it is rain proof. Are you sure it will do?" They were very certain that it would. Damp was a small inconvenience. They stayed for some time. We children were very young. We just accepted their being with us as in the natural order of things.

Our country has in fact always been a community of immigrants, since Roman times and before: Saxons, Angles, Jutes, Vikings, Normans . . . and many, many more since, all of them now part or becoming part of our corporate DNA. The secret of acceptance is always that we come to know people personally—fellow human beings who will add grace and strength to our corporate living.

Let us pray for the peoples and leaders of Finland, Estonia, Latvia, Lithuania, Belarus, Ukraine and Moldova—that form a border between western Europe and Russia—and for all who have come to our country as migrants, refugees or asylum seekers, giving thanks to God for all that they give to us.

22

North Africa and the Sahel: Morocco, Western Sahara, Algeria, Tunisia, Libya, Mauritania, Mali, Niger, Chad

Week after Easter 4

The area is enormous, almost 3,000 miles from west to east, 2,000 from north to south, much of it covered by the Sahara Desert. Most of the peoples of the countries of North Africa live near to the Mediterranean coast. From west to east, the countries are Morocco—which includes the Spanish enclaves of Ceuta (opposite Gibraltar) and Mellila (further east along the coast)—Algeria, Tunisia and Libya. To the south, the Sahara Desert gives way to another vast area, the sparse bushland of the Sahel, much affected by climate change. To the south of Morocco on the Atlantic coast is Western Sahara—the Spanish Canary Islands are to the west—embraced on its southern and western borders by Mauritania. The other countries of the Sahel from west to east are Mali, Niger (watered by the Niger River) and Chad. Morocco is a kingdom of 38 million. Algeria's population is 45.5 million, Tunisia 12 million, Libya 7 million, Western Sahara 626,500, Mauritania 5 million, Mali 21.5 million, Niger 26 million, and Chad 17.5 million. Almost everyone is Muslim, but there is a significant number of Christians, especially in Chad (a third of the population) and some also in Algeria. The Anglican presence is part of the new province of Alexandria, which was inaugurated in 2020. Morocco claims Western Sahara, a claim opposed by its Polisario Front (Sahrawi Arab Democratic Republic). Most of the region was under French rule during the colonial era. The Algerian war of independence lasted from 1954 until 1962. Since the fall of Libyan President Gaddafi, rival factions have vied for power there. Terrorism has become an increasing threat in the Sahel.

Encounters in the desert

The North African coast was home to many notable Christians in Roman times: Augustine of Hippo, Cyprian, Perpetua, Felicitas; these last three were each martyred. Four hundred years later, the whole region had become Muslim. In the eleventh century, the Muslim king of Mauritania, Anzir, wrote to the pope telling him that he had released some Christian prisoners and that he was prepared to free some more. Pope Gregory VII—the remarkable Hildebrand—responded by sending a delegation to Mauritania with a personal letter for Anzir: "God, the Creator of all, without whom we cannot do or even think anything that is good," he wrote, "has inspired to your heart this act of kindness. . . . we and you must show in a special way to the other nations an example of this charity, for we believe and confess one God, although in different ways, and praise and worship him daily as the creator of all ages and the ruler of this world." In expressing his admiration for the king, he concluded, "we pray in our heart and with our lips that God may lead you to the abode of happiness, to the bosom of the holy patriarch Abraham after long years of life here on earth."*

In the modern period, in October 1972, *Guardian* journalist Geoffrey Moorhouse was also in Mauritania, on its Atlantic coast. He was there to start an adventurous journey across the Sahara by camel. In the introduction to his book, describing what happened, he said that he was hoping to explore the nature of fear.** He certainly succeeded in doing that; it proved to be a gruelling and sometimes terrifying journey. He had intended to ride as far as Egypt, but in the end was only able to make it as far as Tamanrasset. He staggered into the oasis some five months after leaving Mauritania.

At almost the same time, two months after Moorhouse's departure, the legendary theatre director Peter Brook set out on another journey, this time with a troupe of actors travelling south by Land Rover from Algeria. His aim was to reach as far as Nigeria. I was intrigued to read

---

* Jacques Dupuis, S. J., *Toward a Christian Theology of Religious Pluralism* (Maryknoll, NY: Orbis Books, 2001), pp. 102–3.

** Geoffrey Moorhouse, *The Fearful Void* ([1974] London: Penguin, 1986).

John Heilpern's book about Brook's project.* In 1970, Joy and I had taken a day trip from Sunderland to see his mould-breaking *Midsummer Night's Dream* at the theatre in Stratford. His idea on this journey was to perform various plays *en route*, his main offering being the Islamic epic *The Conference of the Birds* (see Week 39). Their first production in Salah went well, their second at Tamanrasset rather less well.

Tamanrasset is an oasis in the deep southeast of Algeria close to the Hoggar mountains. It was where the French mystic Charles de Foucauld (1858–1916) had his hermitage, high up on the Assekrem plateau.** Both Moorhouse and Brook made the 50-mile journey from Tamanrasset to see it. During his time, de Foucauld had been a lone presence in the desert, a solitary given to contemplative prayer among the Tuareg. His ministry was later to inspire the formation of the Little Brothers of Jesus, but while there he made little impact. Only one other person was ever with him. Both Geoffrey Moorhouse and Peter Brook, explorers in their different ways of the spiritual life in the wilderness, made their pilgrimage there as an important part of their journeys.

Brook and his company then continued on into Niger. At Agades, they encountered the Perlh (pronounced "pearl") people, a nomadic branch of the Fulani who roam the Sahel with their cattle in search of pasture–increasingly difficult now as climate change is making it harder and harder to find grass. Indeed, there was a severe famine very soon after the actors had passed through. In recent years, nearby Lake Chad has shrunk from its former size of 10,000 square miles to no more than 1,000 square miles at the time of writing. The problem of climate change has inspired a young Chad woman of the Perlh/M'bororo people, Hindoo Oumarou Ibrahim, to become an international campaigner on the issue.***

---

* John Heilpern, *The Conference of the Birds: The Story of Peter Brook in Africa* (London: Faber & Faber, 1977).

** Charles de Foucauld, *Meditations of a Hermit: The Spiritual Writings of Charles de Foucauld: A Hermit of the Sahara and Apostle of the Tuaregs*, trans. Charlotte Balfour (London: Burns & Oates, Washbourne, 1930).

*** Mary Robinson, *Climate Justice: Hope, Resilience and the Fight for a Sustainable Future* (London: Bloomsbury, 2018), pp. 56–70.

The desert—the wilderness—is the place where many find that they encounter the presence of God. It was why both Peter Brook and Geoffrey Moorhouse went there, though they expressed their desire in ways unique to them. It was why John the Baptist made his way there, and Jesus after him (Matthew 4:1–11; Mark 1:12,13; Luke 4:1–13). In biblical times, the wilderness was understood to be the haunt of demons, of evil spirits. It remains a harsh and empty region, starkly mirroring unconscious darkness and fears, an inner void when nothingness threatens. When anyone withdraws into the desert, the dark side of being erupts, sometimes to such a degree that it is very difficult to maintain a sane balance. It was at this point that Jesus experienced the presence of angels, of God the Holy Spirit with him, empowering him towards a new understanding of his vocation and direction. Geoffrey Moorhouse in his prayer of thanks at the end of his book wrote of the newfound sense of peace and way forward as he thought back to his journey.* Peter Brook was particularly impressed by the Perlh people, their myths and the natural pace of their living, the deep meanings in their art and music and dance. He felt they understood naturally what he had been constantly trying to express in his work in the theatre.**

Let us pray for the people and leaders of North Africa and the Sahel, especially for all who meet God when they withdraw into the desert. We pray also for those who work for ecological justice and for all who struggle with the severe effects of climate change.

---

* Moorhouse, *The Fearful Void*, pp. 281–6.

** Heilpern, *The Conference of the Birds*, p. 147.

23

Oceania: Melanesia, Micronesia and Polynesia

Week after Easter 5

The Pacific Ocean is 10 million square miles in size, covering almost half the globe: 10,000 miles from north to south, 12,000 at its widest point from west to east. Oceania is the rather loose name for the region; it includes Australia and New Zealand as well as the 12 independent countries among the island communities. Melanesia is the western-most part, the islands to the immediate east of New Guinea. Strictly speaking it includes parts of Indonesia and East Timor (Week 27) as well as Papua New Guinea itself. Bougainville, currently belonging to Papua New Guinea, voted for independence in 2019. New Caledonia is a French territory. Melanesia's main island countries are Fiji, Vanuatu and the Solomon Islands. Micronesia refers to the many small islands north of New Guinea and east of the Philippines. There are five nations: the Federated States of Micronesia, Palau, Kiribati, Nauru and the Marshall Islands. Guam and the Northern Mariana Islands belong to the United States. Polynesia refers to the islands east of Fiji and includes both New Zealand (Week 45) and Hawaii (Weeks 19 and 26), Samoa (American Samoa is a self-governing island of the USA), Tonga and Tuvalu. Tokelau is part of New Zealand. The Cook Islands and Niue are states in free association with New Zealand. Tahiti with the Marquesa Islands, Wallis and Futura are French. Easter Island (Rapa Nui) belongs to Chile, Pitcairn Island to the UK. The population of Papua New Guinea is 9.5 million; for the rest of the islands it is about 6 million plus, though it is difficult to gauge. For the most part, the region is Christian. The Anglican Church has three provinces: Papua New Guinea, Melanesia and Aotearoa (New Zealand) with Polynesia. Fiji is in this last province.

Prayer and service—Two brotherhoods

It was 1974, and we were staying at the Anglican Board of Mission in Stanmore, a suburb of Sydney in Australia. One morning, a bishop, who was also staying there, asked me if I would join him for breakfast. David Hand was the bishop of New Guinea and saw meeting me as an unexpected opportunity to recruit a priest for a parish he had in mind. He told me about Bougainville, and of problems he was grappling with there, to do with some timber cutting proposal he had been asked to comment upon. He had been reading *Small is Beautiful*, E. F. Schumacher's recently published study of economics,* and as a result had come to the conclusion that the clearing of such a forest was not only bad for the environment but un-Christian. He had done extensive research, had found the project "full of holes" and had circulated his findings accordingly. Then, looking straight at me, he said "What about you coming to Bougainville this Christmas, and looking after a parish there?" It might have been a tempting offer had we not already committed ourselves to doing this very thing, looking after a parish over the coming Christmas in Singapore (see Week 38). He was, I think, somewhat put out to see us wandering about the globe like this, and perhaps thought he should redeem the situation.

We were in effect on sabbatical when such breaks in ministry were unusual. Our bishop John Habgood, the then bishop of Durham, had given us permission to go, and like Geoffrey Moorhouse and Peter Brook a couple of years before us, we had ventured into the wild. We were part of that post-war movement of the young who after years of austerity found themselves able and free to explore the world. Many of us set off on journeys of exploration.

As we had left Los Angeles on this same journey, our plane had been delayed by fog. The airline put us up in one of the airport hotels while we waited for the smog to lift. While we were there, we met a young Tahitian woman, Laurina Suhas, who advised us that when we were in Tahiti, at Papeete we should say hullo to one of her teachers, Frère Dominique

* E. F. Schumacher, *Small is Beautiful: A Study of Economics as if People Mattered* (London: Collins, 1973).

Bénard. The *Lycée* where he taught was run by a Breton Community, the *Frères de l'instruction chrétiennes de Ploërmel*, a lay teaching order based in a region of Brittany. Frère Dominique was Breton himself and by 1974 had already been at the school some 15 years. He entertained us to a meal in our hotel by the sea. We talked together about the French practice of incorporating such distant islands as part of the mother country. He said it was for prestige–a costly prestige, he thought, and against the wishes of many of the people of Tahiti, but he suspected, he said, that they would find life apart from France much more difficult. At the end of our meal, I walked with him onto the hotel pier. It reached out into the quiet of the lagoon, coloured fish darting about beneath our feet; it was easy to see why the French were reluctant to leave.

If we had gone to Bougainville, as Bishop Hand had asked, we would probably have met some of the brothers of another community, the Anglican Melanesian Brotherhood (*Ira Rata Tiriu* in the Mota language). This company of brothers was founded in 1925 by Ini Kopuria, a policeman from Guadalcanal in the Solomon Islands. He, like the Breton brothers, had formed a lay community of men, their purpose to support the local church. The community now has three houses in addition to the main one in Guadalcanal, one in Papua New Guinea and another in Vanuatu. Wherever the brothers worked as evangelists they were supported by the local Christian families, many of them in a kind of Third Order, known as Companions.

Some years later, in 1999, when there was trouble in the Solomons, the brothers played a large part as intermediaries, meeting with the rebels in a peace-making mission. It was at a heavy cost. In 2003, seven of the brothers were killed.* There is a memorial to them in Canterbury Cathedral, an icon to mark their dedication and martyrdom.

In addition to their community life of daily prayer and service, a significant feature of the Melanesian Brothers' rule–of significance not only for them but for the wider Church–is that when they make their final vows, they commit themselves for no more than five years. Then they can leave, and marry if they wish. Many of them do, and some also

* Richard Carter, *In Search of the Lost: The Death of Seven Peacemakers of the Melanesian Brotherhood* (Norwich: Canterbury Press, 2006).

go on to be ordained. Others are allowed to renew their vows for another limited period, and a few stay on for even longer. The majority leave; they take their experience of Christian formation in community into their ongoing discipleship of prayer and service.

Let us pray for the people and leaders of Papua New Guinea, Micronesia, Melanesia and Polynesia, for the Frères of Brittany, the Melanesian Brotherhood and all others who live their Christian lives in prayer and service to their church and community.

2 4

China 2

Rogation Days and Ascension Day

See Week 1 for mainland China. This box is about Hong Kong, Macao and Taiwan. Hong Kong is an island with additional territories in the south of China close to Changzhou (formerly Canton), with Macao a few miles to the south. Taiwan (formerly Formosa) is the large island 100 miles from the Chinese coast, northeast from Hong Kong. Hong Kong's population is 7.5 million, Taiwan's 24 million. There is a Christian presence in both; in Taiwan the Anglican Church is part of Province VIII of the Episcopal Church of the United States. The Hong Kong Anglican Church, *Hong Kong Sheng Kung Hui*, has four dioceses, one of them covering Macao, the former Portuguese territory. Hong Kong was a British enclave until 1997, when it was returned to China, China guaranteeing its autonomy until 2047–since then compromised by changes imposed by Beijing. Taiwan is a part of China, but since 1949 it has been virtually independent and acknowledged as such internationally–especially by the United States. When China became Communist, the ousted ruler Chiang Kai-Shek moved there with his government. China has made clear that it would like to recover sovereignty over Taiwan. Taiwan represented China at the UN until it was replaced by mainland China in 1971. China also lays claim to the Spratly Islands that lie between the Philippines and Vietnam in the South China Sea.

Prayer for a good harvest

It did not feel like good planning to arrive in Beijing just two days before the sixtieth anniversary of the Communist victory of 1949. It meant that much of central Beijing including the Forbidden City—the former Emperor's palace—was closed. Tiananmen Square was still open. I had arrived on the night train from Xian, had gone straight from my hotel by metro to the centre of Beijing and by mid-morning was at the square. Coming up from the underground it felt as if half of China had preceded me there, the crowds were so large, many of them taking "selfies" in front of the portrait of Chairman Mao. I walked slowly around the immense space, right to the far end where Mao's Memorial Hall now is. Crossing the road beyond the hall is the way to the temple of heaven.

Somehow the temple survived the Cultural Revolution. I think it was because the Premier Chou En Lai insisted that it should. It was originally built in the early fifteenth century, a project of the Yongle Emperor of the time, Zhu Di, the first emperor of the Ming dynasty. Each year as the solstice drew near the emperor would begin his preparation for his annual visit to the temple of heaven. He would fast for three days. He and his court would then process in silence and secrecy to the temple. Any of the common people who might be tempted to observe their progress were sternly ordered that they must remain indoors and on no account peep. I made my own way there on foot, also in silence, through a fashionable mall-like area selling handbags and jewellery, to arrive a mile or so later at the temple's enormous park. Somewhere in the middle of it was the temple of heaven. The park in fact is part of the general symbolism of the place, that both earth and heaven should remain fully aligned and one. The temple buildings, the ones on square foundations, symbolized the earth, and the ones that were round, the heavens. The temple's one solitary purpose was to be the place where each year the emperor would come to intercede for the blessing of the Divine on the crops of the land.

The emperor—in his own thinking and that of his people—understood himself to be the "Son of Heaven", the one who in his kingly role should represent the needs of the people before heaven, and in his priestly one, the divine son who could intercede with the divine. Conducting the ritual in precise detail was essential if earth and heaven were to remain truly aligned.

After the emperor's preparatory night in prayer, he would process towards the first of the round buildings, the single-gabled Imperial Vault of Heaven. Here he would meditate on the needs of the country. Then, following an elaborate and precise formula, he would leave the building by the left-hand door—which was reserved for his use alone—his courtiers following him through another door, on the right. The third middle door was shut, always to remain closed, reserved for the use of "the Divine" alone. The emperor would then process along a raised walkway, up the three decorated tiers ahead, towards the climax of his way, the "Hall of Prayer for Good Harvest". Here he would spend a further night in intercessory prayer.

The hall is magnificent; a three-tiered gabled roof, and inside and outside it is decorated in rich colour. Four pillars represent the compass points of the world, 12 more the months, and many more are symbolic representations suggested by the figure nine; the principle is that as nine is the highest single number it can express the hope that here the unity and alignment they seek between the Emperor and the Divine will prevail.

After his night in prayer, the emperor would leave the hall and go back down the pilgrimage route to the large empty platform below; at its centre a round slate is embedded in the stone, marking—so it was understood—the actual middle point of the kingdom. Here he would complete the liturgy.

The Chinese do not refer to God as Person. They speak instead of "Heaven", carefully avoiding any temptation to personalize the divine. They do not speak of "Heaven" as God—very different from Christian theology. Nonetheless, what used to happen at the temple did remind me of the Ascension with its central understanding of Christ as both King and Priest; that empowered by the Holy Spirit we join our own concerns with the prayer of the ascended Christ before the Father, all of us incorporated into the love of God the Trinity for the world.

Being there took me back to the Ovingham Rogation Service that I wrote about at the beginning of the opening essay. Today, as modern people of the west, like the thoroughly practical Chinese, we see problems like global warming and climate change as scientific and technological challenges to be tackled in well-researched ways. Approaching the problems as spiritual issues appears in contrast to be rather old fashioned. Certainly the problems require scientific know-how, but they need so much more. When Pope Benedict XVI addressed the British parliament in 2010, he said that "the world of secular rationality and the world of religious belief need each other and should not be afraid to enter into a profound and ongoing dialogue with each other—for the good of our civilization".* We need both the science and the faith. We hear what is being said by our modern prophets, but have not as yet as an international society fully taken in the seriousness of what they are saying. To achieve the zero emission of carbon by 2050, as they tell us we have to do, is going to require great wisdom and immense spiritual resources. Know-how is great. To have the ability to implement what is needed will only be achieved by faith, prayer, grace and the strength of the Holy Spirit.

Places like the temple of heaven—or indeed Durham Cathedral, or even St Mary's Ovingham, both of which also represent heaven—speak of the sacred, of the fundamental call to align ourselves with the will of God. We are to be at one with the heft of creation, attentive to the underlying order and sacredness, all that we have been given and depend upon. Prayer aligns us with this will, draws us to act in harmony with the needs of the earth and at the same time strengthens us to address and tackle the challenges. Who knows? Something gracious might be the result and at the very least a strengthening by the Holy Spirit to address the severe problems we face.

If our Lord had been in Beijing at the resurrection, he would of course have entered the hall of prayer by the middle door.

Let us pray for the people and leaders of China, that as they seek to align their path with the ways of heaven, we may join with the people and the millions of Christians in China to give thanks for our Lord's intercession for us in heaven, praying that beset by climate change we may endeavour to cooperate with the ascended Lord in doing God's will.

---

* Pope Benedict XVI, "The world of reason and the world of faith need one another", *The Tablet*, 25 September 2010, pp. 29–30.

2 5

Jerusalem and the United Nations

Ascension to Pentecost

Politically Jerusalem is the capital of Israel, but only recently in 2017 has it been recognized as such by the United States. Most embassies are in Tel Aviv. This box looks at the international and religious significance of Jerusalem. In the New Testament, new Jerusalem (Revelation 21:2) is described as a symbol of the coming kingdom, the City of God (Galatians 4:25–26; Hebrews 12:22; Revelation 3:12; Wisdom of Solomon 9:8; Baruch 5:5–6). For many Christians, Jerusalem is also a symbol of Mary, the bearer of the Word of God, and therefore of the Church. By virtue of its history and spiritual significance for Judaism, Islam and Christianity, Jerusalem is an international city. Its name means "Possession of Peace". St Helena, known as "the protector of the Holy Places", visited Jerusalem in 326. The Orthodox, Armenian and Catholic Churches each has a Patriarchate there, the Anglicans a province, the Episcopal Church of Jerusalem and the Middle East. The United Nations and other world agencies for peace are largely in New York and Geneva.

Peace between the religions, peace among the nations

Roger Cohen was for many years a columnist for the *New York Times*. In 2015, he published a memoir about his mother June.* She had suffered from manic depression (bipolar disorder as it is now known) as others in her family had done before her. Her son did not know about this, as is

* Roger Cohen, *The Girl from Human Street* (London: Weidenfeld & Nicolson, 2015).

so often the case in families where there is this disease—a tragic mistake, especially when there are children who tend to blame themselves for what is wrong if no one explains to them what is happening. After his mother's death in 1999, Roger went in search of her, and it was as part of this pilgrimage that he came to Jerusalem.

June's forebears had moved to South Africa from Lithuania—as in fact had so many Jews from Lithuania into the northeast of England. It is the reason why Gateshead has such a leading yeshiva (Orthodox Jewish Seminary). The Gateshead Talmudical College was founded in the 1920s by rabbis from the Novardok yeshiva network in Navahrudak, a city which used to be in Lithuania, but is now in Belarus. The Jewish presence in the Northeast has added considerably to the moral tone of the region, especially in Sunderland where Joy and I used to live when we were in Ryhope.

Cohen entered the Old City of Jerusalem by the Damascus Gate. Almost immediately he came upon three processions.* The first one was a large crowd of Muslims, Palestinians coming up the road from the Al Aqsa Mosque. At the same time, a group of ultra-orthodox Jews were making their way from the Western Wall, the nearest place to the Temple, where they had been praying. And just at that moment a third gathering appeared, this time a band of Philippine Christians walking up the *Via Dolorosa*, one of them carrying a large cross. This last group came to a halt beside the Armenian Church. By now there was a considerable melee. It was quite a task for the other two processions to squeeze past the Philippine group. Cohen reflected that it would not have taken too much for the different groups to have broken into a fight.

The history of Jerusalem would certainly warrant such a view. Simon Sebag Montefiore's recent biography of Jerusalem charts this all too alarmingly.** Whenever stress became too severe, people would side with whichever grouping they felt best held their identity, whether this was a religious or an ethnic one, and conflict would follow. In the Jerusalem setting, this then usually led to even worse trouble. The need for identity

---

* Cohen, *The Girl from Human Street*, p. 276.

** Simon Sebag Montefiore, *Jerusalem: The Biography* (London: Weidenfeld & Nicolson, 2011).

is so fundamental it can at times entirely override existing friendships and lead to tragedy. On this occasion, *convivencia* prevailed, as it does for most of the time. It did when Joy and I were there too.

Joy was in Jerusalem in October 1964. She was on her way back to Northern Rhodesia—to Zambia as it was about to become that very month—to complete her final year of teaching before returning to England to marry me. A few days later, she wrote to me from Tiberias to tell me of her visit to the Tomb of David—the complex of buildings which includes the Cenacle (from *cenaculum*, a dining room), venerated as the supposed site of the Last Supper. In the years before the Six-Day War, which was in June 1967, the Old City was still a part of Jordan, and the roof of the tomb was the nearest place from which Jewish worshippers could actually see the Temple site. This was before there was access to the Western Wall. The day Joy was there she went up onto the roof. While she was up there, she heard a door closing and vaguely wondered whether this might mean she was being locked in—which was what had happened. Unfazed, she decided she would stay put and seize the opportunity for prayer. "As you know," she told me, "I didn't have much of a retreat in England and the quiet time up there served instead. Having just left the Last Supper room, it was comparatively easy to imagine, and meditate on, the last night which Jesus spent before the crucifixion, especially having retraced part of his steps the preceding days." When she left in the morning, the guardian of the building looked surprised. Joy was always adept at extricating herself from such awkward situations.

My own visit had been eight years before in 1956. I was on a weekend visit from Cyprus where I was stationed towards the end of my National Service. Aged 19, I was rather shocked by the state of everything, the untidiness of the Church of the Resurrection especially, shared as it was—and still is—by quarrelling churches. It was the Garden Tomb that spoke most to me; that and the Dome of the Rock and the many other sites we somehow managed to squeeze into our schedule and see during our short weekend. There was certainly little space for the contemplative prayer that Joy had managed to observe.

Jerusalem is a city of so many different peoples and nations milling around together, it illustrates all too well the challenge of how we are to live peaceably together in the modern world. Many centuries earlier, a small group of men and women met there together for prayer. It was the morning of Pentecost, and it was as they prayed that they suddenly experienced within themselves empowering by the Holy Spirit. All of them, despite speaking different languages, found they could understand each other. They knew themselves to be one people. As our Lord had prayed, and as Psalm 122 puts it, "Jerusalem, built as a city that is at unity in itself" (Psalm 122:3, Common Worship Psalter):

> Pray for the peace of Jerusalem: May they prosper who love you.
> (Psalm 122:6, Common Worship Psalter)

We pray for the nations of the world, those working together in the United Nations, for the peoples and leaders of the Holy Land, and especially for those seeking to increase understanding between the great Abrahamic faiths, Judaism, Islam and Christianity: that within the love of God, we might all listen to each other, learn from each other and grow in faith and hope and love. Empower us together to serve the Common Good as we wait for the coming of the heavenly Jerusalem.

26

United States of America 2

Week after Pentecost

For the population and more detail, see Week 19. This box refers to the outlying regions of the States, which include Alaska and in the Pacific Ocean the Hawaii Islands, the Northern Marianas, American Samoa and Guam. The Anglican, Protestant Episcopal Church has two of its nine provinces care for the Church beyond the United States. Hawaii and Alaska are in Province VIII. A number of countries in Central and South America, the West Indies and beyond are in Province IX.

Modern saints caring for the poor

St Paul addresses a number of his letters to the saints, *hagioi* in the Greek, meaning "holy ones", the holy people of God (see for example 2 Corinthians 1:1). Paul referred to them as saints despite their many failures which he talks so openly about, because he recognized them as persons who were in Christ, men and women endowed with the Holy Spirit. A joy of being a parish priest is precisely this, that we minister to a very varied range of people. Some are fairly good, others rather less so, all of them struggling to live their lives as creatively as they can, strengthened by grace and the Holy Spirit; mothers caring deeply for their children, men and women with exacting jobs, people volunteering for works of mercy. All were holy, some of them especially so. In his introduction to the letters of Dorothy Day, Robert Ellsberg quotes Thomas Merton's observation that sanctity is a matter of being more fully human. "This implies a great capacity for concern, for suffering, for understanding, for sympathy and also for humor, for joy, for appreciation of the good and beautiful things of life."* Only a few appear in the lists of saints, but the rest of us are nonetheless the Lord's workers in the Kingdom. The value of making lists of the one or two who are especially holy, despite their often rather obvious personal shortcomings, is that it encourages the rest of us on the way.

Dorothy Day was the founder of the Catholic Worker movement. Living with her, Tamar her daughter found, was demanding. Later in life, her mother's holiness had become too much for her and she broke away from the Church. One of Tamar's own daughters, Kate, the youngest of nine, comments in her biography of her grandmother that having such holiness on your doorstep can be daunting. She also makes it clear how remarkably saintly her mother was too.

Dorothy Day was born in 1898. Her early adult years were bohemian; she lived with different men, was married for a year to one of them, and would dearly have liked to marry Tamar's father Forster if he would only have agreed. He and Dorothy were always to remain friends, and in their later years were close, but they lived separately which was distressing to Dorothy. It was when she first met Forster that she was, at the same time, experiencing a pull towards a relationship with God. It was a surprise and a puzzle to her friends. When Tamar was born in 1926, she arranged that she should be baptized in the Catholic Church. It was not until 18 months later that she herself was baptized.

Dorothy worked first as a journalist, reporting for several small papers. It was while she was doing this that she began to develop a real concern for the down-trodden and vulnerable. She began to wonder if there was anything she could do for them. At the same time, she was feeling uneasy about the direction her life was taking and wondering what instead she should be doing. One day she was reporting one of the 1930s hunger marches, and as she made her way home, feeling downcast by what she had seen, she stopped beside a church, its noticeboard saying it was the church of the Immaculate Conception. It was 8 December, and she knew enough to know that this was the day of its dedication. She decided she

* Dorothy Day, *The Duty of Delight: The Diaries of Dorothy Day*, ed. Robert Ellsberg (Milwaukee, WI: Marquette University Press, 2008), pp. xx.

would go in. Inside, she addressed the Blessed Mother in urgent prayer. "Here I am," she said, "what would you have me do?" It was a moment of grace. Her new way forward was revealed to her.*

A few months later, on 1 May 1933, she and a few colleagues published the first edition of her paper, *The Catholic Worker.* Since it was May Day, with various events happening, they decided to print 2,000 copies; they sold the lot at a penny each. Four months later, the paper's circulation had risen to 24,000. By the late 1930s, it was to peak at 160,000. The first issue had been a joint venture with her supporters, by the second it had become Dorothy's paper, and she was to contribute a regular column for every edition until it closed. When the paper had been going for a year, and knowing what so many of her readers suffered, she opened a home to cater for them. Her daughter Tamar was seven by this time, and she moved into the house with her mother. Many years later Tamar told Kate what it was like. "They were all such wonderful fools," she said, "so full of hope".**

Some 50 years later, when Joy and I were staying in New York, we were shaken by the poverty we saw; it must have been so much worse in the 1930s. What Dorothy and her colleagues did for the poor was demanding. It was her profound and deeply prayerful response to the vocation that she had received.

She and her colleagues faced much hostility. Writing in her diary of the hatred and scorn she aroused, she acknowledged that though like others in her team she found the work hard, she understood that she must see all her clients, whoever they were, as persons better than herself: "which means," she said, "hunting for good points, seeing Christ in them, sowing one's judgement, loving even unto folly".*** There is a marvellous story told of her towards the end of her life, when a diamond ring had been donated to the house. She decided she would give it to Catherine, one of the more difficult and awkward clients they had. Colleagues remonstrated

* Kate Hennessy, *Dorothy Day, The World Will Be Saved by Beauty: An Intimate Portrait of My Grandmother* (New York: Scribner, Simon & Schuster, 2017), p. 66.

** Hennessy, *Dorothy Day*, p. 82.

*** Dorothy Day, *The Duty of Delight*, p. 102.

with her; selling the ring would have done so much more for the poor, they said. Dorothy replied, "Do you think that beautiful things are only for the wealthy? Let Catherine decide what she wants to do with it . . . "*

Dorothy found solace in beauty, the beauty of nature especially. She would often wake up on a morning and reflect on the words of Dostoevsky, "the world will be saved by beauty", the title Kate Hennessy gives to her biography. Her book is also the story of her mother, of the nine children she had and of her marriage to her father David, a violent man, who was often drunk, and quite incapable of holding down a job. As a result, the family was desperately poor. Her parents did eventually separate, but not until Tamar had stood it for a very long time. Later she stopped practising her faith; perhaps it was a necessary step if she was to become her own person. As she lay dying, she spoke to her daughters about this loss of her faith. "You didn't lose it",** her atheist daughter replied. The daughter was right. She knew her mother to be a woman of God.

Let us pray for the people and leaders of the United States of America and especially for the poor, for single mothers, for workers, for all who struggle with poverty and all who work for the Common Good.

* Hennessy, *Dorothy Day*, p. 339.

** Hennessy, *Dorothy Day*, p. 330.

27

Indonesia (including Timor-Leste and Brunei)

Week after Trinity Sunday

Indonesia is a huge archipelago made up of 17,000 islands. The main islands are Sumatra (the sixth largest island in the world), Borneo (the third largest), Java and Celebes. Irian occupies the western half of New Guinea (the second largest island). They lie to the south of Singapore and the Philippines and to the north of Australia. Indonesia has a population of 275.5 million—more than half of the population lives in Java. Timor-Leste, the eastern half of the island of Timor, has 1.5 million; Brunei, a sultanate on the northwest coast of Borneo, between Sarawak and Sabah which are in Malaysia, has 446,000. Indonesia and Brunei are Muslim, Timor-Leste Christian. Indonesia has about 10 per cent Christians, and a few Hindu—Bali to the immediate east of Java is almost wholly Balinese Hindu. The Buddhist population is less than 1 per cent. The Anglican Church is part of the Province of South East Asia. Indonesia, under Dutch rule until the end of the Second World War, became independent in 1949. East Timor was a Portuguese colony until 1975, then, as part of Indonesia, became independent in 2002.

The Buddhist mystical way

In its early days, there was probably a standing cross at St Mary's Church, Ovingham. At least, the church has some carved stones which might have been part of such a cross. To know what a Northumbrian cross would have looked like there are fine examples at Bewcastle and Ruthwell, the first close to the Scottish border in Cumbria, the second roughly halfway between Dumfries and Annan in Scotland. Their relief panels, probably carved by Mediterranean sculptors, illustrate scenes from the Christian story. One panel on the Ruthwell Cross is of Mary fleeing with Jesus to Egypt.

These two crosses are pinnacles of early northern sculpture. At about the same time, somewhere between 760 and 830, in what is now Indonesia another group of skilled sculptors were working in Java. They were designing similar panels for the Borobudur, the huge Mahayana Buddhist temple which stands some 23 miles to the northwest of Yogyakarta.* While the Northumbrian crosses can boast about 40 panels between the two crosses, the Borobudur has 2,672—plus some 504 separate figures of the Buddha. When there was a fear that the Ruthwell Cross might be destroyed by Scottish Puritan iconoclasts, the minister buried it in the vicarage garden. When Java changed its religion from Buddhism to Islam, the Borobudur was simply abandoned to the lush Javanese vegetation which did the hiding for the country.

We were in Java in December 1974, staying nearby in Yogyakarta. We took a rattly old bus to visit the monument. The enveloping greenery is now largely removed, and at the time work had begun on restoration. Parts of it were still in ruins. What we could see was still astonishing. One commentator described the complex as "a manifestation of the Buddha".** Writing to my parents a day or so after our visit, I said it represented "the various stages of growth towards the Buddhist Nirvana".

The Borobudur, built over an actual hill, is surrounded by extensive lake-like paddy fields with mountains in the far distance, symbolizing Mount Meru, the mythical mountain of Hinduism and Buddhism. The building is in effect a three-dimensional mandala; that is, it is not a pattern, like a rose window, on which to focus the mind. Instead, the contemplative is invited to go into its labyrinth-like structure and walk the path, starting from the lowest level up to the "goal" at the very top. The *bodhisattva*, the Sanskrit word for such an aspirant, is called to become a person of ultimate truth, reality and compassion.

---

* Julie A. Gifford, *Buddhist Practice and Visual Culture: The Visual Rhetoric of Borobudur* (London: Routledge, 2011).

** Gifford, *Buddhist Practice and Visual Culture*, p.73.

The central purpose of the Borobudur is to guide souls to a transformation of consciousness, from absorption with the bodily self to becoming someone fully imbued with compassion. As contemplatives embark on their journey, they proceed along the pathway; to their right are relief pictures. Some of these are simply "icons", opportunities to contemplate the Buddha in his own deep stillness, to absorb something of his spiritual strength. The way is a progress of becoming steadily detached from the self, starting at the lowest level, the first of six square platforms, one on top of the other. The lowest platform is now mostly underground. At this level the panels depict sin and its penalties. They illustrate the initial task of any spiritual journey, the purgative way to cleansing and purification. The next two galleries above have reliefs of the way the Buddha himself journeyed, in particular his way before he was actually born. The story is told in parable-like stories or *jataka*, the kind of stories that the Buddha himself used to tell when he was teaching. Many of them feature animals. One is of the monkey and the buffalo. The monkey had met an ogre who was about to eat him. He managed to escape and run to his friend the buffalo to ask for his help. The buffalo, representing the Buddha in an earlier incarnation, offered to give himself to the ogre instead. This so impressed the ogre, he decided to spare them both. The next level going up gives further examples of the way, telling the story of an early disciple of the Buddha. After the square levels, the *bodhisattva* reaches three circular ones, with more illustrations of the way. Finally the contemplative arrives on the roof. This is an extensive platform with an array of latticed bell-like structures each of them housing a Buddha. The Buddhas are partially hidden, the idea being, so Gifford suggests, that pilgrims are reminded of the illusory nature of the self—*bod* in Sanskrit means "self"—which is destined to dissolve away into nothingness. At the centre is a dome or *stupa*, possibly empty as such *stupas* usually are, to depict this disappearance—the end point of self-abandonment, a pure and empty nothingness. At this point, the *bodhisattva* experiences the mystery of spiritual awakening: enlightenment. He or she is filled with compassion. They are now to descend from the heights, go down the stairs to encounter the world and its needs below, to look with compassion on the lost and lonely they find there. It is reminiscent of Jesus coming down from the mountain after the Transfiguration to heal the boy who was suffering from epilepsy (Mark 9:2–29).

At the end of his life, Thomas Merton, speaking at an Asian monastic conference, spoke of having "... now reached a stage of religious maturity at which it may be possible for someone to remain perfectly faithful to a Christian monastic commitment, and yet to learn in depth from say, a Buddhist or Hindu discipline and experience". He quoted St Augustine on the Christian spiritual way of the path from *cupiditas* (self-centred love) to *caritas* (other-centred love).* Similarly, St Catherine of Siena in a meditation towards the end of her *Dialogue* describes her relationship with the Lord as finding herself as one who was "not... for you alone are who you are,... and any being I have I have from you, and you have given it all to me for love".** Her ego was no more, her self had become one with God alone. Awakened, she had become filled with love and compassion.

Let us pray for the people and leaders of Indonesia, for dialogue and meeting between Islam, Hinduism, Buddhism and Christianity, for grace to follow the spiritual path and strength to become loving and compassionate towards all.

---

* Thomas Merton, *The Asian Journal of Thomas Merton*, eds Naomi Stone, Br Patrick Hart, James Laughlin (London: Sheldon Press, 1974), pp. 313, 334.

** Catherine of Siena, *The Dialogue*, trans. Suzanne Noffke OP (London: SPCK, 1980), pp. 273–4.

2 8

Georgia, Armenia, Azerbaijan and the Russian Republics in the Caucasus

Week after Trinity 1

The Caucasus is the mountainous region between Russia in the north and Turkey and Iran in the south that is between the Black and Caspian Seas. The three independent countries south of the Caucasus range are Georgia, with a population of 11 million, Armenia, bordering Turkey, 3 million and Azerbaijan beside the Caspian Sea, 10.5 million. There are seven Russian "republics" north of the mountains. Chechnya is one of these. Georgia is Orthodox Christian; Armenia has its own Apostolic Church, one of the oldest Christian churches in the world. Azerbaijan is Muslim, mostly Shia, as are the republics to the north of the Caucasus. Georgia, Armenia and Azerbaijan were each part of Soviet Russia until its break-up at the end of 1991. Since then, South Ossetia and Abkhasia have become separate from Georgia, South Ossetia after invasion by Russia. The two provinces are recognized by Russia and one or two others as independent but not by anyone else. Armenia claims a separate enclave in Azerbaijan, Nagorno-Karabakh (the Republic of Artsakh), and there was a short war between the two in 2020. Between Armenia and Turkey, there is Nakhchivan, an autonomous enclave of Azerbaijan. To the north, the Chechens tried for independence in a war from 1991 to 1994 and then again in 1999—the capital Grozny was completely destroyed.

Interpreters caring together

The main refugee service in Newcastle is housed in a redundant vicarage. Every room is fully used, so there is no space for a waiting room as such; clients had to wait for their appointments in the main corridor. When I was there as a counsellor, one of my clients always arrived early—as did her Azerbaijani interpreter, Rosa. To the entertainment of us all, my client and Rosa would add a liveliness to their wait by conversing loudly the Russian they both spoke. I used to wonder if this might be the really therapeutic part of our sessions.

Before retirement, I had been the bishop's adviser in pastoral care and counselling in the Newcastle diocese. Work had almost always been with single clients, and there had certainly never been any occasion when I had needed an interpreter. It was different in the refugee service. For the most part, few asylum seekers arriving in Newcastle could speak English, at least not to a sufficient standard for counselling—though almost all of them could speak several languages. For my part, I could manage a little French, but not nearly enough to counsel in it. So interpreters speaking French, Lingala, Arabic, Farsi, Dari, Amharic, Tigrinya or—as on this occasion—Russian were required. I also had to learn how to work with an interpreter. I went on a course in Liverpool to learn how.

Almost all the interpreters I was privileged to work with were extraordinarily skilled at it, enabling the conversation to flow gently along. There was a limit to how many sessions we had with each client—usually no more than eight—but even that meant hours of intense conversation. I found that when there was an interpreter with me, it added a new depth to the encounter. Together we would build a relationship. It needed to be far more than a relationship between the client and me; it had to be with the interpreter as well. Interpreters might imagine before they came that they were there simply to translate what was said, acting as a disembodied voice translating the client's and my words into our two languages, but they were far more than that. The interpreter was another person in the room. She had her own thoughts and feelings about the client, which, added to mine, inevitably affected the dynamic. We were a dynamic of three. Counselling is anyway not about the brilliance of the counsellor's observations, useful though these might or might not be, it is a relationship, and the heart of it is the art of listening. Listening is itself a type of contemplation, a being attentive and wholly present to another, in the process of which both client and listeners—counsellor and interpreter—are a unity together. The ambience allows the client to tell his story within the security of the relationship and know himself heard—and understood. It is this dynamic, far more than any comments I might have felt moved to make, that is the healing factor. Relationship is the primary gift that heals. Simply by being there with the two of us as fellow human beings, the relationship heals.

Work together failed once or twice. There were times when what the client was saying felt incongruent with the tone of their speech and body language, making us both feel uneasy. Whenever I am with a client, I sit roughly at an angle, ten to two, arranging the room so that the light falls on me rather than on the client, so the client can read the way I hear. The interpreter would sit at the client's side. Then I insisted that the client should address her remarks to me, not to the interpreter. Difficult at first, because it isn't easy to speak to someone who is clearly not really understanding what you are saying, but absolutely necessary if I was to grasp two further features: the tone of her speech and her body language. Actual speech counts for surprisingly little in a relationship, despite the need for it. The tone of the voice is statistically three times more significant, the body language five times more. Interpretation adds the speech which then confirms the congruence—or lack of it. Much of what we were told was hard to hear. I had been counselling for almost 30 years before this asylum work and had never heard such devastating stories as these. It inevitably took its toll. It was important that both of us, interpreter and counsellor, should debrief our feelings after our sessions.

It was illuminating at the start of work to see which of the two of us the client would first relate to. If the interpreter was a woman, the two of us would then, as far as the client was concerned, present a parent-like relationship. Sometimes, even a macho Muslim man would relate far more easily to a female interpreter than to me, which spoke immediately of his earlier relationships with women. I remember once working with a distressed adult whose ability to make foolish decisions was such that it was hard for both of us, constituted as we were as awkward parents trying to support a rebellious teenager. We felt we were losing. Another time, a client who had been in prison for several years told us of hearing a muezzin call from his cell. It was like a European hearing church bells, and he was clearly comforted by hearing it. I made some comment about how helpful this must have been. My atheist interpreter was offended. In our debrief afterwards, he rebuked me for my comment. He had nonetheless, I could tell, faithfully interpreted my words.

I felt convicted that I could not speak French better—but my failure in speaking only English did mean I had to work with interpreters like Rosa from Azerbaijan. An added bonus was that she supplied me with an excellent recipe.

Let us pray for the people and leaders of Georgia, Armenia, Azerbaijan and the Caucasus republics of Russia. We give thanks for the gift of the Holy Spirit in helping us to learn the art of listening and hear what people say—whatever their language.

29

Cameroon, Equatorial Guinea, Sao Tomé and Principe, Gabon, Central African Republic and Congo (Brazzaville)

Week after Trinity 2

These countries are south of Nigeria and Chad in Africa, with a rainforest in Cameroon and Gabon. The Central African Republic is to the east of Cameroon; the Republic of the Congo is referred to as Congo (Brazzaville) to distinguish it from its neighbour across the River Congo, the Democratic Republic of Congo (Congo Kinshasa). Sao Tomé and Principe are island states in the Gulf of Guinea. Equatorial Guinea has a mainland base in Rio Muni, between Cameroon and Gabon. Its capital is on the island of Bioko. It also includes the island of Annabon which lies between Sao Tomé and Principe, islands further south in the Atlantic. Cameroon has a population of 28 million, Central African Republic 5.5 million, Gabon 2.5 million and Congo (Brazzaville) 6 million. Equatorial Guinea is 1.5 million and Sao Tomé and Principe 227,400. The population of these countries is predominantly Christian, with a Muslim population of 20 per cent in Cameroon, rather less elsewhere. There is a large number of Muslims in one part of Bangui, capital of the Central African Republic, but overall the Muslim community is no more than 5 per cent–there has been much conflict between Christians and Muslims. When Pope Francis visited in 2015, he went to a mosque. All apart from the island states were former French colonies (Cameroon has a disputed English-speaking region to the southwest of the country). Equatorial Guinea was Spanish and Sao Tomé and Principe, Portuguese. The Central African Republic is the second poorest country in the world after next door Niger.

Fear not the pestilence that stalks in darkness

Brazzaville and Kinshasa face each other across the River Congo—not unlike Newcastle and Gateshead across the Tyne though very much further apart. Even though the Congo is comparatively narrow at this point, it is still almost a mile from one side to the other. A new bridge is shortly to be built.

Seven hundred miles or so upstream, not far from the border with the Central African Republic, there is a tributary of the Congo called the Legbala. This river in Ngbandi means "white river", or as it is in French, *Eau Blanche*, a name that has since morphed into "Ebola". It is this river which has given its name to the new African plague. The disease was first identified in 1976 in the village of Yambuku, a few miles away from the river. Since then, Congo (Kinshasa) where Yambuku is, has had several epidemics and there have been eight more, four in Gabon and Congo (Brazzaville) respectively, though not in the nearby Central African Republic, which given how close it is and how many disasters that country has suffered is remarkable. Infections are like that. When the foot and mouth cattle epidemic ravaged England in the late 1990s, it was first identified in a farm just a mile or so from Ovingham, but it hardly touched our village. Ebola is a lethal disease; the death rate in Congo (Brazzaville) in one pandemic was 75 to 90 per cent of everyone infected, and in Gabon it was 60 to 82 per cent. Recent epidemics in West Africa have killed even more. It puts the Covid pandemic into stark perspective.

The Ebola epidemic began when a four-year-old boy, climbing a tree in his village, became infected by the droppings of fruit bats. Fruit bats, or flying foxes, as they are also called because of their fox-like appearance, usually live high in the canopy of a rainforest. With what Frank Snowden describes as the frenetic pace of rainforest land clearance in this part of Africa to allow for palm oil cultivation, the fruit bats have come down from the tops of the trees to live in the lower branches, so they are much closer to humans.* Fruit bats are immune to the virus; humans are not.

---

* Frank M. Snowden, *Epidemics and Society: From the Black Death to the Present* (New Haven and London: Yale University Press, 2020).

Once infected, the disease incubates for two to 21 days. The infected person then suffers flu-like symptoms, followed by vomiting, diarrhoea, loss of blood, pain and finally a lapses into coma. A few recover, but the majority die. Cruelly, a sufferer who does recover remains infectious and has also to contend with disabling aftereffects. So far it has been controlled locally and has not—like Covid-19—spread worldwide.

Dr Bob Lambourne was a Birmingham psychiatrist who set up a course in pastoral studies in the 1960s. He wrote a number of books about health, his main point being that too much health funding is directed towards acute medicine, and nothing like enough to preventative medicine and public health.* At that time, there was a general consensus among most western experts that infectious disease had become a problem of the past. The situation may have been different in Africa and Asia, but it was supposed concern was no longer needed in the west. It led to a thirty-year lacuna in the funding of public health. It was only after the AIDS outbreak of the early 1980s, and growing evidence that the cutbacks had been a mistake, that there was a change of heart. Planners began to recognize that because of the massive movement of peoples within a global world, any infection suddenly arising could all too easily spread rapidly everywhere—as indeed it has. Compromised immune systems, hospital infections, anti-microbial resistance have added to the danger. As a result, when the SARS and bird flu scares began, countries were ill equipped to cope with the devastation that they caused.

I remember my shock on reading an essay on health in Archbishop Sentamu's collection of essays on the state of the nation in 2015.** It was saying almost exactly what Dr Lambourne had been arguing some 50 years before. We do so want to be cured of our cancers, strokes and heart diseases that we are prepared to spend whatever it takes to solve those problems and baulk at any suggestion that funding should also be given to less glamorous causes like public health—and indeed mental health. Governments know that proper funding of these is far more significant

---

* R. A. Lambourne, *Community, Church and Healing* (London: Darton, Longman & Todd, 1963).

** Kersten England, "Health and well-being in Britain", in John Sentamu, ed., *On Rock or Sand?* (London: SPCK, 2015), pp. 132–59.

for the overall health of a country but persuading the country of this is what is so difficult. The Church could make a start in its intercession by praying for public health and not only for the physically sick and the acutely ill.

In 2009, when I was travelling by train into China (see Week 1), when we reached the border, we all had our temperatures taken. The authorities were looking for signs of the swine flu, which was then the feared epidemic that was afflicting the world. Later, on the same journey, on reaching Cochin in southern India, all of us leaving the plane had to pass through some kind of temperature-taking gadget fixed above us on the airport walkway. Both were necessary exercises in controlling a pestilence stalking in the darkness (Psalm 91:6). Surveillance and contact tracing, backed up by laboratory services and scientists developing vaccines, has since become a commonplace of a corporate response to the impact of a pandemic. Since early 2020 and the Covid-19 pandemic, we cannot any longer doubt the importance of public health (2 Samuel 24:16).

Let us pray for the people and leaders of Cameroon, Equatorial Guinea, Sao Tomé and Principe, Gabon, Congo (Brazzaville) and the Central African Republic and for all afflicted by pandemic disease, for the doctors, nurses and others who care for those afflicted, mentally and physically, but above all for those concerned with public health.

30

West Indies: The Greater and Lesser Antilles

Week after Trinity 3

Christopher Columbus thought he had arrived in India when he sailed the Atlantic, hence the name he gave his "discovery", the "West Indies". The large islands, the Greater Antilles, are Cuba, Hispaniola (divided between Haiti and the Dominican Republic) and Puerto Rico (part of the United States); these are in a line from west to east. Jamaica is south of Cuba with the Cayman Islands to Jamaica's west. The islands to the north of the Greater Antilles in the Lucayan Archipelago are the Bahamas (one state) and the Turks and Caicos Island group. Bermuda is some distance away in the Atlantic. The Lesser Antilles, the many smaller islands, lie from north to south–listed below.

The overall population of the West Indies is about 44 million; Cuba accounts for 11.5 million, Haiti and the Dominican Republic 11.5 million each, Jamaica 3 million. There are 13 island countries overall and 18 dependent territories. Cuba has been communist since 1959; Haiti became independent in 1804. The states of the Lesser Antilles are St Kitts and Nevis, Antigua and Barbuda, Dominica, Grenada, St Lucia, St Vincent and the Grenadines, Barbados, and Trinidad and Tobago. East of Puerto Rico are the Virgin Islands (shared with the USA, who bought their island from Denmark in 1916); Anguilla and Montserrat are autonomous British Overseas Territories with the UK handling defence and foreign relations. Similar arrangements link the several French and Dutch West Indies. France and Holland share one island: St Martin/St Maarten. The other major French islands are Guadeloupe and Martinique; the two which are Dutch are Curaçao and Aruba, both just off the Venezuela coast.

The Roman Catholic Church is dominant in the former French and Spanish territories, in the Dutch and English less so. Trinidad and Tobago, while being mostly Christian, has a significant Hindu population. The Anglican Church is served by the Province of the West Indies.

Nurturing relationships

My mother Ruth died at a comparatively young age, the result of an operation that went wrong. My very bereaved father married again, once more with a gracious partner, Kathleen. Kathleen, at the time, was the headmistress of St Edmund's School in Liverpool. Soon after they married, she became the head of a new school, an amalgamation of St Edmund's with another to become Archbishop Blanch School in Toxteth.

Kathleen was born in 1927 in the Lancashire town of Nelson. Her father owned a mill there. Four years later, in 1931, the great West Indian cricketer Learie Constantine and his family–Norma and their daughter Gloria, aged three–moved into the house next door. Learie had moved to Nelson as the town's cricket professional to play for them in the Lancashire League. The tradition was that each team in the league could employ one professional player. Nelson had made a good move in taking on Constantine. He made such a difference. Between 1929 and 1938, Nelson won the league several times and were never less than second. He was exciting to watch; crowds swarmed to the ground to see him play. The England cricketer Jack Hobbs said of his bowling in a Test match against the West Indies that he was alarmingly fast. As a batsman he could score at speed too. The cricket commentator E. W. Swanton thought that as an all-rounder he was pretty good, but as a fielder he was the best he had ever seen. Understandably, Kathleen has remained a devotee of cricket ever since. In 1965, Constantine was knighted. In 1969, he became a peer.

There was no prospect in 1920s Trinidad that, as a young Black man descended from slaves, Constantine could become a professional cricketer. Still, he was in the 1928 team when the West Indies were touring, and once in England, he decided he would stay. He hoped that his evident prowess as a cricketer might help him to do better. Three years later he joined Nelson.

The family came to love being in Nelson. Constantine was prepared to blame people's initial surprise on their ignorance when they first saw him, but he was shaken by the extent of abuse and prejudice he and his family constantly faced. His first book, *Colour Bar*, describes how it felt. During the war, he was engaged by the government to work as a welfare officer among the increasingly large numbers of West Indians coming to the country. On one occasion in 1943, he and his family were booked into a London hotel. When they arrived, the hotel manager said he could no longer allow them to stay. He explained that some Americans were in the hotel, and he feared they would be offended if they saw the Constantine family. He took the hotel to court—and won. It was an important moment in the battle to improve race relations in the country.

When Gloria married, the family moved back to Trinidad. In 1961, Constantine was appointed Trinidad's High Commissioner (the title of a Commonwealth ambassador) in London. Two years later, he became embroiled in a boycott of the Bristol buses. The city's bus company had refused to employ two West Indian drivers. The result was that, following the example of Martin Luther King in his group's similar boycott in Montgomery eight years earlier, a local campaigner, Roy Hackett, led a boycott of the buses in Bristol. Not long after the boycott had begun, Constantine as ambassador was attending a cricket match between Gloucestershire and the West Indies. He took the opportunity to speak out in support of the boycott. It was not considered appropriate for an ambassador to do such an ungentlemanly thing, to criticize the country to which he was assigned, but as Martin Luther King used to say, when accused by churchmen of making "untimely" interventions: "Frankly, I have yet to engage in a direct action movement that was 'well-timed' in the view of those that have not suffered unduly from the disease of segregation".* Learie Constantine thought the same. Victory in the boycott was announced four months after the match on 28 August 1963. It was in fact the very day when Martin Luther King was giving his *I have*

* Martin Luther King, Jr, *Why we can't Wait* (New York: Signet Books, Harper & Row, 1964), p. 80.

a dream speech in Washington DC. It was an important victory and an important precursor to the British 1965 Race Relations Act.

Crude race relations of this sort may not be quite as prevalent as they were back then, but there are still far too many examples, the Windrush scandal of 2010 being one. West Indians who had been invited to England after the war were suddenly declared illegal and compelled to prove that they had a right to be here. That was bad enough; what is so much more difficult is eradicating the long-held structural attitudes which persist among so many British people, the almost unconscious belief that white people are superior. With the murder of George Floyd in Minneapolis (25 May 2020), in broad daylight and on television in front of the world, the movement that Black lives really do matter made a strong advance. It was a moment for deep soul-searching among all white people—as it is for me, for my readers, for so many white people especially in northern European countries. We all have to address our behaviour and attitudes towards our Black fellow human beings. No one escapes the contagion. It informs the inner prejudice and bias of our culture. In the kingdom of God, we are to nurture our cross-cultural and cross-racial relationships.

Let us pray for the people and leaders of the West Indies and especially give thanks for all who have given so much to the life of our country. May we in penitence confess our racial sins and prejudices and ask God's blessing on all peoples whatever their colour, country or ethnic origin, that together we may be one community within the Kingdom of God.

3 1

Kazakhstan, Uzbekistan, Turkmenistan, Tajikistan, Kyrgyzstan—Central Asia and Mongolia

Week after Trinity 4

The five "Stans" (see Week 20 for the meaning) are the Central Asian countries between the Caspian Sea and the Himalayas, north of Iran and Afghanistan. The River Adamariya (or River Oxus) forms the border between Uzbekistan and Afghanistan, flowing west towards the diminishing Aral Sea. It gives the sometimes-used name "Transoxania" (Beyond the River Oxus) to parts of the region. Kazakhstan is huge, immediately south of Russia. Uzbekistan is to the south with Turkmenistan southwest of it adjoining Iran. Tajikistan and Kyrgyzstan, and indeed Kazakhstan, have eastern borders with China. Kazakhstan at its easternmost point almost touches Mongolia at its most western point—23 miles of a China and Russia border divide the two. Mongolia straddles the Gobi Desert immediately north of China. Populations are: Kazakhstan 19.5 million, Uzbekistan 34.5 million, Turkmenistan 6.5 million, Tajikistan 10 million, Kyrgyzstan 6.5 million and Mongolia 3.5 million. These Central Asian countries (with the exception of Mongolia) were formerly part of the Soviet Union. They are largely Muslim with a good percentage of Russian Orthodox especially in Kazakhstan. Mongolia is almost 55 per cent Buddhist with a small number following Shamanism, and rather less Christianity. The rest profess to have no faith.

The strength to be human

The train from Moscow had picked up a number of passengers in Samara, and we were now just over the Kazakhstan border, at a place called Aqtöbe. I had had the cabin to myself for the first day of the journey, had been joined by Vapa a little before Samara and then in Samara by two more Uzbeks, Navangan and Allerbegan—I hope I have their names correct. They were migrant workers returning home to Tashkent. The journey, 900 miles more to go across the vast steppe lands of Kazakhstan, was to take a further 48 hours. Navangan, the oldest of the three, orchestrated our corporate life, all the time concerned that we should each of us have enough to eat, myself included. It took us nine hours to negotiate the Kazakhstan customs, a further long wait when we reached Uzbekistan—Allerbegan had a television in his luggage, and Navangan a number of things he probably should not have had, and I feared for him when his passport was taken away for examination. He seemed only mildly distressed. Clearly he understood the procedure, that money was needed to ease his passage, no doubt duly supplied, and the passport was soon enough returned. There were still three and a half more hours to go before we eventually ambled into Tashkent. While we may not have been able to talk together, we had nonetheless become a community in our long journey together.

After visits to Samarkand and Bukhara, I flew from Tashkent to Almaty, or Alma Ata as it used to be called, the former capital of Kazakhstan. The new one, Astana, is 600 miles to the north and is now called Nur-Sultan after the former President Nursultan Nazarbayev. My fellow passenger on this flight was a Kazakh lawyer. Seeing the book I was reading, Christopher Robbins's account of his time in the country, *In Search of Kazakhstan*,* she told me that she had attended the book's launch in London. The highlight of our conversation was her idea that we should take three days off each week, one to honour Islam's Friday prayers, another on Saturday for the Jewish Sabbath and Sunday for the Christians. Perhaps we need also to add an additional Monday to accommodate the humanists! "Days

* Christopher Robbins, *In Search of Kazakhstan: The Land that Disappeared* (London: Profile Books, 2008).

off for the pursuit of the health-giving creative things we can do when there is time and leisure to do them," she said. Her words reminded me of Josef Pieper's study of leisure.* Pieper explains that the Greek word for leisure is *scholé* (from which come the English words "scholar" and "school"); the word for work, *ascholé*, the "*a*" turning the word into a negative; "not-work": leisure for the creative things which is thus primary. It bears on a fundamental spiritual truth initially outlined by St Benedict in his rules for a typical day: that time for prayer should be first, time for study second, and only then time for the work that needed to be done. Prayer first, the nurturing of our relationships and for creativity second—and work third! (See Week 16.)

Almaty was the place where the World Health Organization held its September 1978 Assembly and defined what it meant by health: "A state of complete physical, mental and social well-being and not merely the absence of illness and disease. . . . " As many observed at the time, the qualifying adjective "complete" turned the definition into a spiritual and visionary ideal—the coming of the Kingdom of God no less—and surely beyond the powers of any health service to deliver. It was nonetheless a very important understanding. The word "health" in English is derived from the root *hal*, which also underlies words like "whole", "hale", "holy". The drafters of the definition were surely right in seeing that health is first of all a spiritual goal.

The practical problems remained. The following year the Rockefeller Foundation organized a further conference, with the idea of promoting a more achievable programme of action. That perhaps was a necessary practical step, but the declaration nonetheless had said something essential, that health is far more than just "not being ill". Of course health in this sense is humanly unachievable precisely because it is a spiritual ideal; it is a theological vision, more to do with the infinite purposes of God than with a practical humanist programme. But, without such vision, the practical steps that are needed to improve health tend to go awry. A fortieth-anniversary WHO conference was held, again in Kazakhstan, in 2018.

---

* Josef Pieper, *Leisure: The Basis of Culture*, trans. Alexander Dru (San Francisco: Ignatius Press, 1963).

Jürgen Moltmann has defined health as "the strength to be human";* "strength" here referring to the empowering work of the Holy Spirit which gives grace and strength to persons to become human in their relationship with God and each other. As I journeyed through Central Asia with my Uzbek friends and by plane with my Kazakh companion, the two encounters were intimations of the health the Alma Ata declaration was speaking about.

Let us pray for the people and leaders of Mongolia and the states of Central Asia, that in the vision of what it is to be healthy, we may all be given the strength to be human.

---

* See David Atkinson, "Towards a Theology of Health", in Andrew Ferguson, ed., *Health: The Strength to be Human* (Leicester: InterVarsity Press, 1993).

32

The Balkans: Bulgaria, Romania, Slovenia, Croatia, Serbia, Bosnia-Herzegovina, Albania, Kosovo, Montenegro, North Macedonia

Week after Trinity 5

The Balkan states between the Adriatic and the Black Sea form a border area between the east and the west, a tension reflected in its history, especially its religious history. The Danube flows from Hungary through Serbia and then forms much of the border between Romania in the north and Bulgaria in the south before flowing into the Black Sea. Serbia is in the middle of the region, with Kosovo—recognized by almost a hundred countries as independent. Kosovo, with its largely Albanian population, declared itself independent in 2006, but it remains an autonomous region of Serbia. Slovenia, with Italy to the west and Austria to the north, is with Croatia, Montenegro and Albania beside the Adriatic Sea. Bosnia touches the sea at one small point but is otherwise protected from it by a long arm of Croatia. North Macedonia is north of Greece, Albania to its west, Bulgaria to the east. Population is in general declining: Bulgaria 7 million, Romania 19.5 million, Slovenia 2 million, Croatia 4 million, Serbia 7 million, Bosnia 3 million, Montenegro 627,000, Albania 3 million, North Macedonia 2 million. There are substantial ethnic and religious minorities in each of the states, but very broadly speaking Slovenia and Croatia are Catholic; Romania, Bulgaria, Serbia and North Macedonia Orthodox; Bosnia and Albania Muslim. Politically, both Romania and Bulgaria—Bulgaria uses a Cyrillic alphabet—were under the sway of Russia until the 1989 upheavals. Albania had its own separate Communist party until 1990, and the other six republics were grouped together as Yugoslavia until its break-up in 1991 (see below), a process which began with the death of Marshal Tito in 1980. War broke out when the Bosnian Serb army supported by Croatia and Serbia campaigned for a separate Serb part of Bosnia. Peace came in late 1995. Montenegro and Serbia continued together until June 2006 when Montenegro declared independence. Serbia did the same two days later. North Macedonia is called such since the Prespa Agreement with Greece in June 2018. Croatia and Slovenia declared independence in 1991. Bosnia followed in 1992.

Hope for peace in Europe

Yugoslavia became a kingdom after the First World War. After the Second, and the victory of the Communist partisans under the leadership of Josip Broz (Marshal Tito), it became a Communist Republic. Almost immediately, Tito decided he would build a palace in Belgrade as an edifice worthy enough to represent the grandeur of the one state of which he had become ruler. Yugoslavia comprised the six Balkan republics of Serbia, Croatia, Slovenia, Bosnia-Herzegovina, Montenegro and Macedonia. The new building was to house the Federal Executive Council. Tito broke with Stalin in 1948, and this meant that the project had to be put on hold for a few more years; it was eventually finished in September 1961, just in time for Tito with President Nehru of India and President Nasser of Egypt to host the first Non-Aligned Movement of Nations Conference. (NAM meets every three years in the country of the current chairperson–Azerbaijan in 2020.) The building is now called the Palace of Serbia.

I have come to know all this because the Slovenian artist Jasmina Cibic, who lives in London, had an exhibition of her work at the Baltic, the Northeast's "Tate Modern" (The Baltic Centre for Contemporary Art), in the spring of 2018.* The palace features in her film *Tear Down and Rebuild*, which she first made in 2015. It forms the third chapter of her *Spielraum* series. In them, she examines the role of buildings in promoting any ruling group's vision of what they think the future of their

---

* Jasmina Cibic and Una Popovic (eds), *Spielraum* (London: Black Dog Press, 2018).

country should be. The first of the *Nada* films is based on Vjenceslav Richter's design for the Yugoslav pavilion at the Brussels 1958 expo, the expo picturesquely described in Jonathan Coe's novel *Expo 58*. The second is Cibic's fresh take on the composer Bela Bartok's *Miraculous Mandarin* ballet, which was highlighted at the same Brussels expo. Her final film is a reflection on a variety of speeches made by a number of different politicians, the things they tend to say when opening any buildings they have commissioned to effect their political purpose. Their hope, they say, is that the new artworks and architecture will properly express their vision. *Nada* in Croatian means *Hope*; in Spanish, it means *nothing*, a contrast which Cibic explores to illustrate her concern that many of these visionary speeches are in fact vacuous in content, indeed not much more than general expressions of hope.

The Palace of Serbia has six lounges. Each of them is the same size. They represent the equality in status of the six different states in the union. One much larger room was to represent Yugoslavia itself. The different rooms are decorated in art forms deemed appropriate to each particular country. All this became a little awkward when the union fell apart; even more so when eastern European Communism in general came to an end. An independent Serbia did not want to be reminded that it had once been a part of such a conglomeration of states. When Cibic came to make her film in the palace, she was told that she must be very careful not to show any artwork that might offend Serbian sensitivities. What she found herself and thought far more offensive was the extensive array of female nudes scattered around the building, several of them in erotic poses and all of them in plain sight. These were the only women represented anywhere in the building. She highlights her sense of offence at this at the end of her *Nada III*.

The break-up of the Yugoslav federation led to tragedy. Slovenia largely escaped, though there was a ten-day war in 1991. Croatia (Catholic) and Serbia (Orthodox) were involved in the Bosnian (predominantly Muslim) war, and there were terrible atrocities that followed, especially during the siege of Sarajevo and later in Srebrenica. The Balkan States with their volatile history of constant invasion, like so many border countries with different ethnic and religious identities, make the region an apt symbol of the European cause: that of bringing together disparate peoples with a long history of warfare and conflict into one union together. It was the vision of Jean Monet and Robert Schumann after the Second World War, of a European *convivencia*, of a Europe united as one in peace and harmony. While Croatia, Slovenia and Bulgaria are members of the European Union, the other states are in a Free Trade Agreement with the Union.

The Balkan troubles are a challenge to Europe, to the United Kingdom in particular—now that our country has withdrawn from the Union—and we must work out how our country is to maintain and support good relations with our continental neighbours. The Christian commandment is that we are to love our neighbours as ourselves (Matthew 22:34–40; Mark 12:28–31). The Channel Tunnel, and the Mostar Peace Bridge in Bosnia, are important symbols of such neighbourliness, speaking of different peoples coming together in oneness. Can the European Union hold on to its unity? It is a vision which must not be lost.

We pray for the people and leaders of the countries of the Balkans, for dialogue between peoples of faith, Catholic, Orthodox, Muslim and those of no apparent faith, that all may collaborate and develop their corporate vision and work together with God for the Common Good.

33

Vietnam, Laos and Cambodia

Week after Trinity 6

Vietnam and Laos are countries to the south of China with which they share borders. Vietnam stretches along the South China Sea from the Gulf of Tonkin in the north to the Gulf of Thailand. Thailand is to the west of Cambodia and Laos, the Mekong River passing through all three countries to its delta in southern Vietnam. Vietnam's population is 98 million, Cambodia 17 million, Laos 7.5 million. In Vietnam, the majority adhere to Vietnamese folk religion, but there is a significant Mahayana Buddhist presence, and a slightly smaller Christian one, mostly Catholic. Cambodia and Laos are Theravada Buddhist (see Week 38), a large majority in Cambodia, well over half of the population in Laos. All three countries were part of French Indochina–Vietnam was a colony, Cambodia and Laos protectorates, the latter two becoming independent in 1953. The Vietminh, the Vietnamese freedom fighters, defeated the French at Dien Bien Phu in May 1954, and Vietnam became independent after that. The country was then in an almost continual state of war. The United States became involved militarily from 1966 until 1975, when Saigon (now Ho Chi Minh City) fell to the north Vietnamese. Cambodia and Laos were kingdoms until they became communist in the 1970s. The Cambodian Communist Party, the Khmer Rouge under Pol Pot, ruled from 1975 to 1979 and initiated the genocide (the "killing fields") in which a quarter of the population were killed. Cambodia's constitutional monarchy was restored in 1992. Laos was still communist in 2022.

Mindfulness

My twin grandchildren were in Vietnam in 2019. They were struck by the lush beauty of the country and the grace of the people, but were both shocked by the depth of poverty they saw. It is tragic to think that despite years of colonization the people's poverty was still so widespread. And then the Vietnam War! Max Hastings's account of the war makes devastating reading.* In a memorable Passion Sunday sermon when the war was raging in 1968, Martin Luther King commented, "This day we are spending $500,000 to kill every Vietcong soldier . . . while we spend only $53 a year for every person characterized as poverty-stricken . . . which is not even a good skirmish against poverty."** He was speaking of poverty in the United States, but his comments could equally have been said of the people of Vietnam.

The person who urged King to speak out about the Vietnam War was Thich Nhat Hanh, the Vietnamese monk who had come to the United States to lecture at Princeton University. He was to remain all his life a prominent advocate for peace both in the States and in Vietnam itself.

I first came across Thich Nhat Hanh in 1975, when SCM published his *Miracle of Being Awake*.*** SCM at the time was publishing a number of reflections on Christianity and the issues of the day and this was one of the earlier ones about "mindfulness", the Buddhist form of meditation which Thich Nhat Hanh introduced to the west. The concept is expounded in the *Anapranasati Sutra*, one of the Buddhist scriptures (*anaprana* here meaning "breath" and *sati* "mindfulness"); it focuses on the importance of breath control, which is so fundamental to mindfulness and indeed all meditation.

---

* Max Hastings, *Vietnam: An Epic History of a Tragic War* (London: Collins, 2019).

** "Remaining Awake Through a Great Revolution", in James M. Washington, ed., *A Testament of Hope: The Essential Writings of Martin Luther King, Jr.* (London: Harper & Row, 1986), p. 275.

*** Thich Nhat Hanh, *The Miracle of Being Awake: Manual on Meditation for Activists* (Movement Pamphlet No. 30, Journal of the SCM, Dublin, 1975).

Nguyen Xuan Bao (Thich Nhat Hanh is the name given him in religion) was born in Hue in 1926. He entered the nearby Tu Hieu Temple at the age of 16. His novitiate was a long process of induction into the disciplines of *thien*, the Vietnamese word for *chen* (meditation). When he came to the United States on a second visit, the beginning of what was in fact to become a very long exile, he and his nun colleague Chang Kuong began their preparations for encouraging mindfulness in the west by moving in 1982 to the Dordogne in France. There they opened a first monastery to advance his teaching: the Plum Village Monastery. It was to be the first of many foundations.

One example of his teaching that he gives in the *Miracle* pamphlet referred to above is about the right way to wash dishes. "There are two ways to wash dishes", he counsels. "The first is to wash dishes in order to have clean dishes and the second is to wash the dishes in order to wash the dishes." It is the second which is the mindfulness way. It reminds me of a family cycle ride my dad, sister and I once made when I was about 12 and Margaret 10. We were in the Yorkshire Dales, ascending the Kidstone Pass from Buckden, rising up to the moors which separate Wharfedale from Wensleydale. The pass is long, and for most of the way we laboriously pushed our bikes up the never-ending hill. "Won't it be wonderful," I opined, "when we reach the top." My dad, ever the spiritual director, counselled that it would be more important to relish the joys of this particular moment. Very irritating! Yes, but it is the only thing I remember about the trip. These two trivial examples give the essence of Hanh's teaching—we are to abide in the present moment, not in a fantasy future that we imagine might lie ahead, nor indeed in what our memory might trick us into thinking about our glorious past. The truth of this is memorably illustrated in a story from the life of the Roman Catholic bishop of Saigon, Nguyen Van Thuan. He had been appointed bishop just six months before the Communist takeover in 1975. He was imprisoned and held there in solitary confinement for nine long years. He was only released some four more years later; he was in prison for a total of 13 years. On release, he was exiled to the Vatican where he was made a cardinal. On one of his retreats, he told his retreatants how important he had found it to live and be aware of the sacredness of the present moment. "This is the only time we have in our hands," he said. "The past is already gone, and we do not know if there will be a future. The present moment is our great wealth." He said he knew himself buoyed by his membership of the Church, that he had come to learn afresh the nature of his calling, that he was called to be a man of love—especially towards his guards. One of them asked him why. He replied, "Because Jesus has taught us to love everyone, even my enemies. If I don't, I am no longer worthy to be called a Christian."*

Like Thich Nhat Hanh, the French Discalced Carmelite Brother Lawrence learnt much of his spiritual discipline while working in the monastery kitchen. He was alert to God's presence, not just as a person from his past, nor as a possible relationship he might have in the future, but as a real presence now. "The time of business," he said, "does not with me differ from the time of prayer, and in the noise and clatter of my kitchen, while several persons are at the same time calling for different things, I possess God in as great tranquillity, as if I were upon my knees at the Blessed Sacrament."**

We pray for the people and leaders of Vietnam, Laos and Cambodia whose long suffering has been so intense. Let them neither dwell in their past nor pine for their future, but give them peace to abide gracefully in the present moment and spread God's love to all.

---

* Roderick Strange, thinking about Cardinal Francis Xavier Nguyen Van Thuan, "Living in the Present Moment", *The Tablet*, 28 March 2020, p. 7.

** Nicholas Herman (Brother Lawrence), *The Practice of the Presence of God* (numerous editions, 1692), 4th conversation.

34

South India

Week after Trinity 7

(See Week 6 also.) Cochin in Kerala had a Jewish population in the years before Christ, which increased when Jerusalem fell in AD 72. Legend has it that St Thomas came to South India, where he founded the Mar Thoma Syrian Church (MTSC). This is now split into several groups. Two Malabar Churches are in communion with the Church of South India (CSI), which serves the five southernmost states and is part of the Anglican Church. It is the second largest Church in India with a membership of 4 million. The Catholic Church has been in India since the fourteenth century. Christians are above 40 per cent of the population of the Idukki province of Kerala. The Muslim and Hindu populations are also large.

Faith and prayer for unity between churches and people

It was the summer of 1993, and Ovingham was to have a visit from Fr Moni, a presbyter in the Church of South India. He had been at one of the Selly Oak Colleges in Birmingham and before returning to India was to tour some of the Church Missionary Society's supporting parishes. He managed one service with us, but then promptly fell ill with chicken pox. I have always rather dreaded this sort of thing happening when I have been travelling abroad, the embarrassment of becoming a nuisance to some unsuspecting host; actually, in the event, it was a privilege, not least for the long-lasting friendship that developed from it. Moni, as he liked to be called—given his long Malayalam name—was with us for three weeks. Joy and our GP, who came round several times, cared for him throughout. My contribution was slight, not very much more than a daily greeting from the bedroom door.

The Church of South India came into being in 1947. It is a union of the mainstream Protestant Churches brought together on the basis of the Lambeth Quadrilateral, an agreement that stipulates the four Anglican requirements for unity; the authority of the Bible, the further authority of the Apostles' and Nicene Creeds, the dominical sacraments (Baptism and Eucharist) and an episcopal ministry. This last was usually the sticking point in such unity discussions. It was this that scuppered the Anglican–Methodist unity proposals that collapsed so tragically in 1972, a failure that has diminished both Churches since, especially the Anglican. In South India, the Churches managed to agree. They recognized the validity of each other's ministries and ruled that all subsequent ordinations should be episcopal. The new Church was inaugurated on 27 September 1947 in a grand service at St George's Cathedral in Madras (Chennai).

Thirty years later, this was important for us here in Newcastle. Our new assistant bishop was to be Kenneth Gill. In the 1990s, Kenneth had trained as a Methodist minister in Manchester, had opted to work in South India and had then in 1958 been made deacon in the CSI diocese of Mysore. Two years later he was ordained presbyter. Then in 1972 he was consecrated bishop of Central Karnataka, where he was to remain the diocesan for the next eight years. In 1980, he returned to England and came to us in Newcastle. It was a privilege to have him with us. When Joy died, it was he who came to her funeral and gave the blessing.

It was not until 2009 that I was able to visit Fr Moni in Kerala—his wife Christal also and their three daughters, Gifty, Grace and Gladys. I arrived at Kochi (Cochin) airport, only for it to take a further one and a half hours to negotiate the many formalities. It was a relief to find Moni still there, patiently waiting. His parish was in the high hills of Kerala, some distance away. His presbytery near to Kattappana was in the middle of a huge tea garden, the way to it from the road no more than a vague pathway through the bushes. The parish was remote, a beautiful haven in the midst of so many acres of tea garden which stretched far into the rolling hills. The church was next door to the presbytery. On the Sunday, Moni asked me to say a few words to his large congregation, he translating my brief remarks into Malayalam. The kiss of peace was memorable. Each person held their hands in the Namaste position (Namaskar in Malayalam), greeting their immediate neighbour, the greeting passing like a wave from one to the next, a true enactment of their corporate oneness in Christ.

On the drive from Kochi, Moni had shown me the Idukki dam, a great wall in the mountains which holds back a reservoir. A dominant concern during my stay was another dam, the Mullaperiyar, which held another reservoir formed out of the Periyar River. It had been built to serve Madras in the neighbouring state of Tamil Nadu. At the time of my visit the reservoir was 130 feet deep, and Tamil Nadu wanted it to increase to 142 feet, if not more. Apparently the dam was leaking and the local people were concerned. They demanded that it should be fully repaired before any more water was added. At the time of writing, some 11 years later, the problem is still unresolved, not much improved by a Supreme Court ruling in 2014 stipulating that contingency plans should be prepared in case the dam were to collapse. There was a meeting about all this immediately after the service I was at, the concern being precisely this: that the dam might break. Understandably, this was of immense concern to both Moni and his community.

This part of Kerala is a stronghold of Christianity. There are other parts of India where Muslims predominate, but in most of the country, it is the Hindus. Given the immense size of the population, even the minorities are huge: 32 million Christians and some 220 million Muslims. Congress at the time of independence was determined that the country's constitution should be secular, so that no one faith would dominate. Since the election of the Bharatiya Janata government in 2014 this safeguard has been put at risk. Sumantra Bose argues that a deeply religious nation such as India cannot afford to have one faith dominate the country at the expense of the rest.* The different faiths have no alternative, he argues, but to live creatively together.

The twentieth-century ecumenical movement in the Churches was significant for this, a sign to the world as a whole that in this twenty-first

---

* Sumantra Bose, *Secular States, Religious Politics: India, Turkey and the Future of Secularism* (Cambridge: Cambridge University Press, 2018), pp. 273–80.

century there should be a new kind of ecumenical coming together of the different great faiths; that just as St Paul taught that Jews and Gentiles were now one in Christ, so—again guided by Christ—the different faiths should treat each other equally and practise *convivencia*. It is something the world urgently needs. Thy kingdom come, we pray. I cannot remember exactly which Hindu/Muslim clash it was, possibly the ongoing conflict about the Ayodhya Mosque, but I do remember the report that told of a group of Hindus and Muslims coming together after the clash to pray. It was a significant moment.

Thinking of Moni's tea garden church when they offered the kiss of peace, a disparate gathering in a wave of mutual greeting, may the kiss encourage persons of different faiths to do the same—in India especially.

Let us pray for the people and leaders of India, for its large religious communities, that as the Churches of South India have come together and have formed one Church, so the people of different faiths might also come to know, understand and listen to each other, as they work together for the Common Good.

35

The Horn of Africa: Ethiopia, Eritrea, Djibouti, Somalia

Week after Trinity 8

Ethiopia is an inland country in the mountains with a lower region to the south: the Ogaden region. Since Ethiopia broke up with Eritrea, it no longer has a coast, but Addis Ababa, the capital, is linked to Djibouti on the Gulf of Aden by a newly electrified railway. Eritrea is northeast of Ethiopia, Somalia southeast, its northern part on the Gulf of Aden, its southern beside the Indian Ocean. Ethiopia's population is 123.5 million and growing fast, Eritrea 3.5 million, Djibouti just under 1 million and Somalia 7.5 million. Ethiopia and Eritrea are largely Christian, most of them Ethiopian Orthodox. Each country has a large Muslim minority. Both Djibouti and Somalia are almost wholly Muslim.

The Anglican Church is served by the diocese of the Horn in its Alexandria province. Eritrea became a colony of Italy in the late 1800s, Ethiopia remaining independent except for a six-year period when it was ruled by Italy between 1935 and 1941 when the Emperor Hailè Selassie was able to return. The Empire ended when there was a Communist takeover in 1974. There has been much change of government since. There was famine from 1984 to 1985. Since November 2020, there has been new unrest in the far north centred on Tigray. Eritrea remained part of Ethiopia until the end of the civil war in 1991. There have been no elections in Eritrea since, and the country is heavily militarized. Djibouti became independent from France in 1997. Somalia in colonial times was in two parts, the northern part ruled by Italy, the other by Britain; it became one independent nation in 1960 and has had trouble since with drought, famine and ongoing *Al Shabbab* incursions.

Choice after bereavement

The Franciscan friary at Alnmouth in Northumberland stands above the dunes looking out towards Coquet Island and its lighthouse. During Evensong in the winter months, you can see the light sweeping at regular intervals over the waters. It gladdens the heart as it did the hearts of the asylum seekers who had come with us to stay there. Several of us from the Newcastle West End Refugee Service took groups there for weekend breaks, men and women from Ethiopia and Eritrea in particular. They were intrigued by the place, the Muslims among them by the silent breakfasts. Later one of them asked me a question. "When you were counselling me," he said, "you used to ask me some very personal questions. Now it is my turn!" He paused, his eyes agleam. "Are you married?"

I explained that I was a widower.

"So why is it then that you have not married again?"

A fair question! I told him that I had decided not to. I was grateful he had not asked me a few years earlier. Both my father and two of my sisters had each of them married a second time, and so had a number of my friends. Why had I not?

The wife of a priest in Ethiopia faced a similar dilemma. Yetemegnu had been married at a very young age to an older man, a priest, Abuna Tsega, in 1924.* Apparently Tsega had needed to marry if he was to advance his career. He sorted the requirement out by marrying Yetemegnu, who was only eight years old. Twenty-nine years later in 1953, Tsega died. Unsurprisingly their relationship had been distant at the start but had grown much deeper as the years had progressed. They had had their first child when Yetemegnu was 14. That little girl had died. Their second was born five years later in 1935, a son, Edemariam. She was to have eight more children. By these later years, her husband had become an important figure within the government, but then things went badly wrong. He was arrested and imprisoned. To the astonishment of her friends and neighbours who strongly advised her not to do it, Yetemegnu decided she would go to Addis Ababa and personally petition

* "Abuna" in Amharic is the form of address to a priest. It means "Father".

the emperor for her husband's release—which she did, with success! But Tsega had been wounded by his imprisonment. He died soon after. So here she was, a widow at only 37. Should she remarry? There were many who thought she should and many more who wanted to marry her. She was attractive and evidently very fertile. She herself reflected that if she were to marry again, and have more children, her existing children would suffer; they would become secondary to any more children she might have. She could not risk it. Instead, she decided she would become a nun.

She set off to test her discernment, accompanied by her confessor, to visit the monastery of Debra Libanos. This monastery was founded in the thirteenth century and is a shrine to St Tekle Haymanot (c.1215–c.1313), a St Cuthbert-like ascetic whose life had had an immense impact on his fellow countrymen. There are springs near the monastery where pilgrims go to wash and be healed. Yetemegnu went in the hope that once she had been cleansed in the waters, she would be able to see clearly her new vocation.*

Women visiting the monastery today are faced by a large notice at the entrance advising them that they must not enter if they are menstruating. Yetemegnu seems, so her granddaughter says, to have been naked as she queued with the others for the waters. As she stood there, waiting her turn, she discovered to her distress that she was beginning to bleed; she realized she was starting a period. Her confessor standing nearby called her over, and together they walked away. He took her to see an old monk he knew who lived a little way from the monastery. Yetemegnu told this holy man what had happened and how shocked and ashamed she was about it. "Never mind," he said. "It is the devil's fault, not yours. Take courage." She told him that she felt oppressed, that she did not wish to marry again, and that she had thought she ought to become a nun. The old monk advised her to return to the monastery, continue her time of prayer and avoid going to the springs. What has happened, he said, "will not stop you from receiving God". She saw him again as she was leaving. This time he counselled her to forget her idea of becoming a nun. "Be a good Christian," he said, "keep yourself separate and holy and continue to take communion. And go home in peace." It was not what she had

---

* Aida Edemariam, *The Wife's Tale* (London: Fourth Estate, 2018), pp. 173–4.

wanted to hear, but it was wise direction. She was to remain a widow until she died at the age of 97.

My wife Joy had died in 1998. Five years later, I was in Africa, in Zambia and on a bus going from Livingstone to Lusaka. My thoughts were similar to those of Yetemegnu when she went to the monastery; I was asking what direction my life should now take. Should I remain hermit-like? Ought I to marry again? I had with me Una Kroll's *The Anatomy of Survival* in which she describes her own feelings after her husband had died.* She found herself on a plateau, a kind of equilibrium in her thinking, in which she tried to avoid making any decision about her future. At this point, she realized that she needed to decide something: should she remarry or not? She couldn't stay on the fence for ever. I realized I was at a similar impasse. I had been married to a remarkable woman, and yes, I did indeed miss the physical and spiritual intimacy, but I knew enough about myself to realize that to marry again for me would be a mistake. I decided I would remain celibate.

I did not share all this with the asylum seeker, but it was why I was able to answer him with such confidence.

Let us pray for the people and leaders of Ethiopia, Eritrea, Djibouti and Somalia, for those who are hungry and in need and for peace in the country. We pray also for all those who are bereaved and thinking and praying about their future.

---

* Una Kroll, *Anatomy of Survival* (London: Mowbray's Continuum, 2001), pp. 87–90.

3 6

Colombia, Venezuela, Guyana, Suriname and French Guiana

Week after Trinity 9

These countries are in the north of South America. Colombia links with Panama to the west, with Venezuela to its east. The three smaller countries are along the Caribbean coast, each having a southern border with Brazil. Colombia's population is 52 million and Venezuela's 28.5 million. Guyana's population is 809,000, Suriname 618,000 and French Guiana 305,000. All the countries are predominantly Christian, Colombia and Venezuela Catholic with growing Pentecostal Churches (the *Evangelicos*). There is a small Anglican presence, one diocese each in the IXth province of the USA's Episcopal Church. Guyana has one Anglican diocese in the province of the West Indies, and like Trinidad has a substantial Hindu population. Since the 1960s, Colombia has suffered ongoing armed struggles between militias and its government. Peace came in November 2016, but some fighting has persisted. Venezuela has also had a troubled time; the 2019 election result was disputed and several million left for neighbouring countries. Guyana became independent from Britain in 1966 and Suriname from the Netherlands in 1975; French Guiana remains part of France and the EU–the European Space Centre is there.

Problems of addiction

Joe had been something of a trial to people in Ryhope, so people told me when I became vicar there. This was some time in the past; I never knew him. Apparently, he would regularly challenge anyone he met as to whether they were saved, whether they knew Jesus. By all accounts, he was a true Holy Joe, and people would try to avoid meeting him in the street. One or two, so the legend went, complained about this un-Anglican behaviour to one of my predecessors. He decided to visit and learn what Joe's story was. His wife was on her own when he called. He gently raised the issue. "What is life with Joe like these days?" he asked.

"Well!" she said. "It is lovely now!"

"It is?"

"Yes! Compared to what it was. He used to come home every night very drunk—he would grab a knife and chase me round the kitchen. I know he has got God in a big way, but life is so much better."

Joe had apparently been converted by a Salvationist. The transformation had been remarkable. Joe may not have been very adept as an evangelist, but that he was so very much better could not be doubted. Worth a bit of embarrassment, my predecessor thought!

The addictions, whether they are to alcohol as in Joe's case, or to any of the other possibilities—food, gambling, cocaine, heroin—they all appear to offer an escape from some acute personal and unmet need. There is often also a genetic disposition as there is to most disease, and psychological factors weigh heavily and increase vulnerability, but probably the most serious cause is spiritual, an unsatisfied longing for some real meaning and purpose in life. Life in its loneliness and misery becomes all too much. When there are pleasurable and readily available alternatives—drugs etc.—to relieve the pain, it is all too easy to succumb. For many, experimenting with drugs can be just that, a brief exposure! But for any who are prone to addiction, it is dangerous. Recovery is hard beyond words—especially when there are so many who are determined to make sure that they remain addicted.

The Colombian Nobel laureate Gabriel Garcia Marquez was once asked if he would write about his country's cartels, those running the drug trade.* It was the cartels who were the main ones responsible for trafficking, demanding protection money, kidnapping people, and generally brutalizing anyone who might try to oppose them. Some ran private militias. Marquez wrote especially about the Medellin cartel, the largest of the cartels at the time. It was led by Pablo Escobar, a multi-billionaire it was said, his cartel at one stage exporting to the United States as much as 80 tons of cocaine a month. He had tried, Robin Hood-like, to mollify his critics by paying for community projects, but these in no way compensated for the havoc he was causing. Retribution eventually came when he was killed in 1993. The threat of the cartels at the time of writing is as serious as it has ever been, one of the main reasons why so many over the years have tried to emigrate to the United States.

How have South America and the Central American states tried to deal with this? In Colombia, the country was in virtual civil war for years, the army having limited success in containing the problem. An army is a heavy tool to try and deal with something like this; what might have been more effective would have been better intelligence and a strong and efficient police force, had the countries not been so poor. The police were not well paid. They were often badly led.

My personal links with South America are limited, but I suspect that travelling in Colombia is not all that different from going about in Africa. I recall once in Tanzania encountering a police block outside Dodoma, its purpose not to protect the public as I had naively supposed, but a scheme to raise extra cash for the poorly paid police. My host was not at all surprised to be stopped, he simply paid the "tax", which he had ready to hand. It would be easy to say he was just responding to greed—that has to be a factor—but the poverty in the country was a far more serious cause.

In Colombia, many small farmers have to cope with the fact that what they might earn from planting wheat is so much less than they can by growing plants for drugs. Without support and subsidy, the poor are hopelessly compromised. And yet the wonder is that so many, police and farmers alike, do in fact determine to do the right thing, even if they are the losers by it.

---

* Gabriel Garcia Marquez, *News of a Kidnapping*, trans. Edith Grossman (New York: Vintage Pubs., 1997).

Addiction leaves a trail of misery. Here in the Northeast, we have a number of agencies working to help, among them organizations like Drug Addicts Anonymous based on the pioneering work of Alcoholics Anonymous. The treatment is effective because it addresses the spiritual roots of their addictions. All who follow the 12-step recovery programme are supported as they go down into the depths of their despair, to their very lowest point, where paradoxically they discover some higher power drawing them towards new hope and recovery. Not unlike how it was with Joe—no doubt still after his conversion an addictive personality, because such a one does not lose his vulnerability—but this time addicted to something so much healthier, the gospel offering him a new purpose in life.

Let us pray for the people and leaders of Venezuela and Colombia, of Guyana, Suriname and French Guiana, and for all who are victims of the cartels, of violence, of the pedlars in drugs as addicts struggle to find their way through love and care towards hope and recovery.

37

Spain and Portugal

Week after Trinity 10

Spain's population is 47.5 million, Portugal's 10.5 million. Spain has enclaves on the Moroccan coast: the main ones are Ceuta and Melilla. Gibraltar is linked to the United Kingdom. Andorra (population 79,800) is a principality, the princes being the bishops of Urgell, not far away in Spain, and the President of France. Most people are Roman Catholic; the Spanish Episcopal Reformed Church and the Lusitanian Church in Portugal are in communion with the Anglican Church, the diocese of Gibraltar in Europe. Spain is a kingdom and parliamentary democracy. After the Spanish Civil War (1936–9), Spain was ruled by a dictator, General Franco, who died in 1974. The dictatorship ended in 1978. There have been continuing troubles in the Basque country and Catalonia, both regions favouring independence. In Portugal, the *Estado Novo* under the authoritarian rule of Antonio Salazar (died 1970) ended in 1974. The new republic brought Portuguese colonialism to an end.

To behold the fair beauty of the Lord

We were in a Northumbrian village, and it was dark. Very dark! While we knew where we were going, we had little idea where the retreat house we were seeking actually was. I had not been long ordained, and this was a venture planned by our vicar Trevor Beeson: a meeting with his three curates Keith Woodhouse, Peter Stubley and me.* The four of us

* Trevor Beeson, *New Area Mission: The Parish in the New Housing Estates* (London: Mowbray's, 1963)—describes the parish vision of St Chad,

had left Stockton-on-Tees on an evening train for Riding Mill with the idea of walking the final mile to Shepherds Dene. None of the houses we approached admitted to being our destination as we trudged on. Houses gave way to fields which we could not see; darkness wholly enveloped us. Shepherds Dene is set well back from the road. Even if it had been daylight, we would have had difficulty in seeing it—but eventually we saw a light at the end of a drive.

St John of the Cross uses this image of darkness to illustrate his description of the relationship with God. Some writers speak of "the dark night" as if it were a depressive period, an internal struggle during a hard time in life, but essentially John is speaking of something much larger, of the soul's overall experience of darkness on the way. It is especially dark at the transitional moments of the journey towards God. The first of these is when a person reaches that point of discursive prayer and finds that it no longer seems to work. There is no more sensing of the presence of God. Feelings of consolation dry up and everything becomes dry and dark. John speaks of it as a dark night of the senses. At a later stage, when prayer has become very much quieter and indeed contemplative, he describes a second night, a night this time of the spirit when the rewarding awareness of being constantly close to God evaporates. God appears to be absent. All that the soul can do is wait out the absence, in the hope that their closeness will be restored, that light will dispel the darkness. The two nights together form the night of darkness in the relationship with God. John wrote his account of his own pilgrimage in a poem,* which he then expounded in his writings.**

John was born in 1542 to a Converso family—a Jewish family that is, which had become Spanish and Catholic—in Fontiveros, a small place to the northwest of Avila. His father had died when he was three, and his mother, Catalina, possibly of Moorish parentage, brought up her boys, John and his brothers, on her own, somehow scraping enough

Stockton-on-Tees.

* John of the Cross, *Poems of St John of the Cross*, trans. Roy Campbell (London: Collins, Fount, 1979), pp. 10–13.

** John of the Cross, *The Complete Works of St John of the Cross (Three Volumes in One)*, trans. Allison E. Peers (London: Burns & Oates, 1965).

money together so they could live. John entered a Carmelite monastery in Medina del Campo in 1563 and later, in 1572 when he moved to Avila, he met Teresa, 27 years his senior. He was dark in complexion, and small, only five feet tall. Small he may have been, Teresa observed, but to God, she would say, he was great. Teresa was born in 1518 and by the time of their meeting, like John, had started a reform of the Carmelite orders to which they belonged.* Both faced considerable opposition, but they persisted, their reformed communities becoming known as the Discalced Carmelites—discalced because they were said to go "barefoot", though in fact they wore open-toed sandals.

The countryside around Avila is rugged, a terrain of fields strewn with as much rock as there is soil, barren and wilderness-like, symbolic of the ruggedness of the mystical way. Living there must have reminded them of Jesus's experience in the wilderness. The two saints were to write profoundly of their relationship with God through the darkness of their spiritual ways, which in St John's case included a time in prison. St John wrote his dark night of the soul when he was there, St Teresa hers when she was ordered to do so by the authorities, who feared that her spiritual experiences were fraudulent. It was the time of the Spanish Inquisition. Had it been known that both were also partly Jewish they might well have been condemned. The miracle is that they were not. Their writings on the spiritual life are now essential texts of the spiritual way.

In the light of the last vignette (Week 36) about those who supply drugs to disturbed people desperately trying to hide their spiritual distress, there are also some who use them to enhance their spiritual experience artificially, as if spirituality is primarily about this. Teresa herself minimized the significance of her own real experiences.** Both she and John taught that while people do have great moments with God from time to time, such are not essential to the spiritual way; many great Christians do not have them. What is essential is an infinite desire for God, and a willingness to heed Christ's call to love and service.

---

* Carlos Eire, *The Life of Saint Teresa of Avila: A Biography* (Princeton: Princeton University Press, 2019).

** Teresa of Avila, *The Life of Saint Teresa of Avila by Herself*, trans. J. M. Cohen (London: Penguin Classics, 1957), p. 137.

Because they were both so formidable and holy, people were sometimes nervous about approaching them. Years ago, I was again at Shepherds Dene, attending a retreat led by Michael Ramsey, shortly after he had retired as Archbishop of Canterbury. I went to him for confession in some trepidation. John once explained to a woman who had found herself in a similar way. She felt hardly able to approach him with her failures. John, knowing what he was like in himself told her that he could not be scandalized by the faults of others; in fact as a confessor, the more holy, the more gentle.* So it was in my experience encountering Michael Ramsey, another soul full of gentleness and love.

Let us pray for the people and leaders of Spain and Portugal. We give thanks for the mystics and saints who have taught western Christendom about the life of prayer. May we learn to love and serve the Lord, in contemplative silence and loving service to all we meet.

* Thomas Kane, *Gentleness in John of the Cross* (Oxford: SLG Press, Fairacres Publication 92, 1993), p. 1.

38

Singapore, Malaysia, Thailand and Myanmar (Burma) with Nepal and Bhutan

Week after Trinity 11

Singapore is an island state at the southernmost tip of the Malaysian Peninsula in Southeast Asia. Malaysia includes Sabah and Sarawak (and the islands of Labuan) on the island of Borneo. Thailand is north of Malaysia, Myanmar to Thailand's west with northern borders with Bangladesh, India and China. Nepal and Bhutan are Himalayan states north of India adjoining Tibet in China. Singapore's population is 6 million, Malaysia 34 million, Thailand 71.5 million, and Myanmar 54 million. Nepal has a population of 30.5 million, Bhutan 782,500. Thailand and Burma are largely Theravada Buddhist, almost everyone in Thailand, and it is almost the same in Myanmar where Buddhism is the state religion. Malays, about 50 per cent of Malaysia's population, are expected to be Muslim by law. Nepal is Hindu, a republic since 2008. Bhutan is Buddhist and a kingdom. The Anglican Church has two provinces in the region, Myanmar (Burma) and South East Asia, the latter covering Singapore and Malaysia. Singapore, independent since 1965, is now a major international hub. Malaysia is a constitutional monarchy, the kingship rotating between nine sultans. Thailand is a constitutional monarchy. Since February 2021, Myanmar has been under military rule again after a short period of army-dominated democracy.

Stations on the pilgrimage way

It was Christmas Day and I was presiding at the Eucharist in St Peter's Serangoon in Singapore. On the invitation of Bishop Chiu Ban It, I was covering the parish while the priest and his family were on vacation in England. The congregation was large, mostly Chinese with a scattering of peoples from elsewhere, and I had just processed down the nave flanked by servers and acolytes to read the Gospel from the middle: "In the beginning was the Word, and the Word was with God, and the Word was God. He was . . . " (John 1:1) It was at this moment that the doors burst open, and in came the bishop, entourage in support. An impromptu address followed, Happy Christmas to one and all, and off he went—his departure as dramatic as his arrival. Joy thought it rather good. I was a bit put out—and very surprised! That was significant, like the surprise of Christ's first coming. We were about to embark on a pilgrimage when we left Singapore. Perhaps it marked our first station—a station being a pause for prayer and reflection in the course of a pilgrimage. The bishop gone, I continued with the Gospel: " . . . and the Word became flesh and lived among us, and we have seen his glory, the glory as of a father's only son, full of grace and truth" (John 1:14).

A few days later, we left for Malaysia. We travelled to Kuala Lumpur by bus and after a night there, took a taxi—improbably, rather cheaper than the bus—to reach the Cameron Highlands. Joy had been battling with depression in Singapore, having found the heat excessive and living in the vicarage hard. To reach the cool and gentle rains of the hills we hoped would prove a turning point for us all. It did!

The second station was at the local Roman Catholic church on the following Sunday. Going there was to provide further surprise. The priest allowed us to take communion; a nun in the congregation befriended us, and then while walking in the hills, we met Barnabas Lim. Barnabas worked on the nearby Boh Tea Estate, and as we walked by his home, he welcomed us into his home. As a boy blind from birth, he had been educated in Penang, at a special school there. We had heard that there was severe flooding and that the line from Butterworth—a town immediately opposite the island of Penang—was probably closed. "Go to Penang," Barnabas advised, "and introduce yourselves to the headmaster at the school where I used to be. He will help you." William Brohier turned out to be the brother of one of our Singapore congregation, and he did indeed help us. A few days later, we were on a flight to Bangkok, to our third station.

The Ramayana, the great North Indian epic, is known in Thailand as the Ramakien. During our time in Asia, we had seen several renditions of the saga, variously enacted in dance, in relief displays, and now in Bangkok in the long graphic strip which adorns the inner side of the perimeter wall of the temple of the Emerald Buddha. This temple is an astonishing array of colour, a complex of stupas, gold predominating, and at the heart, the stupa of the Emerald Buddha, his form within carved in green jade. Thomas Merton, when he was there, described it as "impressive in a dark, ornate spacious way and the small green Buddha enshrined high up in a lighted niche . . . somehow moving".*

We were there in early 1975 while Fine Arts students were restoring these Ramakien murals. One of them told us that he had been working on just one of them for the best part of a year. The story is of Rama and his wife Sita, of their exile, and of their 14-year sojourn in the forest. While there, Rama's wife had been captured. The depiction spoke to us of Joy's struggles far from home as we travelled through the darker parts of our journey. In the story, Rama receives help from Hanuman–given much greater prominence in the Thai version–and together they rescue Sita. Hanuman is at once a monkey, a god, a successful fighter, and perhaps a representative of the indigenous peoples of India before the Aryan immigration. Merton thought the representation of Hanuman the finest part of the temple.

And so to our fourth station! Flying from Bangkok, we passed over the Golden Pagoda of Yangon (Rangoon). It was clearly visible below. Reflecting on it, we were reminded that even a gentle faith can be compromised when the military become dominant and the leaders especially afraid of any of the minority communities who follow a different faith. Given the troubles of the country, we were disheartened to recall

* Thomas Merton, *The Asian Journal of Thomas Merton*, eds Naomi Burton Stone, Br Patrick Hart, James Laughlin (London: Sheldon Press, 1974), p. 248.

that Britain had ruled Myanmar for so many years and seemed to have left the country a poor legacy. Treating people who are different from the dominant faith community in cruel ways is tragically a worldwide malaise. Even the Bhutanese have difficulty in coping with Nepali Hindus who have moved into their country.

Our flight was to Kathmandu, the capital of Nepal. A visit to the Tibetan Buddhist temple of Swayambhunath, which towers over the city, marked our fifth station, a maroon-cassocked monk prayerfully circumambulating the stupa as he contemplated the mystery.

A few days after our arrival we set out for Nagarkot. We had been told we would be able to see Mount Everest from there. Just off the road from Kathmandu to Bhadgaon we began our climb. As we slowly ascended it was humbling to be passed again and again by children, cheerily asking us for a rupee as they charged past, running despite the loads they were carrying and, as we were told later by a doctor, their many chronic ailments. It was to take the three of us seven hours to reach Nagarkot.

Our final station was the surprise of the view. The silence enveloped us. We could hear voices far away in the distance, a child crying, cows lowing, and beyond the valleys and before us, the mountains. It was majestic beyond words. Joy with her love of the Swiss Alps was deeply moved. We all were. The mountains spoke to her of the majesty of the creation. As she lifted her eyes to the hills, looking for help from the Lord, she contemplated the beauty of God as she recited the beatitudes to our daughter: “Blessed are the pure in heart, for they shall see God” (Psalm 121:1; Matthew 5:8).

Let us pray for the people and leaders of Southeast Asia—Singapore, Malaysia, Thailand, Myanmar, Bhutan and Nepal—that as each of us journey on our pilgrimage of life through the many sufferings there are, may we be open to the surprises of the way, the gifts of grace and strengthening by the Holy Spirit for the way.

39

Iran

Week after Trinity 12

Iran is south of the Caspian Sea, with Turkey and Iraq to the west and the Central Asian countries to the east. Its population is 88.5 million, most of them Shia Muslims. Other recognized faiths are Zoroastrianism, the original faith of Iran, Christianity and Judaism. The Christian community is small, but said to be growing, the largest denominations being the ancient Armenian, Assyrian and Chaldean Churches. The Anglican Church has one diocese which is part of the Province of Jerusalem and the Middle East. The short-lived monarchy came to an end in 1979. It was replaced by an Islamic Republic under a Supreme Leader.

Seven valleys

From Durham railway station, there is a magnificent view of the cathedral and castle, the majestic glory of the one balanced by the grandeur of the other. The castle, now the University College of Durham University, was in medieval times the main residence of the Prince Bishops. The diocese had been constituted a palatinate after the Norman conquest, the Norman idea being that the bishop, on behalf of the king, would be the best person to control the powerful Northumbrian barons and their armies. Bishops, in the medieval period anyway, tended to be as much politicians as they were churchmen, and sometimes rather more the first than the latter—quite happy to recruit St Cuthbert, whose shrine Durham Cathedral had become, as their guardian in times of war. As a border region, there was constant struggle with Scotland, and one of the prince bishops, Bishop Bek, even led a division of soldiers into battle.

Aidan and Cuthbert may have lived in an atmosphere of constant battle, but their understanding of their role was different from this. They were not there to engage in war. They advised the leaders as best they could to live a more spiritual path. The Normans in contrast solved a political problem at the expense of the spiritual.

This is Iran's problem today (in 2022). The country's political life is almost wholly overseen by the clergy. This means that any opposition is construed as un-Islamic, lacking in faith, probably heretical and deserving punishment as such. As a result, a great many Iranians who have come to this country—and it is peculiarly true of Iranians and not of other asylum seekers—have become Christians. Certainly many who have joined us in the Northeast have. In the early centuries of Islam in Iran, Sunni Islam was the dominant faith. After the Mongol invasion, the country became Shia. Any country can shift its spiritual allegiance.

Two great Iranian poets of the past, both Sunni, were Farid ud-Din Attar (c.1145–c.1221) and his successor Jalãl ad-Din Muhammad Rūmī (1207–73). Both were from Khorasan in the northeast of Iran, Attar from Nishapur in Khorasan. They were both *Sufis*, "Islamic mystics" who wrote about the spiritual way. Kenneth Cragg comments of the *Sufi* strand of Islam, that it has the effect of deepening the devotional element of what is in many ways an austere faith.* Attar was a pharmacist, which is what *attar* means, and the author of *The Conference of the Birds*, an epic poem describing the spiritual way; "conference" in this context meaning "gathering".** The birds represent a community of *Sufi* initiates who are about to embark on a spiritual quest.

Their spiritual guide and leader is the hoopoe. A hoopoe features in the Quran as the bird which informs Solomon about the Queen of Sheba (Surah 27:20). Hoopoes do not reach the north of England, though I remember once walking in Ovington and coming across a tree full of waxwings. Waxwings are rather like hoopoes in that they have a crown-like crest. Even seeing waxwings was a rare privilege. At the start of Attar's

* Kenneth Cragg, *The Call of the Minaret* (Oxford: Oxford University Press, 1956), pp. 134–7.

** Farid ud-Din Attar, *The Conference of the Birds*, trans. Afkham Darbandi and Dick Davis (London: Penguin Classics, 1984). See also Week 22.

poem, the assembled birds share their anxieties about the impending journey with the hoopoe. This prompts the hoopoe to tell each of his followers an encouraging story. He wants them to think again about their fears. In one of these, two quarrelling *Sufis* who end up in court are taken aside by the judge:

> "This can't be right," he tells them,
> "For Sufis to provoke a lawyer's fight
> You wear the robes of resignation
> So what have you to do with litigation."*

In this part of the story, the initiates are being instructed about the beginning of the way, about the purgative way. They need to be purged of their sins if they are to cope with the challenges of the way ahead. They are to pass through seven valleys. Their eventual goal is to reach the *Simorgh*—a mythical bird in Iranian lore which, like the phoenix in Christianity, symbolizes the actions of God, essentially the being of God. In the first valley, they will find they must lay aside their former beliefs and certainties; in the second, their previous ways of understanding, so that they will be in a right state of mind to embrace the love that will reach out to them. In the third, they will come to learn that all that they had previously known about themselves is inadequate. In the fourth, that they must develop detachment. By the fifth, their lives will have become so changed they will be open to a love beyond anything that they have known before. But then, in the sixth valley, they will once again become confused and in awe. By the last one, they will know themselves emptied of self, cleansed of all that they have ever been, now simply as nothing before God!

Understandably a number of the birds on hearing all this decide to stay behind. Others set off, but fall by the wayside. Only 30 make it to the end—to gaze on the face of God:

> Their souls rose free of all they'd been before,
> The past and all its actions were no more

* Attar, *The Conference of the Birds*, p. 94.

Their life came from that close, insistent sun
And in its vivid rays they shone as one
There in the Simorgh's radiant face they saw
Themselves, the Simorgh of the world with awe
They gazed, and dared at last to comprehend
They were the Simorgh and the journey's end.*

The name *Simorgh,* as well as describing the mythical bird as a symbol of God and his actions, also means "thirty birds": *Si* "thirty", *morgh* "birds". In seeing the face of God, they also encountered the truth, who they were themselves.

Let us pray for the people and leaders of Iran, giving thanks for Islam and especially for Iran's poets and mystics and those who teach and encourage the faithful to embark on the mystical way towards oneness with God.

* Attar, *The Conference of the Birds*, p. 219.

40

South Africa, Namibia, Botswana, Lesotho, Eswatini (Swaziland)

Week after Trinity 13

South Africa is the southernmost country in Africa. Namibia is on the Atlantic coast south of Angola, west of Botswana, and includes the Caprivi strip, a tongue of land which divides Botswana from Zambia and reaches almost to the west of Zimbabwe. At this narrow end point, and since 2020, the Kalangula Bridge over the River Zambesi links Botswana with Zambia. Much of Botswana, between Namibia and Zimbabwe, is the Kalahari Desert. Lesotho is a mountainous enclave in the midst of South Africa, not far from Durban. Eswatini is between the northeast of South Africa and Mozambique. South Africa's population is 60 million. The populations of Namibia, Botswana and Lesotho are each 2.5 million. Eswatini, which changed its name from Swaziland in 2018, is 1 million.

All the countries are predominantly Christian; a quarter of South Africans belong to independent churches. Namibia is Lutheran, reflecting its past as a German colony before the First World War. A large percentage of the people of Eswatini follow an indigenous faith blended with Christianity. Anglicans in Botswana are in the province of Central Africa; the others are in the Province of Southern Africa. Newcastle diocese has close links with Botswana, and Durham diocese with Lesotho. Apartheid ruled in South Africa from 1948 until 1994. The country is a parliamentary republic with nine provinces. Namibia was ruled by South Africa from 1915 until independence in 1990. The other countries, all former British protectorates, became independent in 1966. Eswatini is an absolute monarchy with a unitary parliament.

Black consciousness

In 1982, three monks of the Community of the Resurrection moved into a derelict vicarage in Sunderland. They had come to live a life of contemplative prayer. I was at the time just leaving Ryhope–on the southern edge of Sunderland–for Ovingham and in need of a spiritual director. I turned to one of the monks there, Fr Aelred Stubbs. He was to accompany me for the next 20 years.

Aelred Stubbs was not long back from southern Africa where he had been since 1959, for several of the years the principal of the Community's seminary in Alice. Like Trevor Huddleston before him,* he had become increasingly distressed by the Church there, the inability of white Anglicans to take even the slightest bit of notice of the much larger Black communities which surrounded them. The gap between the peoples was a chasm. He thought the only way forward would be for the Church to be torn apart and thoroughly refashioned if it was ever to live the gospel as it should. In his distress, he felt the only way forward was to give his whole life to prayer. He had been prevented from returning to South Africa in 1977 so had moved to Lesotho to begin his contemplative offering there. At the beginning of the 1980s, he and his fellow monks were to continue in Sunderland.

In his last years in South Africa, Fr Aelred had written a book about the Black Consciousness activist Steve Biko. In 1988, he revised the book to accompany the 1987 film *Cry Freedom*, and it was reissued as a Penguin paperback.** He had come to love Biko over the years, an admiration which he certainly conveyed to me. He would speak of his "extraordinary magnetism". Physically, he said, "he looked like one of the larger feline animals–a tiger maybe–with an animal grace and an insolent ease and a sense of immense latent power".*** As a leader and pastor to his staff, Fr Aelred thought of him as being like Jesus with his disciples.

---

* Trevor Huddleston CR, *Naught for your Comfort* (London: Collins, 1956).

** *Cry Freedom*, film directed by Richard Attenborough (Universal Pictures, USA and UK, 1987). The story of Steve Biko based on Donald Woods's book.

*** Aelred Stubbs, "Martyr of Hope: A Personal Memoir by Aelred Stubbs CR", in *Steve Biko, I Write What I Like: A Selection of His Writings*, ed. Aelred Stubbs

After the Nelson Mandela generation, Steve Biko was to be one of the most prominent leaders in the confrontation with apartheid. He identified the devastating effects the apartheid policies were having, that it made the Black community think of themselves as inferior, less than they were—as conversely the whites assumed they were superior. As Biko said when appearing as a witness in the Trial of Ideas of nine leaders of the Black Consciousness Movement, his fellow Blacks were a people who had come to believe what was said of them; they felt defeated and miserable; they were without hope!

It may now be not too difficult for most white people to avoid the crude racism of an apartheid system, although there is still far too much of it; what is much more difficult—and I include myself in this—is eradicating racist beliefs from the white unconscious. This is especially true of anyone from the United Kingdom and northern Europe. The only way of tackling the problem is to acknowledge and confess and embrace in all humility the racist ideas that so easily surface from the depths. Biko recognized this white tendency. He saw his first task as one of teaching his people the beauty and honour of being Black, that indeed blackness was a gift from God. "We try to get blacks in conscientization", he told the Trial of Ideas court, "to ... develop what one might call an awareness ... of their situation, to be able to analyse it, and ... provide answers for themselves." Its purpose, he explained, was "to provide some kind of hope". South African society had to accept that Black persons are human. Writing about all this at another time, he said that a Black person "cannot tolerate attempts by anybody to dwarf the significance of [their humanity]".* Basically he was asserting that Black Lives Matter.

There was no violence in Biko's ideas. The violence was in the "system"—as the police and authorities were known by the Black community—and true to form it was the system that exercised violence against him. Shortly before Biko was arrested, he and Fr Aelred had a private meeting. Biko was all too aware that the authorities were closing in upon him, and he took the opportunity, Fr Aelred explained, t open

---

CR, (London: Penguin, 1978, 1988), pp. 174–239, 212 and 181.

* Steve Biko, "What is Black Consciousness?" and "The Quest for a True Humanity", in *Steve Biko, I Write What I Like*, pp. 131 and 108.

his heart and speak about his early life: " . . . it was a confession in the sense that it was a simple telling of the truth about himself. When he had finished there was nothing that needed to be said, but I think that we both sensed, that in this silence after the forthtelling, the path was annealed and the future could be met with a deeper wholeness."* Biko was detained very soon after, in August 1977. Three weeks later the police murdered him. Donald Woods, at the time the editor-in-chief of the East London newspaper, the *Daily Dispatch*, wrote up the story. Much of the latter part of *Cry Freedom* is about the Woods family's risk-filled escape with the book into Lesotho.

Once, when I was in Botswana as part of our Newcastle diocese exchange, Dr Nolwandle Pearl Mashalaba-Moeti and her daughter Kerileng (also a doctor, Kerileng Nomalizo Moeti) entertained me to lunch. Dr Pearl told me the story of her similar escape from South Africa and what it was like encountering the authorities as they crossed into Botswana in 1965. "You have a lot of luggage," the customs official said.

"We are going on holiday," Dr Pearl explained.

"With all these saucepans and pans?"

"We will be cooking in the open air," she said. This seemed to satisfy, perhaps because the children did indeed think that this was what they were about; for their parents it was a nightmare. They made it, and have lived there ever since.

Let us pray for the people and leaders of South Africa and its neighbouring countries, Eswatini, Lesotho, Botswana and Namibia, in thanksgiving to God for the gift of blackness, for grace to end racism, and the strength to work together for the Common Good.

---

* Aelred Stubbs, "Martyr of Hope", in *Steve Biko, I Write What I Like*, p. 221.

41

Japan

Week after Trinity 14

Japan has a population of 124 million. Two thirds of the people follow one or both of the two dominant faiths, Shintoism—Shinto rituals in particular—and Buddhism. The people live mostly in the coastal regions. Tokyo, with the country around it, is the world's most densely populated city. Japan is a parliamentary democracy with a constitutional monarch. The Anglican Communion in Japan, *Nippon Sei Ko Kai*, is made up of 11 dioceses.

Meditation in a garden

The general wisdom when I was working in Sunderland was that building cars in the Northeast was a poor idea—too near the sea, it was said; the salt would corrode the metal. None of this seemed to disturb Nissan; the company was happy to open its vast plant on the outskirts of Sunderland. One of the company's designers bought a house in Ovington. I well remember the deep courtesy the family showed me when I joined them one afternoon for tea. Their young daughter had been attending our Church First school. It took her a mere three weeks to learn our language.

There were several other Japanese firms in the Northeast; Komatsu took over the Birtley earth moving equipment plant from the American Caterpillar Company when I was curate there. Hitachi, with great imagination, built their factory—for assembling their new Azuma diesel cum electric trains—beside the first public railway ever built, the Stockton and Darlington railway, close to the station at Heighington. Japan has had close links with the Northeast ever since the Tyneside Armstrong

Company began building both their navy and—sad to say—the weaponry they required.

The Armstrong skill in making armaments stemmed from the failures that affected the British performance in the nineteenth-century Crimean War. The war had shown just how inadequate British ordnance had become. Sir William Armstrong, the Newcastle entrepreneur, was one of the first of the Victorian engineers to respond. His company was so successful that it was not long before nations from all over the world were flocking to the Northeast, the Japanese especially, to buy ships and armaments. Delegations from Japan would visit the Elswick works in Newcastle, and stay either with Armstrong's managing director Sir Andrew Noble at Jesmond Dene House (now a hotel) or with the Armstrongs at Cragside, near Rothbury. One visitor, Admiral Count Togo Heihachiro, speaking of Japan's relationship with the Northeast in 1911, said: "It is a well-known fact that the name Newcastle is inseparable from the pages of the history of the Japanese navy . . . . A great number of our officers and men have studied in this city."* Another visitor, the Crown Prince, when he came for Queen Elizabeth II's coronation in 1953, stayed with the Armstrong family at Cragside. One of the reasons why so many of them liked staying there was because the gardens were so beautiful. Japanese military men as far back as the eleventh century had always valued the discipline and peace that a well-designed garden could give to the contemplative soul.

Armstrong's original creativity was his invention of hydraulics. The Swing Bridge across the Tyne in Newcastle, built by his firm, is still powered by his original hydraulic machinery. He used it again at Cragside, constructing lakes and water courses to channel the water needed to power the engine making electricity for the house. The engine building was some distance from the house and well beyond the rock garden which is at the front of the house. It was all done to power the new light bulbs which had been invented by his friend, the Sunderland born Joseph Swann. Cragside was the first home to be lit by electricity. All this appealed to his Japanese visitors.

---

* Henrietta Heald, *William Armstrong: Magician of the North* (Newcastle: Northumbria Press, 2010), p. 213.

In Japan, designers distinguish between two types of landscape garden: the first a garden with an attractive view; the second a more elaborate way of capturing and incorporating the view into the garden, making it a *shakkei garden*, as it were "borrowing the scenery"—the meaning of *shakkei*.* It is done by positioning the features of the garden—rocks, boundary fences, gravel, trees—in such a way that they frame the outside scenery so that it becomes part of the garden inside.

The garden creators of Japan say that a garden should encourage meditation, the Zen type of garden in particular. Recently, the gardening guru Monty Don presented two television films about different types of Japanese garden.** On visiting a Zen garden, he asked the monk who was raking some gravel whether he might try his hand. The monk instructed him to breathe prayerfully as he raked so that each action might become a part of his meditation. A Shinto worshipper would be reminded as he meditated of the need for purity of heart, a Buddhist of emptiness, either one encouraged not so much to think discursively about what they were doing, but to be there, free of distractions, open to the real as they contemplated in their hearts the mystery.

During the seventeenth century in Japan, gardens were becoming smaller, especially in the towns. One such popular type was a garden for the tea ceremony; this one also had a spiritual purpose. The path to the tearoom would be made simply, would be rustic in appearance and would usually include steppingstones. The whole way would be designed to remind visitors to shed whatever class status they thought they had. None of them must think themselves superior. To make absolutely certain of this last, the entrance door was made very low so that everyone coming in had to stoop to enter.

Creating a garden to stimulate this kind of spiritual process is an art form. Teiji Itoh recommends that a designer of gardens when first approaching an empty space should first of all sit quietly in front of it and contemplate the expanse—like a sculptor looking at a block of stone

---

* Teiji Itoh, *Space and Illusion in the Japanese Garden* (Kyoto and Tokyo: Weatherhill/Tankosha, 1973).

** *Japanese Gardens*, two programmes by Monty Don, broadcast on BBC 4, 19 and 26 August 2020.

before she begins. Then, the gardener should take tea with the household to listen to what they had in mind for their garden. Only then could the gardener begin to create a new garden which would be right and proper for them.

On the first Easter morning, Mary Magdalene met Jesus in another garden. At first, she thought he was the gardener. She only realized her mistake when Jesus greeted her by name. In fact, of course, she had not made a mistake. She had indeed met the resurrected Lord, the one who was the gardener of the world (John 20:15).

Let us pray for the people and leaders of Japan, that we and they in contemplating the garden of the world may care for it sustainably, and in so doing cooperate with Christ in his work of renewal and re-creation of the world.

42

Turkey, Greece and Cyprus

Week after Trinity 15

The island of Cyprus is in the far east of the Mediterranean, south of Turkey, east of Greece and its islands. Turkey's population is 85.5 million, triple what it was in 1945, though it seems to be levelling off. Greece is 10.5 million, Cyprus 1.5 million, rather more living in the Turkish-speaking northern half of the island. The Kurdish people who live in the far east of Turkey are spread over Iran, Iraq and Syria as well as Turkey and form a sizeable minority. Turkey is Sunni Islam, with also about 10 to 20 million Alevi Muslims. Greece is Orthodox Christian. Cyprus has both Muslims and Christians. The Anglican Church has the one diocese, Cyprus and the Gulf, part of the Jerusalem and Middle East province. St Barnabas was from Cyprus (Acts 4:36). Cyprus became independent from Britain in 1960.

Cooperating for reconciliation

In 1955, EOKA (a Greek acronym for the "National Organization of Cypriot Fighters") began its campaign to oust the British from Cyprus. The island had been under British rule since 1878. The ultimate aim of EOKA was to have Cyprus become part of Greece, but it was first of all campaigning for the island's independence. Once achieved it was hoped that *enosis* (the Greek word for "unity") with Greece would follow.

My final National Service posting was in Cyprus. Our battalion arrived on the island at the end of April 1956. My diary says very little about why we were there. I mention the loss of one of our soldiers in the Troodos Mountains, talk about Lord Radcliffe's work on a new constitution, and say something about the EOKA leader General Grivas; at the time I was really far more concerned about my demob date due in September. I was worried because there were rumours that we might have to stay. President Nasser of Egypt, to the dismay of Britain, France and Israel, had nationalized the Suez Canal. Throughout the summer of 1956, soldiers were being moved into Cyprus in preparation for what looked like a coming fight for the recovery of the canal—which indeed it was. Our camp was in Polis, a small village on the north coast, not far from Paphos. The extensive Troodos Mountains were behind us to the south. I knew our soldiers were patrolling there, but not much more than that. I have learnt since that only one month after we had arrived there had been an operation—Operation Lucky Alphonse—to restrain the activities of EOKA, apparently with some success. As a lance corporal in charge of the battalion's welfare facilities, all this completely escaped me.

Laurence Durrell, the novelist and brother of the zoologist Gerald, who was in Cyprus working as a teacher from 1953 until 1956, wrote about the conflict in his 1957 *Bitter Lemons.** The book speaks of the tension between the Greeks and the Turks, a tension which all too accurately expressed a centuries-long enmity that had existed between Greece and Turkey during the Ottoman Empire years. Cyprus, like a disturbed child coping with quarrelling parents, expresses all too accurately the pains of the relationship.

Independence for Cyprus was to come in 1960. Only four years later, a UN presence had to be put in place to keep the two communities apart. Then in July 1974, the right-wing military junta which had been ruling Greece since 1967 organized a coup d'état against Cyprus and its president, Archbishop Makarios. Its aim was to bring about an eventual union with Greece. Only five days later, Turkey invaded the island and the coup collapsed. While it did have the good effect of ridding Greece of its junta, it left Cyprus in disarray—two halves separated by a buffer "green line", as it was called, a line ever since patrolled by the UN. In August 1995, when we holidayed on the island, the line was still being maintained. It still was in 2022.

---

* Laurence Durrell, *Bitter Lemons* (London: Faber and Faber, 1957).

We had gone to Cyprus because for some reason that year, we had failed to plan a holiday. We turned up at a travel agent and asked them if they would provide us with somewhere—where we could go tomorrow! Larnaca in Cyprus was the response. We went there; we toured the island, visited Polis, the Troodos Mountains—and the highlight, a visit to Pyla, a village in the buffer zone between the two communities. Pyla, or *pula* in the Greek, means "gate" or "entrance", in this village's case the gateway to the Mesaori valley in the northern half of the island. At the time, it was the only place where a pre-partition population of 850 Greeks and 487 Turks still lived together. Our Turkish host in a café there told us how much he valued this unity. We saw the place as a symbol of what we were praying for, that the island might once again become one.

For years, any access between the two communities was virtually non-existent. In 2003, the Ledra Palace checkpoint in Nicosia was opened. I had once been to Ledra Street as a soldier, then reputed to be the most dangerous place in the capital. There I stood, armed with rifle and in uniform, nonchalantly unaware of the danger. Somehow, aged 19, I felt myself immune to whatever risks there might be. There are now several more checkpoints open.

Since 2011, and in a building on the other side of the road from the Ledra Palace Hotel which until recently was the UN headquarters, a new centre, *The Home of Cooperation,* has been opened. It was, and still is, a place where ordinary people of both communities can meet and be together. A UN spokesman, talking about the value of the centre, said: "True peace is not made by politicians, . . . it is between peoples." Lefki Lambrou, a Greek Cypriot, joined the centre in 2014 and became its director in November 2018. She said, "We set the right conditions for everyone to come together." Hayriye Rüzgar, a Turkish Cypriot who is the centre's communications officer, said that her work is to build on the efforts of so many Cypriots over the years who have struggled to bring the island's divisions to an end. "The centre (has) kind of filled a necessity; now this type of work has a home." She added, "Cyprus is too small to be divided."

I remember a local Northeast politician once telling me how much he needed the groundswell of support his constituents could give to him—letters, action from different groups and so on—if he was to succeed in making changes. Change starts with an idea, a person or a group, with someone who has a vision, a surprise perhaps that a way forward has come to mind, that an impossible dream might actually become possible; in Cyprus's case that the island might be reunited again, or at least dispense with barriers. Great ideas start in small ways (Matthew 13:31–32; Mark 4:30–32; Luke 13:18–19).

At the time of writing, it is almost 50 years since the buffer zone was put in place. It is time for a change. There were hopes that a solution might be found in the 2017 talks—but alas, not then! The *Home of Cooperation* stands as an earnest that union will eventually be achieved.

We pray for the people and leaders of Turkey, Greece and Cyprus, and especially for an end to the division between the two halves of Cyprus. We give thanks that we are inspired to think those things that are good and that by God's merciful guiding they may be brought to good effect.

43

Bangladesh

Week after Trinity 16

Bangladesh is almost wholly surrounded by India, Assam to the east, Bihar and Kolkata (Calcutta) to the west, much of it low lying at the "Mouths of the Ganges". Up to 100 miles from the coast, the country is no more than 30 feet above sea level and flooding is constant. In the far southeast, the country has a border with Myanmar. Bangladesh's population is 164.7 million. Almost everyone is Bengali, the vast majority Muslim, with less than 10 per cent Hindu. There is a small Christian presence. Anglicans are part of the United Church of Bangladesh. In 1971, the country as East Pakistan and part of Pakistan, sought autonomy; West Pakistan responded with ferocity and was only finally dissuaded when the Indian army invaded on behalf of Bangladesh. The country became independent in December of the same year.

Giving and receiving for the good of society

Writing in the twelfth century, the great Cordoba thinker Maimonides listed eight ways of giving to the poor. At the bottom of his list, he put giving done unwillingly–giving with a scowl. At the top, the kind of giving that helps a recipient to be self-sufficient. Paul Vallely, who quotes this in his magisterial history of philanthropy, concludes that, ideally, "philanthropy is the understanding that every gift should bind the donor and recipient together in a relationship which also involves the whole of the community".* The thought is a central feature in Pope Francis's 2020 encyclical *Fratelli tutti*, where he speaks of the inherent dignity of every human person, and of the obligation of all in solidarity to be committed to serving the Common Good. The counterpoint to solidarity is subsidiarity, the recognition that many problems need to be tackled at an appropriate level, often at a local rather than a national level.

It was thinking like this that moved the Bangladeshi professor Muhammad Yunus to found his bank for the poor. Yunus was born in Bathua, a village to the east of Chittagong. He was the third of nine children. As a youngster he was a keen boy scout, and through scouting he gathered valuable experience by travelling abroad to jamborees and the like, sometimes to places as far away as Canada and Japan. As an adult, he studied for a BA at Dhaka University, and then went to the United States to do his PhD—he was there at the time of the 1971 Liberation War. When he returned, he became the Head of Economics at Chittagong University. It was there that he began his work for the poor—in the village of Jobra, which is virtually next door to the university campus, itself some distance from Chittagong. Seeing such poverty all around him, Yunus became painfully aware of just how humiliating and degrading poverty can be and, at the same time, how impossibly difficult it was to break free from it. He had an idea as to how he might be able to help.** He began by lending small sums of money to some of the poor women of Jobra. It worked well, and from this small beginning he expanded his vision into what was eventually to become the *Grameen* (or village) Bank of Bangladesh. His practice was to lend money at a low interest rate, almost always to women. He reckoned that it was the women who had the ability to use the money well. He hoped they would be able to develop whatever skills they already had and that their enterprise would increase their wealth. They would then have an income and be able to repay their loan.

Banks had always refused to lend money to the poor because they assumed that whatever they lent they would lose. Money lenders charged

* Paul Vallely, *Philanthropy: from Aristotle to Zuckerberg* (London: Bloomsbury/Continuum, 2020), p. 710.

** Muhammad Yunus, *Banker to the Poor: The Story of the Grameen Bank* (London: Aurum Press, 1998, 2003).

extortionate interest rates, the women then ending up paying back everything they had earned to the lenders. The Grameen Bank, as it gathered experience, learnt that the best way of helping was to insist that women club together in groups of five, who would then support any applicant from their number asking for a loan. Yunus found that well over 90 per cent of such loans were always repaid. His Bank for the Poor has now become one of the largest in Bangladesh. His ideas have in addition spread throughout the world.

Another Bangladeshi initiative was started by Practical Action, the charity that continues E. F. Schumacher's *Small is Beautiful* vision. Hussain Ishrath Adib was the head of its "Programme Implementation in Bangladesh" in the 2010s, and it was his scheme that helped the "Pit Emptiers" as they were called, whose job it was to empty community cesspits. There were still many places without sewers. He concentrated his work in Faridpur, a region to the west of Dhaka. When he started the workers had no protective clothing, they worked with no more than a bucket, and they often had to climb right into the tanks if there were blockages to clear. Disease was rife. They and their families were shunned in their communities. Practical Action, working together with the local authority, decided to provide protective clothing, they designed simple pumps which could clear the tanks, and they further developed a faecal sludge processing plant in which they could convert sewage into fertilizer. The effect on the communities they worked with has been dramatic.

At the southernmost point of Bangladesh is Cox's Bazar. During the same period, more than a million Rohingya refugees from the Myanmar genocide had escaped into camps on the border. They too found themselves facing a similar problem with sewage. UNICEF asked Practical Action if they could help. It was a severe challenge because the country around Cox's Bazar is hilly and the camps very overcrowded. They still managed within a matter of months to install a number of units.

In the northeast of England, we do not know poverty on this scale, but there is evidence that we live in one of the poorer regions of the country. Bishop Auckland, to the southwest of Durham, is a case in point. As the name implies, it is where the bishops of Durham have their home, until recently in Auckland Castle. Not long ago the whole complex of castle and grounds was sold—together with its large collection of Zurbaran paintings—for some astronomical sum to the philanthropist Jonathan Ruffer.* Once purchased, he set about a restoration programme which included Bishop Auckland as a whole. The last time I had been in Auckland Castle, it had been to meet John Habgood, at the time the Bishop of Durham. It was something of a surprise to find myself taking afternoon tea in the same room. I went to see one of the epic spectaculars that are now held in a field beyond the Eleven Arches Bridge, the castle now forming a backdrop to these pageants that portray the history of the Northeast. A local resident, sitting in the seat next to me, was radiant as she told me what all this restoration work meant to her: "How wonderful that this is all happening in our town! I love it."

Let us pray for the people and leaders of Bangladesh, especially for the poor, and for all who give and all who receive and for societies everywhere who gain from this community concern.

* Vallely, *Philanthropy*, pp. 73–8.

44

Russia

Week after Trinity 17

Russia is huge, 6.6 million square miles, the largest country by land mass in the world. It includes Kaliningrad, an enclave on the Baltic Sea south of Lithuania. St Petersburg, also on the Baltic, is 4,000 miles from Vladivostok on the Pacific, which is close to Russia's short border with North Korea. The population—mostly in the west—is 144.5 million and is declining; roughly 40 per cent or more are Russian Orthodox, a third atheist or "other" and about 5 per cent are Muslim—but these are 2012 figures. Soviet Russia lasted from 1917 until 1991. Since then, the Russian Federation has engaged in wars with Chechnya (Caucasus), with Georgia (see Week 28), and since February 2022 with Ukraine, especially the southeast. Crimea was annexed by Russia in 2014. The Kerch Bridge now links the Crimea to the Taman Peninsula in Russia.

Thanksgiving—the heart of prayer

Visitors to Newcastle from London often tell me how clean and attractive they find our Metro. We are proud of it, but in comparison with the Moscow metro it is a simple affair. In Moscow, the stations are dramatic, Arbatskaya especially, a massive space with red marble and chandeliers. Emerging from this station one day in 2009, I came out onto the square which has a statue of the great Christian novelist Fyodor Dostoevsky. It felt astonishing enough to be in Russia, even more to see a statue commemorating one of the great Christian writers. That he was so valued! The square was not far from the Kremlin. There, another surprise! Within its forbidding walls were several chapels—cathedrals as they are known—undisturbed despite the Soviet years. True, it was some 18 years since the collapse of communism at the time of my visit, but these symbols of Christianity had never been removed.

A few days later, I was in a Moscow church for the liturgy. An aristocratic-looking lady was there, tall and elegant as she moved from icon to icon, making her obeisance before each one. She reminded me of another Russian woman, Iulia de Beausobre. I had written about her in an earlier book.*

Lady Namier, as she later became, was the widow of the prominent Manchester University historian Sir Lewis Namier. A close friend of mine, Brian Frost, wrote in a letter to me of "an unrepeatable hour and a half" he had spent "with the 80-year-old saint who has so influenced me". She was born Iulia Mikhailovna Kazarin in St Petersburg in 1893 to parents whom she described as "high-flying idle rich with too much money and not enough responsibility".** In 1917, she married Nikolay de Beausobre, of a Swiss émigré family, hence the name, just two days before the fall of the Tsarist regime. When the Kerensky government was formed, because Nikolay was a diplomat, he and Iulia were moved immediately to the embassy in London. The Kerensky government fell within the year to be replaced by the new regime under Lenin. Nikolay felt honour bound to go back to Russia, asking his young pregnant wife to join him as soon as she could. She fell ill with the Spanish flu as she was returning so that it was some time before she reached Moscow. Not very long after, they had to leave again. Conditions were so terrible, with famine in Ukraine, that Iulia and her husband almost starved. With no milk to feed her three-month-old child, Dimitri died. After a short "exile", they once more went back to Russia, Nikolay again insisting. They survived for some years, but in 1932, Nikolay was arrested. Iulia was arrested five days later.

Their only offence was that they were of aristocratic lineage. She was never to see Nikolay again—indeed it was to be some years before she even learnt what had happened to him. She herself was transferred from

---

* David Goodacre, *Four Ways One Goal* (Newcastle: Leighton Co. Services, 2006).

** Constance Babington-Smith, *Iulia de Beausobre: A Russian Christian in the West* (London: Darton, Longman & Todd, 1983), p. 7.

the Lubyanka to the Boutyrki prison and was there simply informed that as a "terrorist"–their word for her–she must serve five years hard labour in prison.

She was taken to a prison camp in the east, not far from Sarov, the town associated with the seventeenth-century saint Seraphim. He had lived there as a hermit in the woods nearby.* Her fellow prisoners assured her that Seraphim was with them in the woods surrounding their camp. She was housed with some nuns. Iulia's health was not strong. As a child, she had suffered several bouts of life-threatening illnesses, and now in these grim conditions she became so ill that she seemed to be dying. She was almost unconscious when she reached the hospital. In her comatose state, she could hear someone she had known back in the Boutyrki prison telling a story about a woman who had lived in Seraphim's holy woods. It led her to hallucinate that she was that woman searching for her husband whom she still hoped had survived. In her delirium, she dreamt that Nikolay was holding her hand and inviting her to join him before God. The following day she began to recover. When she was back in the prison dormitory, she talked with Mother Theodosia, the Superior of the imprisoned community. She listened carefully to what Iulia had to tell her. She responded, "Even if Nikolay should go . . . , you must always remember . . . those of us who die in Him, now join Him at once. There is no pain for us, only rejoicing. Rebuild your heart into an eternal tabernacle for thanksgiving."**

The authorities decided that Iulia was too ill to remain in prison. After two years, her term was commuted to internal exile. Before leaving, she saw Mother Theodosia again: "Be comforted", she said, "for we are in the care of Seraphim of the Holy Woods, the Intercessor for all who suffer here. Infinite is our joy, incomplete because our brothers beyond the distant border do not deign to understand what it is God wants of us . . . Tell them, not to think of us in paltry terms of transience but of

* Iulia de Beausobre, *Flame in the Snow: A Russian Legend* (Glasgow: Collins, Fount, 1979).

** Iulia de Beausobre, *The Woman Who Could Not Die* (London: Victor Gollancz, 1948), p. 209.

abiding beauty and truth. Tell them."* Once out of the prison, she met a friend who had learnt that if Iulia could find someone to sponsor her, they could pay for her to leave the country. Her childhood nanny, an English woman, raised the £300 ransom required, and Iulia was allowed to leave for London. She was not at all certain that she had been right to do so; she came to interpret that what Mother Theodosia had told her was in fact a call from God. In 1938, she published an account of her experiences in her book *The Woman Who Could Not Die*. It is one of the earliest accounts of the Russian Gulag. She also gave a paper to the students of Lincoln Theological College, which tells her story in a deeper theological way.** She explained that she had toned down her account of abuse in her first book because she did not think that people would actually believe her. She was probably right about that.

Lord, we pray for the people and leaders of Russia and the search for justice and peace. We remember especially all who are wrongfully tortured and abused and all who work with them through the long process of recovery—and give us grace to learn how to build our hearts into tabernacles of thanksgiving.

* de Beausobre, *The Woman Who Could Not Die*, pp. 219–20.

** Iulia de Beausobre, *Creative Suffering* (Oxford: SLG Press, 1940, 1984).

4 5

Australia and New Zealand

Week after Trinity 18

Australia is the sixth largest country by land mass, almost 3 million square miles. Its population, given its fragile ecology, is 26 million, New Zealand 5 million. The countries are predominantly Christian—half the population of Australia are Christian with Anglicans being about 15 per cent of this number. New Zealand is similar, with about 10 per cent Catholics and 10 per cent Anglicans. The Anglican Church of Australia has five provinces; Aotearoa (New Zealand) has one, and it includes the countries of Polynesia (see Week 23) and Fiji (Melanesia).

Land as beloved companion

On my second visit to Australia, I went there via Hong Kong. On the flight from Hong Kong to Sydney, my companion in the next seat was a quarryman returning from a week-long business trip to China. He had been seeking a market for the materials of his Queensland quarry. China is looking everywhere for land and the products it needs for its enormous population. My friend was impressed by what he had seen. I was heading for Eden in the far southeast corner of Australia where I was to stay with Joy's cousin Judith and her husband Chris. Judith was then the Pastoral Leader of St George's Uniting Church in Eden and at the time thinking of embarking on a study of eco-theology. Both Chris and Judith were passionately concerned about the vulnerability of their land. In the end, she was unable to do it because of work and illness; her husband took it on instead, beginning his study by looking at issues of mining and fracking for coal seam gas (CSG).

Eden in 2004 was as its name suggests a beautiful place. Their home nestled among eucalyptus trees, with their peeling bark and dark olive-coloured leaves, sheltering them from the nearby ocean where migrating whales on their way to Antarctica frolicked about. Adam and Eve were not visible, but one could imagine them being there somewhere in the bush. Since the 2019/2020 fires, much of this woodland has been burnt down.

Chris was a scientist by training and work. Taking to theology in retirement he found himself exploring issues in a new way. It would have been equally novel to my quarryman friend and certainly to his CSG counterparts when they were thinking about what they should be doing. CSG questions tended to be practical: would what they proposed doing be feasible? Would it make money? Such questions, Chris admitted, had to be asked, but he now reckoned there were many more: questions of the artist, of the poet, of the theologian . . . .

At an early stage of his research, his tutor suggested he should visit the red centre of Australia, that part of the country which was described by early European explorers as *terra nullius*—the utterly empty and useless interior. It was not how the aboriginal peoples saw it. Chris's journey into the middle of Australia began in Alice Springs. Joy and I had also been there once, in 1974, waiting for a day there for a bus to take us on to Darwin. Before it got too hot, we went to a local museum and saw a number of aboriginal paintings: carpet-like pictures depicting the terrain and the journeys that groups of the people had made through the land. The aboriginals would sing their way past the various stages, assigning to each stage some practical, spiritual significance as they passed. They had uncanny skills in finding their way about, like Polynesians navigating the Pacific. They could read the landscape so accurately that they could orientate precisely where they were. For them, their country was not at all null. It was this kind of meaning that Chris hoped he would discover for himself as his group journeyed southwards to Maralinga and the Great Australian Bight.*

---

* Chris Dalton, *From Terra Nullius to Beloved Companion: Reimagining Land in Australia* (Brisbane: In House Publishing, 2016).

At the end of the journey, he went home via Broken Hill. In a museum there, he saw a nude sculpture by Wendy Martin. It was called *Born into a Landscape*, and on the skin of the model, and on the plinth too, Martin had painted the blue sky and landscape of the Australian bush. It spoke to Chris of the land as a person. In its light, he felt that it was as if CSG were inflicting a cancer on the person of his country. When he got home, he was deeply distressed to discover that Judith herself had developed just such a cancer. It was a crushing blow; it felt to Chris as though he was seeing within her illness the devastating pain mirroring the land he was studying. He wrote a telling poem to record his reflections. Australia's vast interior, he now knew, was not an empty nothing, a nothingness that could be exploited. It was a friend, a beloved companion to be valued.

Chris's study does not prescribe what needed to be done. After all, there has always been mining and quarrying–gold, silver, bronze, iron, tin, lead are the ones listed in a passage in the Bible (Numbers 31:22; see also Deuteronomy 8:9; Job 28:1–10). What is different today is that human depredation has become so vast, it does increasing exponential damage. We cannot, Chris argues, continue to regard the earth as if it was an inanimate object to use as we please. It has its own rights and needs. He quotes a theologian who speaks of it as a sacramental reality, the earth as an objective physical being with its own inward spiritual significance–to which the artist in her art and the poet in his poetry speak.

In addition to these issues, Chris urges that whenever there were proposals like the ones the CSG people were making, everyone who is in any way affected should be consulted; there are questions of health and safety to be considered of course, but also questions of the land itself, what "injuries" might be done to it. This last question is not just about protecting the land, planning for cosmetic improvements once the quarrying is done, important as these are, but much more about the enhancement of the land, the genuine improvements that could be made to honour the land–as a companion loved by God. Chris speculates indeed as to whether land should be given its own legal identity. Apparently New Zealand has done this in one instance: personal status has been granted to the River Whangani to protect it for the future–Sister River, as St Francis would have put it.

In a world seriously challenged by ecological degradation, it is not easy to have hope for the future. With Judith dying so young, and the planet's ills symbolized so grimly, it would have been all too easy for Chris to despair. However, he did not in the short time he himself had left to live. After Judith died, he married again; his new wife was Janice, also a widow. Both of them had lost their spouses, and both had found love together in a new relationship and future. As his and Judith's son said at Chris's funeral, "How good that they had each other." Their marriage had been a fulfilment of hope. Hope transcends the vicissitudes of life so that even in devastating circumstances there are always new possibilities. To extend what Wendy Martin's sculpture had meant to Chris, when setbacks occur as they will in caring for Australia's fragile ecology, hope is always there to refresh the vision.

Let us pray for the people and leaders of Australia and New Zealand, that they may have a concerned relationship with the fragile ecologies of their beloved lands and as wise stewards be creative in their care for them.

46

Poland, Czech Republic, Slovakia, Hungary

Week after Trinity 19

These eastern European countries are the "buffer" states between the Russian-influenced world to the east and the western nations. Poland is the most northerly with a Baltic Sea coast, the Czech Republic and Slovakia are immediately south of Poland, and Hungary south of them. Poland's population is 40 million, the Czech Republic 10.5 million, Slovakia 5.5 million and Hungary 10 million. Poland is strongly Roman Catholic, whereas the Czech Republic has the highest number of atheists in the world after China and Japan. There are still a significant number of Roman Catholics; Slovakia is more strongly Catholic. Hungary is similar to Slovakia. The Diocese in Europe serves the Anglicans in the region. All four countries were part of the Soviet bloc after the Second World War and remained so until the fall of communism in 1989. Poland, led by Solidarity (a free trade union), moved for independence in the 1980s. Hungary tried in 1956 and was stopped by a Russian invasion. Czechoslovakia, the two countries at that time one, tried the same under Alexander Dubĉek in the Prague Spring of 1968, but also failed. The Czechs and Slovaks separated in 1993; each of the four countries is now a member of the European Union.

The dignity of being a person

When human beings are loved, they become persons. The sociologist Peter Berger put it this way: "we become that as which we are addressed".* St John puts it in another: "In this is love, not that we loved God, but that he loved us . . ." (1 John 4:10). Peter Berger is talking about a sociological truth, that outside relationship we cease to exist, St John of the ultimate source of our personhood, the love of God.

Primo Levi, an Italian Jewish writer who was arrested as a partisan towards the end of the Second World War, wrote of what it was like to be treated as a non-person, as a nothing.** When he was about to be transported to Auschwitz, his Nazi captors took a roll call. The corporal in charge marched up to the commander, saluted and shouted, "650 pieces present and correct, Sir!" No one there was a person; they were a collection of objects, sub-human creatures, destined for the slaughterhouse. There are some seriously damaged people who derive sadistic satisfaction from seeing others like this; there are many more who simply go along with it, because they have been ordered to, becoming depersonalized as a result. Deep down we all have these dark inclinations and prejudices, which in times of war surface and can lead anyone to inflict atrocities and cruelty on others. Anger grows and mutates into violence and murder (Matthew 5:21–22,43–44). The Jews of Europe—as well as Black people, and often also women and children—have all too often been treated as if they were inhuman. In the twentieth century, such hatred, a hatred that has grown over the centuries, became the genocide of the Holocaust.

For many centuries, Poland was a place of comparative safety for Jews. Things deteriorated after Poland's neighbours had partitioned the country, but even at the beginning of the Second World War there were 3 million Jews there. Poland was to lose 20 per cent of its population in the war, the Jewish community 90 per cent. Only 200,000 survived to the

---

* Peter L. Berger, *Invitation to Sociology: A Humanistic Perspective* (London: Penguin Books, 1966), p. 117.

** Ian Thomson, *Primo Levi: The Elements of a Life* (London: Vintage, Penguin Random House, 2002).

end, and many of them then left for Israel. The Polish/Jewish population is now between 10,000 and 20,000.

A number of Poles tried to help their Jewish compatriots. Pawel Pawlikowski's 2013 film *Ida* tells the story of Anna, a young woman of 18 who at the start of the film is about to become a fully professed nun.* The abbess tells her that if she is to make a full commitment she must as an orphan find out a little more about herself. She goes to stay with her one remaining relative, her mother's sister. It is only when she meets her aunt that she discovers that she is in fact Jewish—and that her real name is Ida. The two of them go on a pilgrimage to learn more about her early years and what had happened to her parents. A farmer, living in her parents' former home, tells them that her parents had been killed. Later he is prevailed upon to take them to the woods where he had buried her parents. Ida asked him why she was not also in the grave. He told her that he had been unable to kill a baby. Instead, he had taken her to the local priest. And that is how she had arrived at her convent: one representative of an ethnic community who had survived. On their pilgrimage, she had discovered who she was—that she had been "lifted up" from the grave. The film ends with her walking in the wide-open Polish countryside, carrying her few possessions in a small case, into her unknown future.

Ida is a Danish/Polish production. The 2016 film *Les Innocentes* is another cooperative venture, this time with France.** This film tells the story of another convent. It is almost the end of the war, not long after the Russian army had passed by on its advance towards Germany. A French Red Cross unit was stationed not far away. The story is based on the recollections of a French doctor, Madeline Paulice (Mathilde in the film), who was at the time a student doctor with the unit. The film starts with a young novice from the convent running towards the unit to ask for its help. Mathilde, whom she meets, tries to explain that they are not allowed to leave the unit—but then, during a break from her work, as she looks out of the rest room window, she sees the novice kneeling in the snow, apparently praying! Mathilde decides she must respond. Some eight months earlier, the passing Soviet troops had entered the

---

* *Ida*, Danish/Polish film directed by Pawel Pawlikowski (2013).

** *Les Innocentes*, film directed by Anne Fontaine (France, Poland, 2016).

convent and in three days had raped the entire community. They had treated the women as though they were sexual toys, "pieces". Many of the sisters had become pregnant, and they were now about to give birth. The abbess had been hoping that she could keep what had happened secret for the all too plausible reason that her community would be blamed for the outrage; she feared they would be dissolved for breaking their vows. When Mathilde and the novice reached the convent, Mathilde had to perform an emergency caesarean on one of the young women; her baby was in the breech position. Later, when several more of the sisters were about to give birth, Mathilde brought another colleague with her, one of the senior doctors. The sisters were alarmed that he was a man, but reluctantly allowed him to come in—like Jesus, Doctor Joseph was a Jew.

Joseph, who had lost both his parents to the Nazis at Bergen Belsen, had become an atheist, as indeed had Mathilde, but they both responded with love and compassion. When it was all over, the novice mistress, Sister Marie, wrote to Mathilde telling her that though Mathilde might laugh, it was God who had sent her. Mathilde might well have replied that she and Joseph were only doing their duty, and she would have been right. But then, Sister Marie was also right–their care had indeed had a transcendent quality, it spoke of the love of Christ. Sister Marie understood that God had indeed sent them–and, as can all too often happen when the Lord answers prayer, the nuns were at first minded to dismiss God's provision from their presence.

Let us pray for the people and leaders of Poland, the Czech Republic, Slovakia and Hungary and for their peace and security, that each one may be valued as persons of grace and dignity, loved and cared for by Christ.

47

West Africa: Cape Verde, Senegal, Gambia, Guinea Bissau, Guinea, Sierra Leone, Liberia, Cote d'Ivoire, Ghana, Togo, Benin, Burkina Faso

Week after Trinity 20/4th before Lent

The Cape Verde islands are about 500 miles to the west of Senegal in the Atlantic. The other countries are strung along the south coast of West Africa in the order above apart from Burkina Faso, which is north of Cote d'Ivoire and Benin. Gambia is entirely surrounded by Senegal. The population of the 12 countries together is roughly 157 million. Ghana is the largest with 33.5 million, then Côte d'Ivoire with 28 million–the overall population has increased greatly in recent years. The dominant faiths are Islam to the north and Christianity in the south. Anglicans are served by the Province of West Africa. In the past, thousands were trafficked as slaves to the Americas. All the countries apart from Liberia (a country formed by emigrants from the USA in 1847) were colonized, Guinea Bissau and Cape Verde by Portugal, Ghana, Sierra Leone and Gambia by Britain, the rest by France. Sierra Leone was helped by Britain to end a civil war, which lasted from 1991 to 2002.

Blessed are the pure in heart, for they will see God

A service called "The Churching of Women" appears in the *Book of Common Prayer* after the funeral services. I am not sure that I knew it was there until I was ordained. Nothing had been said about it during training, nor had my father ever used it as far as I knew. I was astonished to find on arriving at St Chad's Stockton-on-Tees that every new mother in the community was expected to be churched. It was one of the first services I took. Both of us were very nervous: the mother kneeling at the altar rail, while I stood in front of her mouthing the words of thanksgiving—which is what the service is about: thanksgiving for safe delivery. Not that this was the reason she had come. Not the main one anyway. She was there because she had to be "churched" if she was to be able to visit her Nan, possibly even her Mam; Northeast culture insisted she be purified before she went.

When Mary was purified in the temple, in obedience to the prescription in Leviticus (Leviticus 12), she brought two pigeons as a sacrifice and prayed that she would be cleansed after giving birth. There were rules too for cleansing after menstruation (Leviticus 15:19–33), partly to do with hygiene but much more to do with spiritual cleansing after the discharging of blood. The tendency in a patriarchal society is to regard bodily and fleshly discharges as a woman's misfortune, something that marked them as being inferior to men. Equally, if a man had sexual desires, then it was the woman's responsibility to safeguard her chastity; even if a man overpowered her and raped her, she was to blame. Nonetheless, while Judaism required that boys should be circumcised, it did not require it of girls. If the term "circumcision" is used of female genital mutilation (FGM), it is a mere euphemism, it does not excuse the abuse. It is not a requirement of Judaism, nor of Islam, nor indeed of Christianity! It is a cultural phenomenon designed to deprive girls of sexual pleasure and prevent them wandering from their men.

Female genital mutilation is an excision of the clitoris and, in most forms, of the labia as well. The practice is widespread in the Horn of Africa and across large swathes of northern and western Africa—which is how I came to know about it. Newcastle now has a large community of West Africans, especially from Guinea and Côte d'Ivoire. Women told me of how their men had insisted that they be "cut" before they could be married. Several had fled their country as a result. Mothers, who had themselves been mutilated, shared their concerns lest their daughters be forced to suffer it also. A UK Act of Parliament was passed in 2003 forbidding FGM in this country and also elsewhere. It does not seem to have stopped the Home Office from denying asylum to girls who have come here to avoid it. Officers simply say they do not believe that their fear is real. Since 2003, there have been very few cases under the Act.

The 2004 Senegalese film *Moolaadé* is a powerful story about this.* It is the story of Collé, one of the wives of a Muslim husband in a small village in Burkina Faso. Seven years before, she had refused to allow her daughter to be "purified", as the village elders thought she should be. At the beginning of the film, we see several girls aged between four and eight being made ready for this ritual mutilation, described throughout the film as "purification". Four of the girls escape and take refuge with Collé. She invokes the *Moolaadé,* a sacred word carrying such power it forbids any person outside her family from entering her compound. It provided sanctuary for the children, like the knocker on the main door of Durham Cathedral did for wrongdoers in medieval times. The film is not only the story of Collé's immense courage and leadership in fighting the custom; it speaks of a new awakening among the rural women of West Africa, that the custom needs to stop.

FGM is not so much about purification as about the cultural abuse of women. Cleanliness is of course necessary and important for health—though as a pathologist friend who worked for a time in West Africa used to tell me, too much sanitation is damaging to the auto-immune system. Spiritual purity is not about physical hygiene. It is to do with the direction of the heart towards God, the orientation of the whole person, the more human the better, to the contemplation and love of God. We are all of us, after all, bodily human beings. Blood circulating, wonderfully functioning fluids of all kinds moving within to ensure our health, all of it essential and valuable. Purity is about the heart. The beatitude which

---

* *Moolaadé*, Senegal film directed by Ousmane Sembane, Bambara and French (Artificial Eye DVD, Burkina Faso, 2004).

refers to it says: "Blessed are the pure in heart; for they shall see God" (Matthew 5:8).

Let us pray for the people and leaders of the countries of West Africa, for all who work to end the abuse of women by FGM, for the welfare of women and for girls everywhere, that all of us, women and men, may be pure in heart.

48

Sri Lanka

Week after Trinity 21/3rd before Lent

Sri Lanka is an island southeast of India; it is almost tied to Tamil Nadu in India by the "Adam's Bridge" in the Gulf of Mannar. Its population is 22 million; 75 per cent are Sinhalese, most of them Theravada Buddhist; 11 per cent are Tamil living in the north, who are Hindu. The Lankan Moors (just under 10 per cent) are Muslim. The rest are Christian, mostly Roman Catholic. The Anglican Church is divided into the Jaffna diocese in the north which is in the Church of South India, and the Colombo and Kurunegala dioceses which are in the care of the Archbishop of Canterbury. Conflict between the Tamils (the Liberation Tigers of Tamil Eelam, who fought for independence between 2006 and 2009) and the rest of the country led to about 100,000 deaths. On Easter Day 2019, an Islamic group attacked churches and hotels. Political turmoil has continued.

Listening and truth

Towards the end of the Second World War, two emissaries from Poland came to England. They had come to warn the western governments that Poland's Jewish population was being systematically murdered. Michael Evans, reporting about this in a *Times* article of 5 June 2005, said that the British official who first heard their story refused to believe them. Would it not, he said, be so much simpler to shoot the Jews rather than starve them to death. He noted too that the report had come from suspect Jewish sources. It is similar with officials listening to asylum seekers today, or hearing that a bishop has been abusing ordinands, or that a Christian pioneer is molesting women. The story is too difficult and appalling to hear. The tragedy is that in their report—and in each of these examples—they were in fact telling the truth.

Human rights legislation allows asylum seekers to settle in this country provided they can meet the necessary requirements—a process that is constantly changing. At the same time, there is a general perception that a country cannot cope with too many asylum seekers, so politicians expect their officials to take a tough line. In recent years, a hostile environment policy and ever fiercer laws have made the process even harder. Applicants have a mountain to climb if they are to succeed in proving that they have a right to be here.

When asylum seekers first meet a Home Office interviewer, the latter is likely to be listening rather more to the political line they are expected to take than to anything the person happens to be saying. In fact they may not really hear anything. If they do grasp it, their programming will ensure that they will not believe it. It is rare for someone to be accepted on a first encounter. Most of them, at some time in the future, will have to face a judge to learn whether their plea is to be allowed. James Hanratty is one such judge. In his book, he tells the story of a Tamil from Sri Lanka who appeared before him.* The defendant had told the court that he had been badly burnt by his captors, and that he was frightened that if he were to be returned it might happen again. Judge Hanratty asked for a report on the burns. No one had actually thought to have one done. So, would the defendant, the judge asked, be willing to show the court where he had been burnt? He would, he said—and showed them his hands and his feet. He won his appeal.

Every so often, in my work with asylum seekers, I would write a report for one of these judicial hearings. I did so once for another Sri Lankan. I had to explain to the client that it would not count as corroborating evidence; I could not check on the veracity of all that he had told me. The report was simply a witness to our conversation. He could show the report to the court if he so wished. The court in this instance accepted it, and clearly it helped in their decision. I was not quite so successful when I appeared as a witness with other asylum seekers, a couple this

* James Hanratty, RD, *The Making of an Immigration Judge* (London: Quartet Books, 2020), p. 154.

time, some of the first clients I had worked with. In the court, I ventured the opinion that my clients were suffering from post-traumatic stress (PTSD)—flashbacks, nightmares, etc. "Are you a psychiatrist?" the judge asked. As the judge made clear, I did not have the authority to say that.

My colleagues and I used to explain to asylum seekers when they talked with us that apart from writing a report at the end of our work, we would be unable to help them with their asylum application. Our role was to listen, to offer a quiet and calm space in which the asylum seeker could tell us their story. Within the relationship, my role was to listen. It required concentrated attention, a listening beyond what they were saying to their feelings and levels of stress, to the reasons they had for coming to see me. From the clients' point of view of course, if they were to recover from whatever trauma they had suffered, they had to tell me the truth. No use to them if they didn't do that! Only the truth heals. On most occasions, the healing work had little to do with whatever I might have said, it was far more to do with their slow telling of their story. They were often able to recover those parts of it that they had forgotten, the listening giving them the space and time to do so. In the telling they would then be able to reorganize all that had happened into a new pattern of understanding which they could comprehend. Trauma has this effect of blanking out parts of the story; it causes experiences to disappear from consciousness, leaving in their place a jumble of vague and disorganized memories. Telling the story allows them to recover these and so find peace. If listeners are hostile, the blankness caused by the trauma simply increases. It is only when someone is heard that they can come to experience healing.

The Refugee Service allowed us to offer up to eight sessions, eight hours in all—occasionally longer, but often not so long. For those who were psychologically strong, this was enough; for those who were not, it was at least a beginning.

If a court does in fact refuse permission to an asylum seeker this rarely means that they are sent away. Most immigrants who come to this country, or indeed any country, stay where they have arrived.* This

---

* Randall Hansen, "Migration to Europe since 1945: Its History and its Lessons", *The Political Quarterly*, special issue, 2003, pp. 25–38.

has always been the case. The elaborate methods we use to keep them out are largely political, ways of persuading the general public that the authorities are doing something to restrict the numbers that are coming. On the whole, they try to keep quiet about their failure. Once here, of course, immigrants contribute enormously.

Let us pray for the people and leaders of Sri Lanka, for the healing of relationships between the different ethnic groups and faiths in their country and for all who seek asylum in a new place, especially those immigrants who have joined us here in the British Isles.

49

The Andes: Ecuador, Peru, Bolivia

Week after All Saints' Day (30 October to 5 November)/4th Sunday before Advent

Ecuador, north of Peru, south of Colombia, with Peru straddles the Andes mountains. The Galapagos Islands, which belong to Ecuador, are 600 miles to the west in the Pacific Ocean. Bolivia is south of Peru, its western half in the Andes mountains–its administrative capital La Paz is about 11,000 feet above sea level–with an eastern lowland adjoining Brazil. Ecuador's population is 18 million, Peru 34 million and Bolivia 12 million. The great majority are Roman Catholic among a larger population of Christians. Peru and Bolivia are single dioceses in the Anglican Church, while Ecuador is in Province IX of the Episcopal Church, USA. The Communists in Peru, the Shining Path, fought for control between 1985 and 1992. Ecuador recognizes the rights of nature in law.

A healing ministry

We often had visitors to our vicarage in Ovingham from tourists who were visiting the church. They usually came for information about the great wood engraver Thomas Bewick, who is buried there. This new visitor was from Ecuador. He had come to learn about his grandfather, Frank Hastings, who had been the Vicar of Ovingham for some 23 years and had in later years emigrated to Ecuador. It was interesting to reflect that in his day the parish had been little bigger than two villages and outlying farms with a population of about 600, and he was full time. Thirty years later, the parish was four times larger, and the vicars were part time. My immediate predecessor had taught in a nearby school. I combined the role with diocesan work as the adviser in pastoral care and counselling–which also at first included encouraging the ministry of healing.

I was keen to start a healing ministry in the parish. An opportunity came when a woman telephoned from Middlesbrough–some 30 miles from the Tyne Valley: "Could I come to your church," she said, "and be healed of my cancer?" In some trepidation, I invited her to come and meet me and tell me what she had in mind. She came, and we agreed a date for a healing service in a few weeks' time. In the meantime, she agreed to prepare herself by opening her heart to the Lord in penitence and love, trusting that she would receive the healing she desired. I thought it would be a fairly private occasion, but come the day, she arrived with most of her family and relations. They were joined by rather more than I expected of our own congregation. It was a stirring occasion. She, and indeed most of her family, all received the laying on of hands and anointing. I heard later that it had been an enriching experience for them all, that together they had experienced the healing presence of Christ in a deep and meaningful way. She was not in fact healed of her cancer. The days following the service were gentle for her, days of grace as she moved quietly towards her meeting with the Lord in a gracious dying.

The Church as the body of Christ is called to heal. The Eucharist and Anointing with the holy oils are the two main healing sacraments and the laying on of hands is a further following in the way of Christ. Together with the gifts of listening and counselling–the two that are the most important in mental health care–they are the ways the Church extends Christ's healing touch towards the sick. A few people also have particular gifts of healing: Juan Martin de Porres Velasquez (born in Peru in 1579) was one such and Isabel Flores de Oliva (born 1586) another. They were lay Christians, both of ethnic parentage, *mulattoes*, as persons of mixed race were called in Peru, contemporaries and friends of each other who cared for the sick in different parts of Lima. They are now both buried in the great monastery church of Santa Domingo in the city. Isabel–later known as Rosa of Lima and a patron saint of the country–modelled her life on Catherine of Siena, and she like Catherine was a third-order Dominican. Martin's path was different.

Martin was the son of a Spanish nobleman and a freed Black slave, Ana Velasquez. Ana was clearly a loving mother—though I have to say Martin's biographers do not paint her as such—like the Moroccan mother of St John of the Cross, who also had to bring up her two children (both sons in her case) largely on her own. Ana and her son and daughter were poor. Nonetheless, for them to turn out as they did, her love and care must have been greater than her critics supposed. She endowed them both with a profound love for God. From the beginning Martin was a free spirit, a person of prayer, who did what he thought was right, regardless of the consequences, which could not have been all that easy for Ana. In his teen years, he acquired some medical skills and learnt about the healing properties of herbs, all from a local barber surgeon. At the age of 15, he tried to join the Dominican Community of the Holy Rosary—another name for the Santo Domingo Monastery—but was told that he couldn't because he was Black. He persisted, however, and finally managed to persuade the community to take him on as a servant. It is why he is always depicted in stained glass windows with a broom in his hand. He remained as a servant for the next eight years. At the same time, during these eight years, he was quietly developing a healing ministry. People from all walks of life began to seek him out, all of them coming to the monastery to plead for healing from him. Eventually the prior decided he must ignore the country's racist strictures, and he admitted Martin to the community as a lay brother.

His new position was not to the liking of some of the other brethren. They mocked and abused him. He in response bore their behaviour without complaint. It was how things were, he told himself: their problem, not his. In himself, he was his own person, deeply conscious of the love of God for him and that he was called to be a caring healer. There was one occasion when a scruffy beggar, mugged and badly injured outside the monastery gate, banged on the door to ask for help. Martin had been taking people into his own room to heal them but had been ordered to stop doing this. On this occasion, he disobeyed. He brought the beggar in and cared for him. When the prior later remonstrated,

Martin replied, "Please do set me straight, for I am greatly puzzled. Was it really wrong to put charity before obedience?"*

Not many of us have gifts such as Martin had. Certainly I do not, beyond the gift of touch that we all have as human beings. But, like all ministers of the gospel, each of us has the additional gift of the Holy Spirit to pass on God's healing. I remember in the early days of ministry as a hospital chaplain, laying hands on some who were dying, strongly commending them to go forth from this world in the name of God their creator, only to have them promptly recover. One of our Ovingham congregation told me of his joy when he had found himself healed at one of our services. That was the infinite graciousness of Christ! More often persons were not actually cured but found themselves in a deeper relationship with Christ. They had received grace and strength from the Holy Spirit. They had grown in prayer. Others had learnt to value more the caring hands of their doctors, nurses and the many others who were mediating the love of God towards them. Spiritual healing is primarily about this: about being ushered into a new relationship of love with both God and their neighbour; sometimes they also experience a remarkable physical or mental healing.

Let us pray for the people and leaders of Peru, Bolivia and Ecuador, that learning from the examples of St Martin de Porres and St Rose of Lima, we may minister the healing touch of Christ to all who turn to Him.

---

* Claire Huchet Bishop, *Martin de Porres, Hero* (Boston, MA: Houghton Mifflin Co, 1954), p. 82.

50

The Philippines

Week after 3rd Sunday before Advent

The Philippines is an archipelago of 7,641 islands east of Vietnam, north of Indonesia and south of Japan and China. The main islands are Luzon in the north with Manila, the capital, and Quezon City next to it. Mindanao, autonomous since 2019, is the most southerly. Samar, referred to below, is in the east, north of Mindanao. Palawan is in the far southwest, north of Borneo, the Sulu Sea to its east. The rest of the islands are gathered around the Sibuyan and Visayan Seas. The population is 115.5 million and growing. Most of the people are Catholic, but there is a sizeable Muslim minority, especially in Bangsamoro, Mindanao. The Anglican presence is the Episcopal Church in the Philippines. The islands were colonized by Spain in the sixteenth century, handed over to the United States at the end of the nineteenth and became independent in 1946.

Fasting

Manila in the Philippines may be some 11,000 miles from Lima in Peru, but there are links between the two. Both were ruled by Spain in the sixteenth century and both countries honour the memory of Rosa de Lima and Martin de Porres. Santa Rosa City in Laguna is named after Rosa, and the Medical School of the St Thomas Catholic University in Manila after Martin. Martin is also said to have bi-located to the country, as Ezekiel did to Jerusalem (Ezekiel 8:3; 40:2–4), journeying there in a spiritual dream-like pilgrimage. People said, so his biographer observes, they saw Martin there when he was actually still known to be in Lima.*

The second link is that both countries are on the same Ring of Fire, the horseshoe line of volcanoes and earthquakes that circles the Pacific basin from the Andes to the Philippines and Indonesia. The region is equally subject to typhoons—as hurricanes are called in the Pacific region—devastating storms with winds exceeding 100 mph that cause havoc in their wake. Typhoon Haiyan, or Yolande as it was also called, was one such in 2013.

It started in the Pacific on 2 November, reached Guiuan at the southern tip of Samar on the 8th, destroyed almost 90 per cent of Tacloban City in Leyte and killed more than 6,000 as it passed through the archipelago. Eventually it subsided and became a tropical storm on reaching Vietnam. Winds of 145 mph were recorded, one gust reaching 195 mph. I remember once going to Edinburgh and walking up from Waverley Station to find myself so buffeted by the gale that I could hardly stand. Compared to Haiyan, a mild affair! Nonetheless, I went straight back down and caught the last train running that evening to Newcastle. The Philippine people regularly cope with typhoons, but Haiyan was particularly bad.

In response, the Christian Aid chairman Rowan Williams—the former Archbishop of Canterbury—urged supporters to offer a monthly day of prayer and fasting for the people there. The idea was that it would serve also as a prayerful way of preparing for the UN Climate Change Conference which was to be held later that year in Lima. As I was writing this in November 2020—during the first lockdown of the Covid-19 pandemic—the current Archbishops of Canterbury and York were inviting the churches to do something similar, urging us to consider a Thursday fast as an assist to our prayer for the nation.

The archbishops' letter was like Joel's call to his people to fast when Judea was being invaded by locusts (Joel 2:15—see the opening essay above). They were calling on the Church to make a small sacrifice as an add-on to their prayer. There is a story in the Bible about a similar

---

* Claire Huchet Bishop, *Martin de Porres, Hero* (Boston, MA: Houghton Mifflin Co, 1954), pp. 105–6.

request, when the Jewish people were threatened with genocide. Queen Esther (4:15–17) was herself Jewish, and she was asked by her uncle Mordecai to speak to the king about this. She said she would if as a preparation her people were to offer three days of prayer and fasting. If they would do that, she said, she would feel the more able to risk her own life and approach the king uninvited, something not permitted even to the queen. Similarly Jesus, before he began his ministry, fasted for a long period in the wilderness (Matthew 4:1–11).

Dag Tessore in his little book about fasting explains that its ascetical purpose is to help persons open their hearts before the Lord.* In the early Church, it had a threefold purpose: to strengthen self-control, to increase spiritual insight and to help persons identify in some small way with the struggles the people they were praying for were having. This feels appropriate enough to the Philippine situation. In 2016, 25 per cent of the population had less than $2 a day to live on.

Fasting practices over the years have varied considerably. Sometimes Christians have fasted from food and drink altogether. More often—especially in corporate settings—they have adopted a simpler vegetarian diet, like Daniel (10:3) when he cut out meat and wine for three weeks. Others have favoured a stricter vegan diet, removing dairy products altogether and limiting their eating to a single meal in the afternoon, or at the end of the day. This was the practice taken over by Islam in its Ramadan discipline of eating only when it was dark. Perhaps, now that so many are already either vegetarian or vegan, some new disciplines are required: for example, abstaining from television, social media and the like or, as Isaiah strongly emphasized (58:6–9), giving time to helping others in need.

Fasting in the way the early Church did as a spiritual discipline to enhance their prayer was a way of identifying with others who were suffering. Jesus emphasized that whatever we do it should be done quietly (Matthew 6:6–18). And it should not be extreme! A couple of nuns once asked Dorothy Day if it was true that she managed to live on the sacrament

* Dag Tessore, *Fasting*, trans. Frank Johnson (London: New City, 2007), pp. 13–14.

alone—as is sometimes believed of saintly people.* "Hell no!" she said. Fasting is not about being heroic. It needs to be sensible. It needs to remind us that many people go hungry on a daily basis and that western eating patterns are often harmful to the environment. I remember when Oxfam, I think it was, invited people to fast for a couple of days and give the money saved to the poor, that we tried it one weekend in the parish and found it a valuable exercise. An essential thing is simplicity. I was struck when reading Jay Rayner's book that even he, *The Observer's* restaurant critic, a carnivore as he describes himself, argued that it would be good to have one if not more vegetarian days each week.**

Islam has its valuable Ramadan month, a discipline which my Muslim friends tell me they find very helpful. The secular world favours January as a "dry month". Christians have Lent. These are all disciplines we need to recover.

Let us pray for the people and leaders of the Philippines as they cope with so many natural disasters and troubles. We pray especially for the poor. Give them and all of us wisdom to contain our greed, grace to live simply and strength to deepen our relationship with God and our love for the poor and starving in our prayer and fasting.

---

* Kate Hennessy, *The World Will Be Saved by Beauty: An Intimate Portrait of My Grandmother* (New York: Scribner, Simon & Schuster, 2017), p. 85.

** Jay Rayner, *A Greedy Man in a Hungry World* (London: Collins, 2013), p. 217.

5 1

Congo, Rwanda and Burundi

Week after 2nd Sunday before Advent

The Democratic Republic of the Congo (Congo Kinshasa) is a huge country centred on the River Congo with a narrow seaboard where the Congo enters the Atlantic. Uganda, Lake Tanganyika and Zambia are to the country's east, Angola to the south. Rwanda and Burundi are small mountainous countries, Rwanda beside Lake Kivu and Burundi beside the northern stretch of Lake Tanganyika. The population of the Congo is 99 million and expected to increase, of Rwanda 14 million and Burundi 13 million. All three are predominantly Christian, mainly Roman Catholic. The Anglican Church has a province in each of the countries. Leopold II of Belgium took over the Congo in 1884/5 as his private fiefdom. There were so many people killed and other atrocities committed that the country of Belgium assumed control in 1905. The same happened with Rwanda and Burundi. Congo gained independence suddenly in 1960, Rwanda and Burundi a little later in 1962. Rwanda and Burundi are peopled by the Hutu (over 80 per cent), Tutsi and Twa ethnic groups. Tensions between the Hutu and Tutsi flared in the Rwandan genocide of April to July 1994; 800,000 were killed.

Ordination and beginnings

On 30 June 1960, the Congo regained its independence. Very soon afterwards, the Katanga pedicle to the southeast of the country declared itself independent, it was thought with the support of the departing Belgian government. The Congo crisis had begun. All of these June 1960 events happened at the very beginning of my ministry–I was made deacon on 12 June of that year. It was a dark time for the Congo, made worse when the new prime minister, Patrice Lumumba, who had been refused help by the west, looked to the Soviet Union for help as well. The consequences for Lumumba were dire.

Writing a year after the Congo crisis had begun in his seminal book *Persecution 1961*, Peter Benenson explained why; the powerful United States and the Soviet Union were each determined that Africa should be ruled by their particular ideology and not be seduced into following the ideas of the other.* Given that communist-leaning leaders were already active in several of the African countries, the alarm of the States was considerable. What Benenson particularly noted was the effects of all this on political activists of the time. Lumumba, even though he was the legitimate prime minister, was kidnapped and held captive. Benenson was determined that something should be done for the many other activists being similarly detained. After publishing his book in April 1961, he launched and founded Amnesty International on Sunday 28 May of the same year with a major article in *The Observer.* The book itself is largely a collection of essays about a number of such activists. His plea was that they should either be released or, if that was not possible, be allowed to go into exile. One was Agostinho Neto, a leader in neighbouring Angola, another the Filipino agrarian reformer Luis Taroc.

I was to learn far too much about the experiences of persons like them, especially those who had fled the Congo, in my work with asylum seekers: the beatings by the police, some so severe they had to be admitted to hospital; the rapes of women; families attacked by intruding militias; murders of loved ones; soldiers, many still children, made to tramp the vast country in drugged and fugue-like states so they could commit atrocities without feeling anything. So many died! An organization like Amnesty International was desperately needed.

It so happened, to add a personal note, that on the very same day of Amnesty's founding, 28 May 1961, six of us, young deacons who had trained at King's College, London, "a group of callow youth", as one of my colleagues described us, were ordained in Durham Cathedral. It was Trinity Sunday, the day on which ordinations in the Anglican Church used to take place. It felt personally significant for us to think that such

* Peter Benenson, *Persecution 1961* (London: Penguin, 1961), p. 12.

an important international beginning should have happened on that watershed day in our personal lives.

One of the tasks that came my way some 40 years after this, after I had retired, was a request to find out how many ethnic community churches there were in Newcastle. It turned out that there were 17, plus some smaller groupings, and probably some more I did not discover. Many of them were from West Africa, the Congolese notable among them. Large numbers of the Congolese have settled in Newcastle, despite coming from one of the warmer parts of the world. The result is that they have several churches.

There was one such that met in the United Reformed Church in central Newcastle. I had been introduced to it and its pastor, Papi Eva Likofo, by my multi-lingual Rwandan friend Musa Hassan Ali, who often used to interpret for me when I was counselling asylum seekers. Pastor Eva had his office in an African enclave in a shop behind the Byker Wall, and when I visited him there, he gave me a video of his ordination. It had been conducted by his church's bishop, Apôtre Tambu Lukoki. It was a joyous occasion, the congregation and ministers moving together with that grace and dignity that is so natural to an African community, the congregation at one in their participation in the ceremony. The ordination itself included an anointing. The ministers stood over the candidate, one of them holding a full flagon of Tesco oil, in preparation. It looked as if oil was not only going to flow down to the collar of his clothing, as it did onto Aaron's (Psalm 133:2–3), but much beyond. In the event, when the moment of anointing arrived, only a little was used. More surprising was a drama soon after when the apostle suddenly and with élan slapped Eva smartly across the face. It was certainly a surprise! Also a sacramental moment, a Pentecostal shock. Eva fell to the ground, slain in the Holy Spirit—the phrase used by Pentecostal Christians when someone is overcome by the Lord and collapses. He lay there, still, not moving—to rise from the ground to receive the greetings and hugs from both ministers and congregation. Newcastle has been blessed by the arrival of such Congolese and their vibrant culture. Eva and his church were at a moment of new beginning.

In the same year of this ordination of Pastor Eva, those of us who had been curates with our vicar, Trevor Beeson, in 1960 and 1961—and later—were compiling a *festschrift* to honour his eightieth birthday.* We used it to explore the many and varied ministries that each of us had done since: working in television, writing about censorship and vocation, developing pastoral care and counselling, working in industrial mission, ministering in a new town, acting as chaplain in a local authority. It was significant that all of us had developed special interests in addition to our general ministry as priests. Trevor wrote in the original book: "it would be nothing less than tragic if an attempt was to be made to reproduce a Victorian church tradition in a new area."** True then; even more so now! The Church of England still seems to hope it can recover its Victorian authority. Newcastle diocese alone has lost more than half of its full-time clergy and is losing more each year. What then is the Holy Spirit saying to the churches (Revelation 2:7 et al.), the Church of England in particular?

We are like the Congolese Church, at a new beginning. Whatever dark times there are ahead we have to pass through them if we are to reach a new resurrection. In the meantime, we are to listen in prayer.

Let us pray for the people and leaders of the Congo, Rwanda and Burundi—that after so much trauma each country may come to new beginnings and new hope. We pray for the ethnic churches of the Northeast together with the rest of the churches and the Church of England in particular, that all of us may listen in prayer to what the Holy Spirit is saying to the churches.

* *New Area Mission and Beyond: Essays in Honour of Trevor Beeson*, ed. Derek Jones (privately published, 2006).

** Beeson, *New Area Mission*, p. 15.

52

The British Isles

Week after Christ the King

Ugglebarnby—referred to below—is a small village very close to Whitby in North Yorkshire. The United Kingdom's population is 67.5 million; Ireland 5 million. In common with Europe in general, the majority are post-Christian: humanist and secular together with the established Church of England, the disestablished Church in Wales and the (Presbyterian) Church of Scotland. There are five provinces of the Anglican Church: Canterbury, York, Scotland, Wales and Ireland. People of other Christian denominations and other faiths are well represented in a multi-cultural society. The Republic of Ireland is strongly Catholic, though there has been a significant loss of confidence in the Church following the recent child abuse scandals. The impact of the sectarian troubles which ended with the Good Friday Agreement (10 April 1998) can still be felt.

Evening prayer in Ugglebarnby

In 1945, immediately after the Second World War, my family moved from Bradford to Coniston Cold in the Yorkshire Dales. We were at the time a family of six, our parents Norman and Ruth and four siblings aged from three to nine. Two more were to be born a decade later. Each year in the late 1940s, we went on holiday to Sleights, a village in the Esk Valley a few miles inland from Whitby immediately below the North York Moors. We used to camp in a field to the right of the road from Sleights to Grosmont, just past a distinctive terrace of five cottages, looking oddly out of place in such a rural setting. Our parents slept in our caravan, the rest of us in a bell tent purchased from the naturalist Romany. We used to splash about in the river below the site, played endless games and had a wonderful time amongst the cows and sheep. On Sunday mornings, we went to St Ninian's Church in Baxtergate, Whitby, a high Anglican enclave which my father liked and thought we should experience: very dark and gloomy! The church is still there, but more recently became home to a schismatic traditionalist group who preferred to pray in Latin. In the evenings, our parents went to Evensong, either in Sleights or Ugglebarnby—since 1829, the two villages had been in the same parish. Ugglebarnby is apparently named after a Nordic warrior called Uglu Barbur. I remember well my mother talking about their visits to the church there. She was always deeply moved by the way the elderly vicar used to read the lessons; I have never forgotten how she used to speak about it.

Almost 50 years later, Joy and I were again in Sleights—this time as part of a 1994 sabbatical. Our daughter's parents-in-law had their retirement home there and had allowed us to stay in it for a fortnight of the sabbatical. Another visit to Ugglebarnby was high on the agenda, and as soon as we could, Joy and I went there to see All Saints' Ugglebarnby. It is one of the original churches of the parish. The current 1872 building replaced a Norman chapel of 1127. It stands in the middle of the village, surrounded by its churchyard and the few houses that make up the village. On the day we were there, the churchyard was guarded by geese and sadly it was locked, but with a notice on the door: "Evening Prayer will be said here on Wednesday", adding the date of the coming Wednesday and the time. Come the hour, we were still making our way up the hill out of the valley which divides Ugglebarnby from Sleights, a more exacting climb than we had anticipated; we were late. We barged in to find two men just beginning the office. Seeing a congregation so surprisingly appear, they graciously began again. At the end, they told us that they did this every Wednesday afternoon. It was their regular offering for the community as well as for themselves. Joining them was a high point of those sabbatical days. There were four of us in our group for prayer that afternoon, one more than the two or three stipulated in the gospel (Matthew 18:20). The Lord was with us as we held the community in prayer.

—

This is the final vignette of our year-long tour of the world. You, as reader, have joined me in visiting the various countries of the world. It feels appropriate in this day and age that we finish the pilgrimage in a remote church in a tiny hamlet in the north of England. It was sad that it was not open. A key was available, we were told, but it would have been so much better had it been open; visitors could then have shared the village's church, local villagers could have come in to pray quietly. Of course, it does not matter where one prays, but an ancient sacred space where people have prayed for centuries adds a depth and a companionship to the encounter with God. A church is a symbol of God's presence at the heart of a community. It did not matter that when the four of us said Evening Prayer together, there were only a few of us. The Anglican Church in England is small, much smaller now than it was when I was first ordained, and it is becoming smaller. Perhaps it does not need to be so big in the modern world. The Church's vocation of witness and prayer in the twenty-first century does not require large numbers to be fit for purpose. Only a remnant is needed for the real spiritual work we are called to do: empowered by the Holy Spirit holding our world and wider community together with the ascended Lord before God the Father.

The Church has a vital vocation to hold the people of our country, indeed the people of all countries, in prayer before the Lord. It is after all the merciful God who is eventually going to establish the kingdom. It is the Lord, who with strength of arm will scatter the proud, cast down the mighty from their positions of authority, lift up the down-trodden, and fill the starving with good things. Let us magnify the Lord in thanksgiving for this.

There are probably far more than we realize (1 Kings 19:18) who are doing this already, but a few are enough. Your kingdom come, Your will be done as it is in heaven.

Let us pray for the people and leaders of Ireland, Northern Ireland, Scotland, Wales and England: that as we come to the end of this year of intercession, we may give thanks for all that God has done and is doing in our world, that empowered by the Holy Spirit, we may join with our Ascended Lord as he holds the needs of the world before the Father.

Select bibliography

Baelz, Peter, *Prayer and Providence* (New York: Seabury Press, 1968).

Black, Ian, *Intercessions for Years A, B and C* (London: SPCK, 2009).

Brown, Rosalind, *Prayers for Living: 500 Prayers for Public and Private Worship* (Durham: Sacristy Press, 2021).

Chaplin, Doug, *Leading Common Worship Intercessions: A Simple Guide* (London: Church House Publishing, 2009).

Chapman, Raymond, *The Intercessor's Guide* (Norwich: Canterbury Press, 2007).

Clements-Jewery, Philip, *Intercessory Prayer* (Aldershot: Ashgate, 2005).

Ferguson, David, *The Providence of God: A Polyphonic Approach* (Cambridge: Cambridge University Press, 2018).

Greig, Pete, *God on Mute: Engaging the Silence of Unanswered Prayer*, second edn (Colorado Springs, CO: David C. Cook, [2007], 2020).

Kelsey, Rob, *Praying for the Earth* (Durham: Sacristy Press, 2021).

Kramer, M. J., *The Canterbury Book of New Parish Prayers: Collects for the Church and for the World* (Norwich: Canterbury Press, 2021).

Moore, Gerard, *Lord, Hear Our Prayer: Praying the General Intercessions* (Strathfield, Australia: St Paul's Publications, 2008).

Pritchard, John, *The Intercessions Handbook: Creative Ideas for Public and Private Prayer* (London: SPCK, 1997, 2011).

Sayers, Susan, *Prayers of Intercession Book 1 and Book 2* (Stowmarket: Kevin Mayhew, 1997).

Sayers, Susan, *Prayers of Intercession for Common Worship* (Stowmarket: Kevin Mayhew, 1999).

White, Vernon, *Purpose and Providence: Taking Soundings in Western Thought, Literature and Theology* (London: T & T Clark, 2018).

Two sample intercessions

The two are built on a couple of the vignettes. The first is the twenty-eighth vignette in some detail in the **Preparing the petitions** chapter; the second is the vignette for six months before. They take the theme explored in the vignette and the region highlighted and suggest petitions which might be offered in other sections of the prayer.

The two are designed to be used with one of the two forms provided on pages 281 and 282 of *Common Worship: Prayers for the Church of England* (London: Church House Publishing, 2000). The first is 215 words, which with versicle and response and whatever additional collect or concluding prayer is added, make it roughly 250 words. The second is shorter, but not by much. It is good to allow time for silence too.

Petitions 1: The Caucasus

To go with the form on page 281

Let us pray with the Orthodox Churches of the Caucasus, the mountainous region between the Black and Caspian Seas; for the Orthodox Churches of Russia and Georgia, the Armenian Apostolic Church and the Muslim Communities especially of Azerbaijan. We remember also our fellow Orthodox Christians *(here in ...)*, and we pray for good relations and understanding between our local Churches and the Muslim *Umma* (or "Community") here.

Let us pray for the peoples of the Caucasus region–Russia, Georgia, Armenia, Azerbaijan–and for their leaders. *(Mention whatever is currently happening: at the time of writing for example, the war in Ukraine.)* For those damaged by conflict, for those who seek asylum away from their country, for wisdom in those who devise national policy and for all who seek to create harmony between different ethnic peoples in this country.

We pray particularly for persons seeking asylum in our city, for agencies that work with them *(name a local Refugee Service)* and for those acting as interpreters. We pray for our city in its role as a "City of Sanctuary" *(if this is the case?)*, for those who administer justice and exercise authority in local tribunals.

We pray for those whose health has been damaged by ill-treatment and for those who help them *(a Rape Crisis team, Freedom from Torture).* We pray for all who suffer from mental health issues and all who are frightened. Here in our own church community, we pray for the sick: *(limit the list to about five)* and all who care for them.

We pray for all who have died, especially those who have died in times of conflict.

Petitions 2: Brazil

At the time of writing, the journalist Dom Phillips and the Brazilian advocate Bruno Pereira were both murdered in the Amazon Rainforest. These petitions are designed to go with the form on page 282.

In giving thanks for all we receive from South America, especially from those from there who live here among us. We pray for the people and leaders of Brazil, the great cities of Sao Paolo, Rio de Janeiro, Recife and Manaus. Let us pray especially for all who seek for a just policy of care for the Amazon Rainforest.

We remember the Churches of Brazil, the Roman Catholic Church, the Pentecostal Churches and the Anglican Presence there *(a particular diocese and bishop?)* and our Church here in ... (*A church and congregation with whom we are praying this week.)*

Jesus said, "Blessed are the Poor." As we pray for the poor, we give thanks for all they teach us by their way of living about the dignity of life in the face of misfortune. We pray for government in its provisions for the poor, for good practice and justice between rich and poor, for the Church and charitable agencies *(name one: Crisis for example)* in their works of mercy. We pray especially for good, prudent and honest practice among those who lend money, especially banks and micro-credit schemes.

Especially we remember all who have given their lives in the service of the poor and down-trodden *(i.e. the two men mentioned above—together with those who are sick and have died in the congregation).*

Index of countries

References are to the chapters, not to the pages.

Thematic Index

References are to chapter numbers.

Lightning Source UK Ltd.
Milton Keynes UK
UKHW021548300123
416188UK00009B/425

9 781789 592610